July 31, 2020

Shelly O'Hara
6101 E Bellevue St Apt 221
Tucson AZ 85712-5165

Dear Shelly,

I sincerely appreciate your prayer and partnership with Alpha Ministries.

As always, I am humbled by the Lord's guidance and provision for Alpha Ministries, supplied through your friendship and partnership as we serve Him together.

Please find enclosed with this letter our newest book My Father's Business: Making the Most of His Must. You are receiving one of the first copies from the press. In this book I share some deeply personal testimonies of His faithfulness and lessons I have learned over the years walking in my father's and heavenly Father's footsteps.

I hope you are encouraged by the story of how the Lord led my parents, my family and the ministry of Alpha Ministries up until this day. May you be strengthened in your journey with the Lord. I pray that through the reading of this book, God will so inspire you through His Holy Spirit to be the love of Christ to those around you. Thank you for helping us continue proclaiming the truth of God's Word—even in the midst of this global pandemic—and impacting lives around the world for Jesus Christ!

Your friend and fellow servant in the Lord Jesus Christ,

Brother Bennie
Alpha Ministries

P.O.Box 4563 - Lynchburg, VA. 24572-4563 434-546-3069 AlphaMinistries.com

MY FATHER'S BUSINESS

MAKING THE MOST OF HIS "MUST"

Brother Bennie

Lynchburg, Virginia

PRAISE FOR
MY FATHER'S BUSINESS

"It is with enthusiasm that I recommend *My Father's Business*. I have personally known the Mathews family and their faithful service in ministry for at least five decades. Their zealous commitment and integrity toward loving God, loving people, and the Greatest Commission remain unquestionable. The miraculous testimony of Brother Bennie and his pioneering missionary parents, Cherian and Grace Matthews—who, in brokenness, forsook all and by faith picked up their cross to follow Christ into the front lines of Gospel proclamation—will inspire and give every reader a clearer perspective to better understand what it means to live a Kingdom-consumed life, invested solely in eternity."

—Dr. Ajay B. Pillai
Director & General Secretary
India National Inland Mission (USA)

"Deeply inspiring and motivating. From 'none of my business' to decades of the 'Father's business,' Brother Bennie's journey witnesses the transformative power of the Gospel of Jesus Christ. For the Kingdom's business, let's GO share the love of Christ in India and China, the two most populous nations in our 'Father's world.'"

—Dr. Bob (Xiqiu) Fu
Founder & President, China Aid

"Brother Bennie is a man of God with an incredible gift of faith. Hebrews tells us "that without faith it is impossible to please God." The proportion of Bennie's faith is greater than anyone I have ever met. *My Father's Business* is the story of how Bennie has trusted God and become a person in whom He is well pleased. Bennie's life serves as a challenge to all of us to trust God and see His hand meet all of our needs."

—Pastor Butch Pursley
Senior Pastor, Maranatha Bible Church

"It gives me great joy to attest that this book, like its author and the ministry he leads, is the genuine article (1 Peter 1:7). This is the kind of authentic, unexaggerated, and God-glorifying testimony of faithfulness we should be reading. You will be inspired by the exemplary faith and faithfulness you encounter in these pages as you meet wonderful Christian brothers and sisters who joyfully pay any price to serve the Lord in difficult and dangerous circumstances."

—Cole Richards
President, The Voice of the Martyrs-USA

"Everyone who desires to be about their Father's business should read this book and gain a wealth of wisdom to build their faith to greater heights than ever before. Some of the stories will make you cry with joy as you see the faithfulness of God to a family that has sacrificed so much for the furtherance of the Kingdom. Your faith will soar as you plainly see what our great Lord can do with dedicated saints who follow Christ. I highly recommend this book. It will be a great resource and support for anyone that is about His Father's business."

—Dr. Dale Carver
President and Founder
GRAB (Gospel Reaching All Borders) the World Ministries

"The call to follow Christ is a challenge to lay down one's life—to live close to Golgotha. Yet what is inspiring about Brother Bennie's life and the stories in this book, of how God has revealed Himself in him and through his remarkable family, is to see resurrection power at work, time and again. His example moves and inspires. Through his story, I am left looking upward, to give thanks for Bennie's faithful testimony."

—David Campanale
International Broadcast News Reporter, The United Kingdom

"The title *My Father's Business* is a beautiful play on words. At the age of 12, Jesus told Mary and Joseph that He "must be about his Father's business." The story of Alpha Ministries is the story of sacrificial love and enduring obedience to the call of the Heavenly Father upon the Mathews family as they have generationally determined to be about the Father's business. But the "family business" of global evangelization has not come without a price. *My Father's Business* is the story of light chasing darkness, truth battling demonic strongholds, and the Lordship of Jesus Christ. I know the work, and I know the workers. And I can testify that they, above everything else, are about 'the Father's business.'"

—Dr. Dan Reichard
Far East Regional Director, Advancing Native Missions

"If anyone knows how to be about the Father's business, it is Brother Bennie. His walk with God is exemplary, his demeanor is humble, and his passion for the Lord is amazing. His new book will help us all focus more clearly on what it means to be about the Father's business. Don't miss it!"

—Dr. Ed Hindson
Dean Emeritus & Distinguished Professor of Religion,
Rawlings School of Divinity, Liberty University

"*My Father's Business* is an intimate, powerful, and inspiring memoir of Brother Bennie. With a touch of candor, Bennie writes about his quest for Christ-likeness in the 'real' life of a leader. He brings in his smallest and biggest experiences to engage us with exciting content that stretches our faith and strengthens our character in the pursuit of our Father's mission. Bennie weaves the ordinary stories of his joys and struggles into a tapestry that is utterly captivating to read."

—Dr. Finny Philip, Ph.D.
Author of *The Origins of Pauline Pneumatology and Editorial Director Christian Trends* & Board Member, Lausanne Movement International

"As one who has 'suffered for the sake of the Gospel,' it is my honor and privilege to call Brother Bennie my dear friend. Bennie's Father's 'business' is a total commitment to our Savior, Jesus Christ, and His finished work on Calvary. The spread of this 'business' has come at a great cost to their family! I am always amazed at the called-out few who work in hard places, far from comfort and safety. I am glad this heroic story has been written. I know it will encourage us, in turn, to see where we belong in our Heavenly Father's business! I recommend it heartily."

—Gracia Burnham
Author of *In The Presence of My Enemies* and *To Fly Again*
& Missionary, Ethnos360

"This book is a must-read! Acts of the Apostles today. The story of Papa and Mama Mathews is an example of a modern-day apostolic couple. They remind me of Priscilla and Aquila, the couple from the book of Acts. Just like them, Cherian and Grace Mathews have welcomed, housed, fed, taught, and impacted thousands of lives. In one of the hardest harvest fields on the face of the earth, they haven't just kept their faith despite the struggles, hunger, and rejection for over 50 years, but because of their faith, they were able to birth a move of God. Their lives are a testimony of conquering faith and having the true fear of God. And our almighty Father and King has shown Himself faithful on their behalf all the way. It is amazing to see how these seeds of faith are also manifesting through their children, which we are able to witness so vividly in our greatly appreciated friend Brother Bennie."

—Hrvoje & Ise Sirovina
Intl Gemeinde
Germany

"I first met Bennie at the turn of the new millennium in the historic city of Amsterdam. We were among the 10,000 evangelists who gathered to be encouraged to continue the work that Christ began on earth at His first coming. We quickly became good friends, especially when we realized that we both entered the 'family business' as pastors' sons. This book helped me understand more fully what a wonderful legacy we pass on to the next generation as we serve the Lord wholeheartedly as a family. And it is yet another testimony of how God's promise to Abraham continues to be worked out across the face of the earth, that through his faith "all the families of the earth will be blessed" (Gen. 12:3). May this book inspire you to likewise be about our Father's business in these urgent days, to bring the Good News of His unfailing love to all the families on this earth!"

—Dr. Jonathan Wong
Convener of Lay Leadership Training
Diocese of Singapore (Anglican)

"Proverbs 18:6 says, 'humility comes before honor.' That verse describes my good friend Brother Bennie. Bennie has been honored to be chosen as the leader of the amazingly far-reaching and effective Alpha Ministries, because, in his humility, God has given him wisdom and great favor in dealing with people and conveying to them His love and plan. My family always looks forward to having Bennie in our home because his humble spirit provides us an example of what can be accomplished through a man when he steps out of the way and lets God's light and power shine through. The book you are about to read will tell you a wonderful story of what God has done and is doing through a family that humbled itself and has continued to allow God to work through it. It's a marvelous story."

—Nathan Sanders
Businessman

"Do you ever wonder if God can use you? Have you ever wondered how to find your place in God's plan? My friend Brother Bennie wrestled with those questions. This book tells the gripping story of how God worked in Bennie's life to bring him to the forefront of spiritual advance in India and Africa. Bennie knows how to see God's fingerprints in the circumstances of life. I found this book highly inspiring because it reminds us that God still speaks to His children today. Read *My Father's Business* and then get ready for your life to change. May God use this book to raise up a new generation of men and women ready to do His will, no matter what it takes, wherever He leads, whatever it costs."

—Dr. Ray Pritchard
President, Keep Believing Ministries

"What happens when we decide to sell out completely and be committed to our Father's business of reaching the lost for Christ? In his new book, Brother

Bennie shares the deeply moving stories of the challenges his mom and dad faced and how God performed miracle after miracle when they relocated to an unreached region to preach the Gospel. In circumstances of severe hardship and persecution, God proved Himself to be faithful again and again. Having personally ministered in many different mission fields, I can say without hesitation that I have never known people who were more dedicated to the call of God and to raising up pastors and frontline leaders than the Mathews family. If you want proof that God honors sacrifice and that He responds to faith, read this book. If you desire to know whether or not prayer still works, open its pages and see the answer for yourself. But if you read it, be ready to be challenged—even changed. You cannot read *My Father's Business* and remain unmoved."

—Dr. R. Heard, Ph.D.
Founding Pastor, Inspire Church

"Having been to the areas of the world where Brother Bennie serves his Savior, I know the difficulties of doing ministry there. It takes a special breed, with a special calling and God's anointing, to be effective. When my wife and I first met Brother Bennie, and the following year his father, I could not believe the scope of their vision. I thought to myself, 'This can't be done by mortal man'. Yet today, 56 years later, the world is seeing the fulfillment of their vision. Alpha Ministries started with nothing and has done without for so long that the only answer for what their ministry has accomplished, and is accomplishing, can be attributed to the direct favor of God. This book *The Father's Business* is a mere glimpse into the life of sold-out, selfless servants of Almighty God and an inspiring example of what you, too, can do to bring men to Jesus. If you want to have your passion for the lost reignited, read this incredible account by Brother Bennie of sacrifice, faithfulness, and victory."

—Richard Headrick
President & CEO, The Headrick Companies

"Dr. Cherian Matthews remains a rare icon in the business of our Heavenly Father. His obedience to the call of God to leave the comfortable, familiar, and known environment in Kerala, South India, to go to the unknown, unfamiliar, and hostile environment in the North to spread the Good News of Jesus Christ inspired his wife and six children to follow in his footsteps. He has indeed commanded his children to serve God by his own example of obedience to and trust in God. The blossoming of Alpha Ministries is an eloquent and glowing tribute to his and his wife's faithfulness to God. That same faithfulness has trickled down to their children. May the Lord continue to prosper Alpha Ministries and use the ministry to advance our Father's business in the 10/40 window."

—Dr. Ruth C. Onukwue
Harmony Christian School, Restenburg, South Africa

"An applause from Heaven. I congratulate you, Brother Bennie, for articulating through this book your life journey with a focus on the eternal destination adopting a lifestyle of Christ-likeness. This book is truly an applause from Heaven, a testimony of the grit and courage of your parents who poured themselves as a drink offering for the cause of the Kingdom. In this book, we learn the flow of many dimensions of ministry forging ahead in spite of an environment of resistance to the Gospel. My prayer is that *My Father's Business* becomes an inspiration to many people to become an instrument in the hand of God to bring His Kingdom on Earth."

—Shekhar Kallianpur
Spiritual Philosopher & Author, Bombay, India

"Brother Bennie is the real deal. There are many today that speak the language of sacrifice, daily dependence on God for their provision, and living courageously by faith in God; however, precious few Christians consistently live these out. Brother Bennie is one of these precious few. *My Father's Business* walks us through Bennie's and his parents' adventure following God, and there isn't a dull moment in the whole book! It's incredibly encouraging to see a man whose life is absolutely in line with what he professes to believe. Bennie's life story serves as a fine example worth imitating as well as a megaphone shouting out just how good and mighty the God we serve is."

—Spence Hackney
Founder & President, Proclaim Interactive

"Without a doubt, one of the most unique and gifted spiritual giants I have been privileged to walk with is not one from the past, not one I have read about, but one I have walked with among the living. I have seen his dependence upon the Lord to provide for his every need, whether it be in the villages of India, the orphanages of Burma (Myanmar), the churches of Kenya, or the confines of his own home. I have personally observed a life of commitment that our Heavenly Father has miraculously blessed. By reading *My Father's Business*, you will be walking with a living, breathing spiritual giant. Brother Bennie, one that I am proud to call a friend, will inspire you to put your total trust in the One who will make a way when there seems to be no way. Praise the name of our blessed LORD!"

—Pastor J.D. Surbaugh, Jr.
Senior Pastor, Temple Baptist Church

"What a great title for a book, and an even greater pursuit for life. My appreciation for this theme begins with my own story, growing up in a pastor's home, much like Brother Bennie. I watched my father love God, and I learned to serve from his example. I love Jesus and His church — not always the case with pastors' kids — because of my father's character. But he never pressured me to follow in his steps; rather, he encouraged me to follow in my Father's steps. Brother Bennie and I both learned how to "be about our Father's business" from our earthly fathers, who have both gone to heaven. But this calling is not just for those in the pastorate — it's for every Christ follower. All of us, like Peter, James, John, have been invited to "drop the nets" of our earthly family business and to follow Him! You'll read about the faithfulness of both of our fathers in this book, but more importantly, you'll be encouraged to step into the Father's business for yourself."

—Dr. Matt Willmington
Executive Pastor of Ministry, Thomas Road Baptist Church

"I so appreciate Brother Bennie's willingness to honestly share both victories and defeats—the times he saw God work mightily and the times Bennie argued or complained. Bennie's story challenges each of us to surrender fully to our Father's plans for us, plans far greater than any we could make for ourselves."

—Todd Nettleton
Host, The Voice of the Martyrs Radio

"This incredible testimony, shared by my close friend and ministry partner of over 20 years, is raw, genuine, and vulnerable. Prepare to be convicted as you read about the victories and challenges of a family committed to their faith despite severe persecution. You will be both amazed and appalled by the stories shared, and inspired by how hearts and lives can be saved when you put your business in your Father's hands."

—Dr. Vernon Brewer
Founder, World Help

MY FATHER'S BUSINESS

MAKING THE MOST OF HIS "MUST"

MY FATHER'S BUSINESS
MAKING THE MOST OF HIS "MUST"

ISBN number: **978-0-578-23265-2**

Cover and Interior Design: Peter Roark at Roark Creative, www.roarkcreative.com

Printed in the United States of America.

Published by:

Alpha Ministries
P.O. Box 4563
Lynchburg, VA 24502-4563
434-929-2500
www.AlphaMinistries.com

CONTENTS

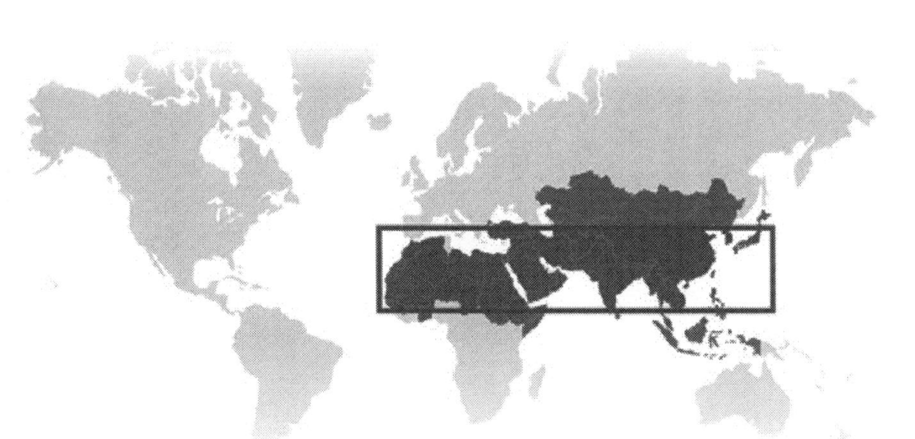

This book is dedicated to the thousands of frontline messengers who are working hard every day to make Jesus known in the 10/40 Window, many of whom are doing so without great fanfare or much financial reward. It is also dedicated to my parents' pioneer support team: my Uncle Daniel and Alikutty Mathai, Pastor CA Varghese and Aunt Moni Varghese, and the great Ammai Annamma and Uncle Thomas Mathai. One hundred percent of the royalties from this book will go directly toward training and providing for our frontline messengers in the 10/40 Window.

ACKNOWLEDGEMENTS

I cannot say thanks enough to each and every person who has made such a great impact in our lives over the years and have made this book possible.

I am grateful to many others who have helped me complete this book as well. I would first like to thank my wonderful and loving wife, Lina, for always being supportive of me and on-call with me to finish the task to which He has entrusted us. You are a God-sent mountain of support and strength in my life. I love you, and I love our children, Faith, Laramie, Ben, Elizabeth, Joy and William. Each of you has shown your love and support in the way you have consistently encouraged me to be available to God at all times. Thank you for standing with me in our commitment to reach this generation for the Lord Jesus Christ.

And of course, I thank my mother and father, whose faithfulness, persistence, sacrifice, and commitment to God and His people led me to a relationship with Him and made me believe I could do anything with His help. I must say thanks to my brothers and sister, Finny, Denny, Davis, Jimmy, and Lovely, and the rest of the Mathews family, including every child whose encouragement enabled me to persevere in the task that God has set out for me. My heartiest debt of gratitude and love to my affectionate mother-in-love, Mrs. Thresia Augustine, for her prayers coupled with an always encouraging attitude.

A lot has been accomplished toward the goal that God has set before us because of the concerted efforts of the entire A-Team led by my friend and brother, Pastor Nathan and Ammravati, Davis and Anila, Shiny and Toms, Sunita and Steven, Joel and Shalomi, Kartik and Sara, Ashish and Jennifer, Selvan and Selvi, Subodh, Yogesh, Bablu, Akash, Ragu, Prabu, Nepo, Sheikh, Toni, Leon, Raja, Sheelas, as well as hundreds of our frontline messengers.

I also want to thank my colleague Kelly, a God-sent blessing, who keeps the frontline team pressing forward in action, and "the maintenance guy and friend" Brian. No words can suffice to express my gratitude to you both.

Thanks also to friends Dr. Heard, Isa and Harvoje, Nathan and Judi, Ben and Linda, Richard and Gina, Dustin and Mitchell, Rich and Margaret, Dwight and Cindy, Mike and Connie, Spence and Tara, Mike and Mo, Jeff and Rashall, Pastor J.D. and Barbara, Blair and Angie, Glenn and Diane; without all of you, it would have been impossible to be where we are today.

Thank you, Heather, for helping me craft this book and turning my ideas and stories into reality. Your willingness, joyful spirit, and burden for Asia and the work of Alpha Ministries has blessed this book. Lina, Joy-Ruth, Lynn, Greg, and Tomi, for your help with editing to complete this work. May the Lord continue to bless all of you.

I also want to thank friends of Alpha Ministries and their families for their friendship and partnership, standing in the gap and lifting our hands to be victorious. And there are all of you—so many, who pray for me regularly and encourage me in a multitude of ways. I thank my church family in Baroda, India, and Madison Heights, Virginia, who helped me along the way. There are far too many to mention here.

Finally, a special word of thanks is directed to all unnamed others whose works, giving, and prayers continue to make the native church-planting movement a reality. I wish I could salute them all. Together, we give all the glory to the Lord of us all.

To Him alone—our Jehovah-Jireh, our El Shaddai—be the glory forever. Shalom! May God richly bless you!

Some names in this book have been changed or omitted to protect the privacy of the individuals concerned.

INTRODUCTION

The first memory I have of my father is seeing him pressed up against a wall, one hand of a militant religious fanatic gripping his neck while the other punched my father repeatedly in the face. My mother, having recently given birth to her third child, a daughter, stood helplessly nearby with tears streaming down her face. She pleaded with the man to stop as she held her newborn in her arms, while my terrified four-year-old brother clung to her legs. My Aunt Alice grabbed the fanatic's arm, trying in vain to stop his brutal attack. As the fist swung back again, my father held his Bible quietly in his hands, allowing the painful blows to land.

I was only six years old at the time, but I decided back then that my father was incapable of protecting himself, his family, or me. I was too young to understand the biblical concept of "power made perfect in weakness" or the strength it took to offer grace to those who neither wanted it nor deserved it. To me, my father's superhero status was very well hidden, and it took many years for me to fully comprehend the Holy Spirit power that enabled my father to respond the way he did.

I spent the next few decades of my life determined to take what I felt was his vacated place in our family. I endeavored to fill his shoes by earning the money we desperately needed and providing the protection I had always wished he would provide. I knew my father's God was real, but I wasn't interested in his particular brand of faith. In my young eyes, my father knew nothing about business or the "real world."

After all, my father's only "business" was preaching the Gospel of Jesus Christ. Every day, he traveled from town to town on a bicycle that doubled as my family's only method of transportation for 18 years. When he would reach a new town, he would hand out Gospel tracts, host and serve new believers, and preach to his countrymen (most of whom worshipped 36 million other gods and goddesses) about the one true God. Eventually, my father started a church, and a Bible institute and IMPACT leadership training was born. The results of that training by 2013 would include 27,000 trained and equipped frontline messengers, 16,000 church-planting stations, over 700 orphaned and impoverished children housed and fed in children's homes, and countless thousands attending children's Bible classes or clubs each week across Asia and Africa. His work overflowed beyond the borders into Nepal, Burma, and Africa.

As I said, it would be decades before I would realize and understand the true power and integrity of my father. As a small boy, I was so heavily focused on the growing pains that accompany a start-up family ministry that I could not picture the glorious future my father and his God could clearly see. Their business made no sense to me. It generated no money and made me unpopular with my friends. In fact, it made our entire family look foolish to everyone around us. The people in town knew us as the "South Indian priest with all the children" or the "Hallelujah man with all the children." I have to admit that I struggled through intense embarrassment over the ministry.

As a result, I resolved to follow a different "business plan." I set my eyes on money and worldly success and focused all my efforts on achieving those goals. Although my motivation was generally to support my family, I knew to a very deep level that my true motives were self-serving. Like the words of Frank Sinatra's song,

I decided I would do it "my way."

What about you? How have you spent your life doing business? Have you done it your way? Have you focused on success and on planning and working toward what you must do to achieve it? What is your business plan? Many people want a business plan that will give them:

A good job
Security
A nice home
A comfortable income
Good health
A beautiful, educated, talented/athletic family
Friends and popularity

People who have these things are often respected by the world and regarded as "successful." When I was growing up, my father rejected this sort of plan. He possessed none of the things listed above (except for the beautiful family, of course) and worked by a completely different business plan:

> *But in all things we commend ourselves as ministers of God: in much patience, in tribulations, in needs, in distresses, in stripes, in imprisonments, in tumults, in labors, in sleeplessness, in fastings; by purity, by knowledge, by longsuffering, by kindness, by the Holy Spirit, by sincere love, by the word of truth, by the power of God, by the armor of righteousness on the right hand and on the left, by honor and dishonor, by evil report and good report; as deceivers, and yet true; as unknown, and*

> *yet well known; as dying, and behold we live; as chastened, and yet not killed; as sorrowful, yet always rejoicing; as poor, yet making many rich; as having nothing, and yet possessing all things.*
>
> **—2 Corinthians 6:4-10**

This Scripture is the opposite of the average business plan. Things like hardships, hunger, and beatings do not sound like a plan for success, but rather one for failure. However, that is the life I remember from my childhood. It was, and is, my father's business. He learned it from his Heavenly Father and was gracious enough to teach it to me.

Jesus understood. Jesus was also about His Father's business. It was the only plan that made sense to Him and the one for which He would give His life. As an adult, He knew hard work, sleepless nights, and hunger. He was homeless and a man of sorrows, yet always rejoicing. He was poor, yet made many rich. As Jesus told the young man on the road to Jerusalem, "Foxes have holes and birds of the air have nests, but the Son of Man has nowhere to lay His head" (Luke 9:58).

By the common measurements of man, Jesus' earthly life was a failure; "though He was rich, yet for your sakes, He became poor, that you through His poverty might become rich" (2 Cor. 8:9). However, no man can be said to have had a greater influence. "And having been perfected, He became the author of eternal salvation to all who obey Him" (Hebrews 5:9).

Jesus' life was spent doing nothing but contributing to the most significant business the world has ever known…His Father's!

It took a long time, but I eventually came to appreciate and understand the importance of dedicating my life's work to God. Today, I happily work for both of my fathers—my earthly father and my Heavenly Father. It is a business I would not trade for anything. Looking back, I see now that in the moments where I thought we had nothing, we truly possessed everything. My father knew. It was his business to know, and nothing could beat it out of him.

This is my story of picking up his business.

PART ONE

NONE OF MY BUSINESS

Even as a 12-year-old boy, Jesus demonstrated the maturity it would take me many years to find. Luke 2:41-49 tells the story of Jesus, the carpenter's son, recognizing His true profession and the moment it became clear that He would take after His Father.

> *His parents went to Jerusalem every year at the Feast of the Passover. And when He was twelve years old, they went up to Jerusalem according to the custom of the feast. When they had finished the days, as they returned, the Boy Jesus lingered behind in Jerusalem. And Joseph and His mother did not know it; but supposing Him to have been in the company, they went a day's journey, and sought Him among their relatives and acquaintances. So when they did not find Him, they returned to Jerusalem, seeking Him. Now so it was that after three days they found Him in the temple, sitting in the midst of the teachers, both listening to them and asking them questions. And all who heard Him were astonished at His understanding and answers. So when they saw Him, they were amazed; and His mother said to Him, "Son, why have You done this to us? Look, your father and I have sought You anxiously."*
>
> *And He said to them, "Why did you seek Me? Did you not know that I must be about My Father's business?"*
>
> **—Luke 2:41-49**

Jesus knew that the work of His Heavenly Father was more important than any other. It was obvious from childhood to adulthood that His primary concern was His Father's business. Today, many Christians justify their choices and lifestyles to merely sprinkle aspects of their faith into their business of choice without ever really investing in the Father's business at all.

I was one of those Christians.

Since then, I have learned that the secret to leading a truly successful Christian life is to mind more of God's business and less of my own. My father knew this secret, but it took me many years to discover it. I stubbornly traveled my own path toward the life I thought I wanted until God graciously brought me around to His way of doing business. By His grace, I have never turned back.

CHAPTER 1

THE HERITAGE

His [Jesus'] parents went to Jerusalem every year at the Feast of the Passover.
Luke 2:41

The Son of God started His life on earth as the son of a man—the son of a good and faithful man, it seems. We do not think much about Joseph, Jesus' earthly father, until Christmas time, and then, he is usually forgotten until the following December.

However, what we know of Joseph shows that he was a man of great character and integrity. He made the difficult decision to stand up to his family and his culture by marrying a woman of whom they did not approve. He obeyed the law when the government required everyone to travel to the town of his heritage for a census, though it was inconvenient with a wife nearing her due date for her firstborn child. When he, Mary, and a very young Jesus were forced to flee to Egypt as refugees, Joseph learned a new language and found a way to support his family in a new land. He continued to worship his God though they were foreigners in a country historically hostile to his people and his faith. Through difficulty, hardship, inconvenience, and pain, Joseph did his best to make wise and necessary decisions for his family. Even by the time, Jesus was 12 years old, Joseph was still leading his family in righteousness, going up to Jerusalem as all faithful Jews did during Passover. The earthly heritage he left his son was one of obedience, faithfulness, and courage.

When I think of my father, he is not so different. Born Cherian Mathews, son of a farmer and brother to eight siblings, he was raised in the southern part of India, where tradition shapes the attitudes and culture of people in a way that runs deep into the core of who they are. Rich in history, the tales of the region that my father was raised in say Thomas the Apostle (doubting Thomas) was martyred in Southern India and that the 12 disciples, desiring to preach the Gospel to the uttermost parts of the earth, divided the world into sections and cast lots to determine who would go into each part. Thomas traveled farthest of all the disciples to the east of Syria and is said to have landed in India. Can you imagine how long it must have taken him to travel to India in those days? Even though he is nicknamed "Doubting Thomas," he was also called Jesus' twin because he imitated the Lord (John 20:24). He was so close to Jesus; he was willing to go and die when they learned about Lazarus's death:

> *Then Jesus said to them plainly, "Lazarus is dead. And I am glad for your sakes that I was not there, that you may believe. Nevertheless, let us go to him."*
>
> *Then Thomas, who is called the Twin, said to his fellow disciples, "Let us also go, that we may die with Him."*
>
> **— John 11:14-16**

Thomas was the first person to address Jesus as, "My Lord my God." He knew He was the Messiah. Thomas had a passion for imitating Jesus as if he were his twin. Eventually, despite his momentary doubt, Thomas's heart connected with his Lord, and his faith took him to the uttermost. His boldness and passion drove him to travel the farthest distance and share the good news. It is said that he founded the Church of Mar Thoma (still in existence today), that he was killed by four soldiers with spears, and is believed to be buried in South Indian soil. Accordingly, the Syrian Orthodox Church has been an influence in southern India for nearly 2,000 years. Today, if you laid a stick across a map of India, you would see that nearly 85% of all Christians live in the south, and only 15% live in the north.

My father, like his father, grandfather, and great-grandfather before him, grew up in the Orthodox Church and was considered to be a "Christian" by his culture's definition. Without any doubt, he would have continued in that tradition, had God not shown him another way.

ACCEPTED AND THEN REJECTED

One day, as a young man, my father left his home to go for a job interview. While waiting for the bus, the only means of transportation available to him at the time, he heard a random group of people singing and clapping farther up the road. Out of curiosity, he went to investigate and found a group of excited believers in Jesus talking about their faith in a way my father had never heard before. Their music and vibrant passion for what they believed intrigued him and created within him a great excitement for God that he had never experienced. He missed his bus that afternoon but could not have cared less. That very day, my father gave his life to Jesus Christ and vowed to follow Him for the rest of his days.

Later that evening, when he returned home, my grandfather began to inquire about the job interview anxiously. "I did not go," my father told him, and cheerfully explained that he had received something much greater than a job. He had received new life in Christ.

His father, a traditional Orthodox Christian, was unimpressed, to say the least. "They are radicals," he said of the believers my father had met. He warned his son to stay away from them. As a farmer with nine children, my grandfather needed as many of his children to contribute to the family income as possible. There was no time or tolerance for messing around with a radical religious life.

My father, a man of honor and integrity even then, agreed to continue working for his father on their farm as a way to honor him but would continue to meet with his new Christian friends often. As he grew in his faith, he learned much about the Word of God and discovered that the Bible said he must be baptized as a means to publicly profess his faith, and so he was.

The news of his baptism reached my grandfather before my father had the chance to explain what his baptism meant rationally. Furious, his father met him at the door that day and began to exclaim, "I heard that you had done this disgraceful thing—is it true?"

"Yes," my father answered. "I have trusted in God, and I was baptized."

"You have humiliated me and defiled my name in this community," my grandfather spit at his son. "I cannot take you into my house!"

"I'm sorry you feel that way," my father answered with great courage and conviction, "but this is biblical. What am I supposed to do?"

"Wash it off with hot water," my grandfather demanded. "If you wash it off right now, I will take you back into my home and receive you again as my son."

My father confidently stood his ground and refused.

"Then I'll have nothing to do with you," my grandfather said resolutely. "From this point on, you have no family. Who will allow their daughter to marry you? You will never have children. You will have nothing but your radical religion. Get out of my sight." The door to my father's family slammed shut at every level, and he was left holding only his Bible. My father turned and walked away.

PURPOSE DRIVEN CALL —A MAN NAMED MATTHEW

The Lord called my father, and he left everything, just like Matthew 9:9, and never looked back. The scripture says, "Jesus walks on, he sees Matthew, who is also called Levi, sitting at the tax office." Jesus extends a wonderful invitation to him: "Be my follower." Matthew, the tax-collector, left his table and his lucrative trade, to become almost a beggar, sustaining himself on the sometimes meager contributions made to his Rabbi or Master. For Matthew, following Jesus was a considerable sacrifice; if this courageous decision was a failure, he could not go back. He did not give up collecting taxes for the Romans on a whim and expect ever to return. Matthew burnt his bridges to follow Jesus and never looked back. Having responded to Jesus' call, Matthew would spend the rest of His life learning God's truth, implementing its principles, and partnering with God in the expansion of His eternal kingdom. "No one can come to me unless the Father who sent me draws him" (John 6:44).

Like Matthew, my father left everything, took up the Bible, and followed Jesus to the new life. Having responded to Jesus' call, my father would spend the rest of his life learning God's truth, implementing its principles and spiritual practices of prayer, servanthood, generosity, contentment, and encouragement. The changed life displayed God's power and revealed His purposes. My father cared more than people thought was wise, risked more than what was safe, and dreamed more than was practical. He lived this way because he had no joy outside of knowing Jesus and serving Him.

Along with Paul, he could confidently say, "But what things were gain to me, these I have counted loss for Christ. Yet indeed I also count all things loss for the excellence of the knowledge of Christ Jesus my Lord, for whom I have suffered the loss of all things, and count them as rubbish, that I may gain Christ" (Philippians 3:7-8).

PURPOSE DRIVEN WOMAN —THE GIFT OF GRACE

My father's new friends cared for him and found a place for him to stay. It was like the early church period that we read about in Acts 4:32-35:

> *Now the multitude of those who believed was of one heart and one soul; neither did anyone say that any of the things he possessed was his own, but they had all things in common. And with great power, the apostles gave witness to the resurrection of the Lord Jesus. And great grace was upon them all. Nor was there anyone among them who lacked; for all who were possessors*

> *of lands or houses sold them, and brought the proceeds of the things that were sold, and laid them at the apostles' feet, and they distributed to each as anyone had need.*

Before long, my father learned about a nearby Bible college through his association with his new church family and eagerly yearned for a formal education in the Word of God. He eventually enrolled there and began taking his first steps toward the lifelong ministry that awaited him.

Although his earthly father had cursed him, his Heavenly Father had blessing after blessing in store for Cherian Mathews. One of those blessings was a beautiful young woman named Grace. She had been raised in a loving home with parents who honored God.

God began drawing Grace to Himself early in her childhood through signs and visions. At the young age of five years old, she saw a divine vision sent from God; it was Jesus, up in the sky, inviting her to follow Him. Later, when she was eight years old, she saw the words, "I am the Light of the world; follow the Light," written in fire on the wall of a room where she was resting. She always remembered those visions and spent her life following Jesus, the Light. She was fully surrendered to Him, lived by faith, and prayed daily.

My mother and father first met while they were attending the same Bible college. The dating culture in India, specifically in those days, was very different than the dating culture in the Western world today. Young men and women did not just meet each other and fall in love. A wedding in the traditional Indian sense was more of a business transaction than a romantic affair. Families haggled, negotiated, gossiped, and involved themselves in every area of the happy couple's lives. The bride and groom's feelings for one another or romantic interests were not nearly as important as the respective family's opinions of one another.

That cultural tradition is why my grandfather thought he had cursed my father to a life with no family of his own and excruciating societal exile. My grandfather knew that no respectable Indian family would let their daughter marry a man who had been rejected by his own family for following a radical religion. However, my grandfather did not know the Bible and, because of that, did not understand the story of Joseph and his brothers, and what the Scriptures said about their actions: "But as for you, you meant evil against me; but God meant it for good, in order to bring it about as it is this day, to save many people alive" (Genesis 50:20).

Grace's parents, on the other hand, had been praying that she would marry a godly young man who would willingly guide her as a spiritual leader and care for her the way Christ cares for His church. If they had met my father's family as Indian culture typically dictates, they probably would not have given their daughter to a man raised under such dogma and blatant lack of spiritual fullness. But, God is the one who orders the steps of man, and in sending my father away from his family, my grandfather actually freed him to marry this beautiful woman of faith.

In 1963, my mother's parents were more than happy to give her to my father in marriage. One year later, I came along to make them parents for the first time and to put their faith to the test in an extremely tangible way. I will tell you much, much more about that in the chapters to come. First, let me tell you about the amazing foundation God created in this simple Indian couple of great faith and obedience.

My parents have both been deeply involved in God's business and were known to always serve Him in singleness or marriage, with children or without. Their reputation has always been as people of service, people who gave, people who cared for others. Their desires in every circumstance have been for evangelism and for reaching others.

JUST A FEW LOAVES AND FISH

Just as obedience to God's Word was always at the forefront of my father's heart, service to Him was always in my mother's. She knew how to feed and to take care of people better than anyone I knew, so that is precisely what she did. That is what her life was about. Growing up, she cared for her three brothers, one sister, and many others within their community. She had a love and a natural gift for the ministry, so when she was grown, God gave her to my father. Together, they made an outstanding team, where my father acted as the heart of the ministry, and my mother the backbone.

When they were first married, my parents served the Lord in the South Indian state called Kerala. My father was working with a church in a nearby village, and my mother, as always, was serving alongside him. Both of them believed mightily in the God of the Bible, the God who does not change, the God who still works miracles, the God who is always on time!

In 1963, there was an evangelistic crusade held at their church, and many prominent speakers of the day were invited to come and preach. The congregation of the church was made up of about 40 people, most of whom were laborers in a nearby tea plantation. As the date of the crusade drew near, a strike was declared at the tea gardens where most of the church family was employed. Finances had already been tight, and cash flow in the church had slowed from a trickle to a standstill. There was nothing to be collected for the crusade, and the situation began to look bleak.

The day of the crusade arrived. The community was excited, and the crusade team, made up of perhaps 40 to 50 people, was ready to see God work despite the difficult financial circumstances. My mother was working in the kitchen with four or five other women from the church where they were tasked with preparing lunch for the entire crusade. However, there was a problem there was no food available to be prepared for the crusade at all.

My mother responded as she always did: in prayer. She gathered all the women in the kitchen together to intercede on behalf of the difficult situation, and then, they took the largest cooking pot they had and placed it over the fire. As they filled it with water, they continued to pray, asking God for a miracle. One of the women produced a few packets of rice that some children had placed in the offering at Sunday School. It was barely half a kilogram (about two cups), not even enough to feed a handful of people, but they put it in the large pot of water and continued to pray. Some other ladies went to a nearby forest to pick some wild spinach and began cooking it as a side dish. While they prepared it, they prayed.

Soon it was time to eat. When my mother and the other women went to the large rice pot, they saw that it was filled to the brim! The entire crusade team and all the workers ate well that day. The God who fed the multitudes in Israel 2,000 years earlier with five loaves of bread and two fish fed a body of believers gathered for the Kerala crusade in India in 1963 with half a kilogram of rice. This was indeed a miracle of biblical proportions.

Later that year, my parents were traveling together to a Bible school in Pampadi, Kottayam, for a few months of Bible training. When they first set out on the trip, my mother thought my father must have been carrying money for the journey—but my father thought my mother had it. They did not discover their misunderstanding until they were already at the bus station far from home.

When they realized what had happened, they saw they only had 75 paise (barely a penny in U.S. currency), not enough to make it even halfway to the Bible school. It wasn't even enough to go back home, and even if they could, their relatives had made it difficult for them to leave in the first place, so they knew going back was not an option. God had called them to go, so going forward was their only choice. They sat for a few minutes to think, but more importantly, to pray.

My father suddenly said, "There is a pastor I know staying nearby. We should go and see him." Within the culture of believers, then, very much like the early Church in Acts chapter 2, it was common for Christians to meet the needs of one another. They understood that Jehovah Jireh, the God who provides, is the one who provided everything they had and that often times, He would use what He had given them to provide for others. My parents were hoping that this pastor could help them get to Pampadi, Kottayam.

When they reached the pastor's house, they found his wife weary and tired in the kitchen. Her three children were sitting on the floor in the room where the pastor held church services. My mother knelt down beside the children to inquire why they looked so sad and weary. Their eyes were swollen from crying for a long time.

"Why are you crying?" my mother gently asked the oldest one. He sniffled and wiped his eyes. He was about eight years old.

"My mother hasn't given us any food to eat. We did not eat breakfast, and we did not eat lunch. We haven't eaten anything all day, and we are hungry."

My parents immediately realized that this pastor and his family did not have anything at all, not even food to feed their children. My mother took the 75 paise out of her handkerchief and handed it to the oldest boy, telling him, "Go now, go quickly and buy some rice."

My father prayed for the pastor and his family so that God would strengthen them, encourage them, and bless their ministry. He and my mother then returned to the bus station, without any money at all, and sat down to wait and pray.

All of a sudden, they saw a man frantically waving his arms from one of the bus windows. Confused, they looked around to see if he was waving at someone behind them, as they had no idea who he was. The man continued to point and wave, calling to my parents. The bus was in a waiting lane, and the driver had gone for a tea break, so they finally went to speak to the man.

As they got closer, the man got very excited.

"Do you not recognize me?" he said to my mother. My mother confessed she did not. "That doesn't matter," he said. "I am your relative." He went on to explain how they were related and talked about family and about God. Before long, the driver returned from his tea (not an extremely uncommon occurrence in India), and the bus was ready for departure. The man blessed my parents, laid his hands on them, and prayed for them. Then, as he was leaving to go on his way, he handed my mother a handkerchief as the bus pulled away, and he was gone.

Inside the handkerchief was enough money to go to the

Bible school and back, meeting all of my parents' expenses along the way. It was truly a miracle, and my parents learned in a very incredible way that day that they could never out-give God. The little they had given by faith was returned to them in double measure. They were aware that Jehovah Jireh was on their journey with them, for they had seen Philippians 4:19 come to life: "And my God shall supply all your needs according to His riches in glory by Christ Jesus."

STRANGERS IN A STRANGE LAND

My father had officially dedicated his entire life to full-time ministry in 1961. At that time, the Holy Spirit clearly spoke to his heart and told him that, like Abraham, he would have to leave his family, his land, and go to a place God alone would show him (Genesis 12:1-3). To man's way of thinking, what God asked Abraham to do was extremely difficult, but God had plans to greatly bless him and his generation.

Just after I was born, God fulfilled that prophecy in my father's life.

Although my mother and father were faithfully serving and enjoying a fruitful ministry in South India, my father knew in his heart of hearts that God had called him elsewhere. In North India, the stakes were high for those who decided to proclaim the Gospel, and the unfriendliness that missionaries and pastors would receive was not something to take lightly.

In India, there are 15 major languages spoken along with 1,500 dialects, with each state having several languages of its own. These languages are not like accents or the regional slang of the English language to which the people living in the United States or Great Britain are accustomed. These are languages completely different from one another. So, when an opportunity to participate in a language-training program in Itarsi (North India) became available to my father, he had to make the very difficult decision to leave my mother and me in Kerala to go and get trained. He understood that this was God opening up an incredible opportunity for them and for the calling on his life to be fulfilled.

He was gone for several months and was often unable to communicate with my mother at all due to the fact that communication by mail was very difficult in India in those days—plus, my father's schedule was extremely rigorous. My mother, who was expecting her second child at that time, decided it was time that the family reunite once more and be together, so she made plans for us to go to him. She sent him a letter telling him that we were on our way and began making the arrangements.

By faith, she said good-bye to her family and friends, and we boarded a bus bound for a town from where we could make a connection to a train heading to Itarsi. However, once we reached the town, she only had seven rupees left due to the unexpected expenses of the trip. I was just 18 months old and fully dependent on my mother for any need I had. I became hungry upon our arrival to the town that day, but my mother did not have money to buy food for me with enough left over for the train tickets. We sat down on a bench at the station, and she prayed. "I'll just wait here and see what God will do," she thought.

Soon, a family friend of ours named Pastor P. M. Philip was passing by and noticed my mother and I sitting at the train station looking visibly troubled. He chatted with my mother and asked if she had been able to purchase a train ticket. She felt embarrassed to tell him that she was unable. After making some casual conversation with my mom, he said good-bye and was on his way. My mother, still without a ticket, was very worried but attempted to strengthen herself with the promises of God and remain calm.

Just before the train arrived at the station, another family friend—this time, a man who happened to be a well-known businessman—hurriedly approached her.

"There you are!" he exclaimed happily. My mother was surprised because she knew of no reason that he would be expecting to see us at the train station. Through her confusion, she was able to muster up a soft smile to cover the initial shock in her facial expression. He laughed and began to explain what had happened. Earlier that morning, he was praying, and God spoke to him three separate times, telling him he had a ministry to do at the railway station. He had already come to the station several times but had found nothing out of the ordinary and had returned to his office, confused and doubting. When he arrived at the station for the fifth time that day and found us sitting there, he knew that God had sent him to minister to my mother and me.

After hearing my mother explain the difficult situation we found ourselves in, he immediately purchased our train tickets and some food for me without hesitation. He then gave us money for our journey and sent us off with a blessing. He praised the Lord all the way back to his office, just as my mother praised the Lord all the way to Itarsi.

Due to the difficulty in transporting mail in India, the letter my mother had written to my father informing him we were coming to be with him arrived the same day we did. Astonished, he rushed to the railway station to pick us up, surprised, happy, and concerned all at the same time. "What are you doing here?" he said to my mother while embracing his bride. "Why did you just leave like that? I don't have anywhere for us to live." As another answer to prayer, Dr. Kurien Thomas, the founder of Central India Bible College, was gracious to accommodate our family with housing at their campus.

The following week at CIBC, they had their Annual Fellowship Conference and Convention. My parents planned to wait until the conference was over before making a concrete future plan on where they would move. At the conference, they were fortunate enough to meet Pastor K. T. Thomas. My parents had previously heard of him and his ministry in Delhi and were very much aware of the work he was doing. They also were able to meet another acquaintance named Pastor C. J. Mathew from Ahmedabad.

Being so far away from home, in distant North India, they were blessed to encounter these mighty men of God. My parents had the opportunity to share their heart's cry and burden for the people of North India. They took their time to carefully articulate their heart's desire to reach and help those spiritually lost in North India. The new friends were deeply moved by the testimonies of bold acts of faith and how God moved and worked so miraculously with my mother in providing for the three-day journey by train to come to Itarsi. It was an awe-inspiring moment for Pastor K. T. Thomas and Pastor C. J. Mathew. Deep down, they knew the Lord was with my parents' vision and mission to share the Gospel of Jesus Christ. Together, they were able to pray and share a lot during that week at the conference. Pastor K. T. shared the need of the Gospel in Baroda and mentioned that one of his distant relatives named N. M. Thomas was living in Baroda at the time. Pastor C. J. was ministering in Ahmedabad, which was only 120 kilometers away from Baroda. So Pastor K. T. suggested my parents travel with them to Ahmedabad. This afforded our family an opportunity for stability, as my mother and I would stay with Pastor C. J.'s family until my father could go to Baroda and find a suitable place to settle.

PREPARING TO LAUNCH —TO THE UTTERMOST (ACTS 1:8)

My parents clearly saw that God was orchestrating this plan. The Lord was also providing a pioneer field, the first contact who knew the town they wished to work in, the opportunity to secure a proper living arrangement, and the ability to establish a church. My parents traveled with Pastor K. T. and C. J. to Ahmedabad. The following Sunday, my mother and I attended the Sunday morning church service at Pastor C. J.'s church. They asked my mother to share her testimony about how the Lord had graciously provided for all of our needs. After the service, my mother was able to meet one of her distant cousins and aunts at church. They were very excited to meet her and to hear about the call my parents had on their lives for the unreached region of North India. They were kind enough to invite my mother to come and stay with them until my father returned from Baroda.

While living with her relatives in Ahmedabad, my mother thought, "I should not be living 120 kilometers away from my husband since God has called us to Baroda. I should join him and be his helper!" Feeling led by the Lord and wanting to serve Him and her family well, she felt led to travel to Baroda to join him. With a lot of bravery, my mother boarded us onto the first train to Baroda. My mother's aunt was very gracious to her and gave her 30 rupees for the journey. That was a lot of money in those days and would act as a tremendous blessing for the trip. She had no fear despite the fact that she was pregnant and traveling with a young lad of only 18 months old. Her mind was set to be with her husband, and she knew her calling.

When we arrived at the Baroda station, she realized the local people spoke a different language, and she was unable to understand or communicate with them. She cried out to God in prayers as she waited anxiously at the station. She knew the Lord would answer her prayer, and He brought a young man who spoke my mother's language, Malayalam, to help us. My mother explained that my father was living with N. M. Thomas, and the man knew where he lived. She was amazed to see the faithfulness of God once more. We took a rickshaw through the town and reached N. M. Thomas's house, where my father was residing with other bachelor friends. My father did not know what to do about this situation, but he totally understood my mother's desire to keep the family together. Though he was very excited to see us, he was even more concerned about our lack of housing. My mother understood the problem and suggested he look for houses in the neighboring town that she had just traveled through on the train. Taking her advice, they visited the new town and were successful in finding a house that could accommodate us all.

While this occurrence seems to be extraordinary to most people, to my family, it was total dependence on God and a testament to my mother's incredible amount of faith.

Like Joseph, Jesus' earthly father, my father married a woman no one in his family expected him to. She was willing to travel while pregnant in order to stay close to her husband, and although they ended up living in a state that was hostile to them and to their faith, my father showed himself to be a man of tremendous character. He learned a new language (no easy task for anyone) and worked hard to provide for his family as he continued to worship God, following Him in all areas of his life.

Both of my parents were committed to the business of their Heavenly Father. The heritage they established, even before the arrival of their children, was one of obedience, faithfulness, and courage.

With such a foundation, it would seem nearly impossible for me to stray and create difficulty in my own life.

However . . .

CHAPTER 1

APPLICATION POINTS

Are you about the Father's business, or do your own affairs seem to get in the way?

Many books have been written and seminars held for those seeking to know the secret to a "successful Christian life." However, one needs to look no further than Jesus. He modeled the secret for us throughout His earthly life. The secret is simply learning to focus more on God's business and less on our own.

Jesus knew the work of His Heavenly Father was more important than any other.

The Lord's primary concern, even as a young boy, was His Father's business. Jesus was raised by earthly parents who had also learned to be about God's business. Joseph left his children a heritage of obedience, faithfulness, and courage.

Even if you did not come from a Christian family, it is not too late to focus on the Father's business.

Remember, the day my father was baptized, his father completely cut him off from the family, calling him a disgrace. My father walked away with nothing but his Bible, and for the rest of his days, he demonstrated a life surrendered to Christ.

When you face challenges, do you focus on the challenge or on the Father?

When you focus on the problem, you will become overwhelmed in the details and can miss what God is about to do. You will be prone to take matters into your own hands, or worse, throw in the towel. Wait. Pray. Trust Him.

When you're about the Father's business, He provides the wages—the needs are met.

Time and again, I saw my mother pray and wait, and God sent the answer. This very same God is ready to do great things in your life as you surrender to Him and trust His leading in every detail.

CHAPTER 2

CHILDHOOD

And when He was twelve years old, they went up to Jerusalem according to the custom of the feast.
Luke 2:42

Mary and Joseph went up to Jerusalem at Passover-time to obey the teachings of the Law. It was not simply a custom; remembering the miracles God had performed in the days of Moses was foundational to their faith. Too many Hebrew generations had forgotten Moses' words of caution, and Israel had paid for their memory lapse with decades of captivity and foreign occupation. Jesus went up to Jerusalem with His parents to learn the practices and traditions of Judaism, just as Mary and Joseph had with their parents when they were children. Worship was a family affair, and in my home, it was no different.

My parents did not have traditional "jobs" like my friend's parents. There was no office or factory to head to in the mornings, no regular paychecks, and no holidays. Their life was ministry, and ministry was their life. They were called to work in the field that Jesus said was "white unto harvest," and my siblings and I had no choice but to follow them into that field whether we shared their vision and passion or not.

For me, it was a mixed experience. I saw God constantly at work and was able to witness Him provide for us time and time again. I never doubted the Bible stories my mother read to us throughout my life and knew that the lessons found in them would greatly benefit me if I chose to apply them. Life without the Bible or without prayer was foreign to me, but as a fish with no appreciation for water, I was not thankful for the life-giving power of the faith that surrounded me. Many times, in fact, I resented it.

However, God's faithfulness is not determined by our own. He is faithful, no matter how faithless we are, and His goodness is not diminished by our sinfulness. As a child, I was continually exposed to the goodness of God, and what I was able to witness would shape and mold me forever.

NEW IN TOWN —LAYING DOWN OUR LIVES (JOHN 10:11-15)

When my parents first moved to Baroda, they felt the weight of being strangers in a strange land in the fullest sense. While the majority of southern India claims to be Orthodox Christian, the faith of northern India is Hinduism, and my parents were considered to be outcasts even before they ever had a chance to begin developing a Christian community of their own.

Hinduism began around 1500 BC when invaders from the West conquered the Indus Valley civilization singing Vedas (songs about sacrifices to gods and the relationships between god and man). Those Vedas formed the basis for Hindu literature. Hinduism has no one founder and no single unifying philosophy or tradition. It is a religion with millions of gods and goddesses. Ancient tradition shows that there is one deity for each individual Hindu. The belief system, with its unique culture and worldview, greatly impacted my parents as they began to interact with the people of North India. Their pantheistic way of life was so contrary to Christianity!

Many Hindus worship their own village god or goddess. In that way, Hinduism is lived out on more of a local level than a universal level. While the gods and goddesses they worship are distinct from one another, there is also a belief that every deity is a manifestation of one god, Brahma. In fact, Hinduism teaches that all living souls are part of Brahma, like drops of water in a great ocean, and that each soul goes through several life cycles or reincarnations. Finally, through their good deeds and faithfulness to Hindu teaching, Hindus reach a new level of existence called moksha, and their souls dissolve into the universe.

Because Hindus believe in reincarnation, they believe in a hierarchical caste system. The life circumstances one is born to represent the consequences (for good or bad) of a life lived before the current one. This is why Hindus are vegetarians—they believe every living soul has landed somewhere on the reincarnation continuum, and humans in this life do not want to end up as someone's hamburger in the next. They call the impersonal force in the universe governing this process karma. As a result, if a Hindu is in need, it is common that other Hindus feel no compulsion to help him.

There are five classes in the caste system: three which cower beneath those above them while they lord over those below, one that is above all, and one that is untouchable. Therefore, to pity or to help the poor (the untouchables) is uncommon because Hindus assume they are being punished for a previous life by the situation they have been born into. Those who are rich and powerful are respected, for surely (again, Hindus assume) they must have lived very good lives before they were born.

THE HUMBLE BEGINNING —HOW SHALL THEY HEAR? (ROMANS 10:17)

For my parents, who grew up in southern India in an area predominantly influenced by the Christian faith, this drastic move to a state where 0.5% were Christians held unanticipated blessings and difficulties. My mother and father had been concerned that as southerners, it would be difficult for them to find a home in the north and dreaded the possibility of being severely discriminated against because of their faith. They knew northerners were very strict about the caste system and would never rent a house to a family that was considered to be from a lower caste. But when the people in Gujarat saw that my mother was very fair and beautiful, they assumed she was a Brahmin, the highest of all, castes. Because of this assumption, they rented a one-room house for our family. Though we were very poor, there was no issue renting the house. The only requirement was that we could not eat meat, a standard requirement of the Brahmin Hindu sect.

My parents "had nothing and yet possessed everything" because their joy was always in sharing the Gospel and serving the people. My mother made roti (Indian bread) using an empty oil bottle as a rolling pin because she did not own any kitchen utensils other than a couple of pots. During the day, my mom and dad walked many miles in the hot sun going to the villages passing out Christian tracts. I can only imagine how difficult it would've been for my mom, who was pregnant to manage a little boy (me), barely 2, alongside her. I received my missionary training very early in life. At the end of the day, she would stop to collect sticks for fuel in her now empty bag and vegetables on her way home. She built a low fire over two bricks where she cooked in the corner of our home. My mother had a special way of putting food on the table somehow, even when there was no money. Guests were always welcomed and served food even when we didn't have enough, but God always met the needs in a miraculous way.

Not long after we got settled into our little rented home, I began to often ask for meat, as we only ate vegetarian foods. When we lived in the south, our family ate meat dishes like most other families in the region. As a growing two-year-old boy, I loved meat, and I could not understand why my mother would not cook it for me. So I kept crying, "I want meat! I need meat!"

My parents, wanting to provide meat for their only son, were worried whether or not they could even find meat in a *strictly* vegetarian area. The only way to buy it would be to go into the Muslim neighborhood and possibly risk being seen. So my father hushed me and said, "I'll get it for you tomorrow." His promise quieted me for a little while, but the next morning I still wanted meat. Day after day, I would cry, and day after day, my father would hush me, saying, "I'll get you meat tomorrow."

But I was a stubborn little boy. Several days went by—I continued to beg. One morning, I cried louder and louder, and no amount of shushing would calm me down. My mother missed meat dishes too, and so she did what she always did: she prayed.

Suddenly, as if on cue, two pigeons flew into our house. Quick as lightning, my mother shut the door. My mother caught and killed the two pigeons and praised God for His amazing provision. She swiftly plucked the feathers, washed the birds, and cooked up a delicious pigeon curry. For two days we enjoyed that meat, and I was a very happy boy. Neighbors would pass by our house and say to my mother, "Your cooking smells so good!" She would smile and thank them and leave it at that. They had no idea why "dishes from the south" smelled so aromatic.

Late that first night, my mother and father snuck out into the darkness. They stealthily carried rolled-up newspapers with the feathers and bones of the pigeons securely tucked inside. They walked an incredibly long distance to dispose of them secretly, but it was worth it. A meat curry may seem an insignificant thing to some, but my parents knew it was a provision straight from the hand of God. Again, Jehovah Jireh provided exactly what our family needed just when we needed it. He is an on-time God!

> *Are not two sparrows sold for a copper coin? And not one of them falls to the ground apart from your Father's will. But the very hairs of your head are all numbered. Do not fear therefore; you are of more value than many sparrows.*
>
> **—Matthew 10:29-31**

THE HAUNTED HOUSE —MAKING HIS NAME GREAT (MALACHI1:11)

Before long, my brother Finny was born, and after him, my sister Glory. When she was three years old, she suffered from typhoid and pneumonia and went to be with the Lord. Our family greatly grieved her passing—it was our first heartbreaking loss on the mission field. Over the following years, my three other brothers were born, followed by another sister. Life in Gujarat was not easy; days were full of both blessings and heartaches, and as a growing family, each member felt the pains and trials of life in North India in their own ways.

With the size of our family increasing rather rapidly, my mother and father knew that one room would no longer be able to contain us all. My father also wanted to start a church and needed space for a congregation to gather, and our current home was just not going to be able to provide that. One day, while my parents were out in the village, passing out tracts, my mother saw an empty house. It was a bigger home than ours, with at least two rooms inside and a veranda, so my mother went to inquire about it, hopeful that this could be the house we had been waiting for.

"That house?" The landlord shook his head. "There is an evil spirit in that house. No one will live there; it is cursed."

My mother stood up tall and looked him in the eye. She nearly scoffed: "We don't worry about evil and those sorts of things. We'll take it."

The landlord knew that no one else would rent the house. However, he was afraid that once my mother met the evil spirit, our family would leave, so he dropped the rent to less than one-third of the regular rate and said, "If you want it, it's yours."

The landlord, along with all of our other neighbors, thought our family was delusional for agreeing to rent the house. My parents thought the landlord was crazy for giving it to us at such an affordable price, but ultimately, they knew our getting the house had less to do with our neighbors' fear than it did with God's provision. God had arranged exactly what we needed. Being about the Father's business came with some very nice benefits.

It was a bigger home, somewhat like a bungalow, with two 10-by-10-foot rooms and a veranda. Both the kitchen and the bathroom were indoors, which was not very common in those days. When pastors and other guests stayed with us, they slept comfortably in the veranda and had plenty of room to spare.

The five of us boys—Bennie, Finny, Denny, Davis, and Jimmy—shared one room. We slept like slices of bread, all in a row, and my parents stayed in the other with my sister, Lovely.

The landlord may have been crazy for renting the place at such a low price, but as my family would soon learn, he was not wrong about the evil spirit. Spiritual battles certainly took place in that house while we lived there. Several times when my parents were praying to Jesus, they would see scary-looking images of gods and goddesses—blue-skinned women with many arms or men with animal heads standing before them. One of the worst experiences was when my uncle felt as though he was being choked by an invisible power. He was on the floor, turning blue, as my mother rushed to him and sat beside him. She rebuked the evil spirit in the name of Jesus Christ and prayed over him. Immediately, the spirit left, and my uncle got up. My mother, however, was not lying when she had told the landlord that her family did not worry about evil spirits. Like the Apostle Paul, she could confidently say, "I know whom I have believed and am persuaded that He is able to keep what I have committed to Him until that Day" (2 Tim. 1:12). God made that haunted house a good home for us, despite the intense attacks we felt from the enemy frequently.

Our next-door neighbor happened to be a Hindu "pujari," a temple priest. Most Hindus in that area were unfamiliar with Christianity, so because my father was a holy man, they called him a priest as well. So the two "priests" lived next to each other. The actual similarities between them, however, stopped with the titles.

Since the pujari represented the Hindu people to their gods, the people in our town always wanted to stay in his favor. They thought the pujari had "tantric," evil powers that could cause harm or bring good to the worshippers depending on how he perceived them. The local traditional worshipers require people to bring gifts like coconut, apples, and bananas—and sometimes watermelon and milk—as offerings. Each idol requires a different kind of gift or offering to appease their gods or goddesses. The pujari's family never went hungry. We would sometimes stand outside and watch as they were showered with gifts from local villagers. The pujari would receive so many coconuts that some would roll into the back yard and go completely unaccounted for. Sometimes, when they had a hand lorry-cart full, they would call the local vendor and sell those to him. The coconuts would go back on shelves, and worshipers would buy them again. This was not an unusual practice at temples and other houses of worship. In fact, some mosques in the area even sold sheets that had been used to cover dead bodies.

Even though our neighbor had an abundance of food and resources and knew that my family lacked basic necessities, he never even considered sharing with us. He and his family assumed we were going through the curse of karma, paying for our sins from another life. Since we were Christians, he considered us a lower class of people and did not understand that we had chosen to follow the living God who paid the price for our sins—that we followed Him whether we had food or otherwise. We may not have always eaten good food as we would have wanted to, but God never failed to provide us with what we needed. (Although, there were times I felt I would really have liked one of the coconuts.)

The priest and his family would regularly ridicule us, not only for our belief and life, but also for the fact that we had moved up from the south. They made fun of our accents and our heritage, calling us names like "Madrasi," the Indian equivalent of "rednecks." We spoke differently; we believed differently and altogether lived differently. My family was never like everyone else's.

SHOUTING IN THE DARK (PSALMS 42:3)

Growing up in that neighborhood was difficult. All the homes were very small and close to one another, so there were no secrets. Everyone could hear and see their neighbors' lives happening through open windows. My brothers and I would spend the evenings playing cricket or tag in the streets with neighborhood kids, and as the sky would turn from light blue to orange to nearly black, our parents would stand on their porches and yell for their children to come home. As our playmates ran home for dinner, my brothers and I would go home, too, but it wasn't to eat. It was to get our Bibles and pray. Oftentimes, there was no food on the table. I would feel so upset and embarrassed because there never was a certainty or stability in our lifestyle. *Why did we have to be so different? Why could we not be like everyone else?*

I respected my father and was scared of even looking him in the eye when I was angry. I remember one evening when the sun was nearly gone; I switched off the light in my room because I felt like the darkness gave me the courage to speak my mind. Angrily I proclaimed, "Our family is a dysfunctional family!" Thankful for the darkness that hid my anger, I tried not to imagine my father's face as I continued, "Can you hear the neighbors? They all call their children in to have dinner. And what do we have? We have prayer!"

Just then, my father's voice, hard as steel, calmly cut through my "cloak of darkness": "Be quiet and turn on the light, Bennie. You will pray." I turned on the light, and I prayed, but I did not like it. Once again, it only reminded me of how odd we were.

SEEKING LOST SHEEP FOR THE SHEPHERD (LUKE 15:3-7)

My father's ability to go the distance and persevere in the midst of great hardship and difficulty has been one of his greatest attributes throughout his life. His incredible capability to not give up, along with his determination to be used by God, has been the reason the ministry has flourished so significantly over the years. Having grown up in a farming family, he was trained from an early age to start his days off very early and work extensively throughout the day. This developed within him a physical endurance and stamina that would continue to serve him well throughout the entirety of his life.

These incredible character traits and attributes kept him moving onward in ministry, even when his only tool to spread the Gospel was a bicycle. Later in his life, after years of being faithful with what God had provided him, the Lord gave my father a motor vehicle that was able to exponentially increase the extent of his influence. His zeal for the work of God was catapulted to new heights, while his ability to travel long distances and cover many homes only increased. His much younger coworkers and partners in ministry would joke about how they could hardly keep up with him. Even into his 70s, my father would go on extensive missions with a deep sense of duty and enthusiasm to continue spreading the Gospel to a lost and hurting world.

Even today, years later, stories of our ministry are often told by believers in remote parts of the world—about how my father would show up in villages on his bicycle ready to preach, teach, and spread the Word of God. Mr. and Mrs. Sutariya gave us a specific example of this when they told us about a time they were employed by the ONGC, a government oil company, which was quite a distance from where our home used to be. They said, "Your father would ride a bicycle and come to visit us in the company quarters where we stayed. And then," Mr. Sutariya continued, "I would take him with me to visit homes of people that I knew so he could share the Word of God with them and pray for them."

This couple eventually introduced my father to the families of Mr. Franklin and Mr. Pinto. It took over three decades for spiritual fruits to come out of the relationships my father established with these families, yet he continued to tirelessly visit and pray for them. For years, they would live their lives simply as nominal Christians with no relationship with the Lord. But today, we are thrilled to say they are strong, believing families, and their children know the Lord as well and serve the Alpha Church in Baroda.

Mr. and Mrs. Sutariya are much older now, struggling through different physical conditions and homebound. Their hearts are still moved as they share stories about my father's dedication, his passion for helping lost souls, and his zeal to reach the unreached. All of this was a result of pushing the bicycle wheels to go long distances and being relentless in the pursuit of souls, without getting disappointed by lack of fruit in the short term.

Our upbringing as children was steeped in spiritual training. While we had next to nothing in terms of food and clothing, there was no lack when it came to the spiritual nourishment brought through prayer and Bible study. These important disciplines and spiritual treasures held priority over everything else. I don't remember my father or mother ever checking our grades to see how we were doing, or scolding us for low grades. Those things were not considered the main priority in my household. However, when it came to waking up in time for the early morning prayer or the reading and memorizing of scriptures, it was always a must.

THE BOOTCAMP & LAUNCHING PAD (PSALMS 119:54)

Our first Bibles were the hard-bound English King James Translation Bibles published by the Gideons. We each had our name written on the inside of our copy as well as on the sides. Reading God's Word was always an important part of our daily existence. Being that all of my brothers and I slept in one room on the floor while our sister and parents slept in the other, each morning, my father's 5:30 a.m. wakeup call was nothing that could be avoided.

Along with his voice calling out our names to wake up was the sound of him splashing water with a cup in his hand. My siblings and I all knew that splashing sound was the ominous precursor to getting sprinkled. If the sound of his voice and the splash of his water cup didn't wake us up, we would receive a dousing of cold water that was guaranteed to get us out of bed.

After we had gotten out of bed each day, we would start with praise songs and prayer all before our morning ablutions. This was a routine established all throughout our early days.

While this was beneficial to our spiritual growth as children, it also acted as the major tool we used to learn to read English. While we could have much easily read the Bible in any other language, mom wanted us to learn English. And so our Bibles were English Bibles that also became educational resources. Little did we know at that time that our family would eventually migrate to the United States. In fact, when we moved to the U.S. and met other people from India, they were quite impressed with our English-speaking abilities. They often asked how we had learned the language so quickly. God has a way of thinking so much further in advance than we ever could.

I remember getting a large Living Bible translation—I don't know where it came from, but it was a treat. Davis, my younger brother, usually carried this special Bible to church. Something that brought him some self-esteem and pride as a little boy was reading from it during our church services. In most churches in India, the speaker only says the reference. He was usually the first person to open to that reference and read it out for all to hear. The simple language of the Living Bible stood out to the congregation and impressed my father, who would ask him to read it again.

Sunday evenings were times set aside for evangelism. My father would lead us out on the streets to distribute tracts and to sell small packets of Gospel literature. When there was a crowd, we would all sing songs of praise before preaching to those assembled, many of whom appeared to be bewildered by the strange-looking people and message. I would always stay behind my brothers and make sure we all returned home safely.

Back in those days, when someone gave us an acoustic guitar, my brothers took to learning how to play. This quickly became a novelty where we lived and provided an amazing resource for us to evangelize. Many kids would gather around the guitar wanting to touch it. Once the guitar playing and songs stopped, the kids dispersed. This was where my brothers learned to preach the Gospel. Our home was our Bible school, and the streets our training ground.

Growing up, my father's rules and laws always annoyed me, and I always followed the rules grudgingly. I just wished I had a normal family and a normal life like everyone else.

THE BOOK THAT BROUGHT BREAD (MATTHEW 6:34)

My parents were not able to enjoy financial security or the simple peace of mind that came with having a stable, monetary support system. Without a church or community of believers backing their ministry, they did not receive regular monthly support to meet our growing family's most essential needs. They embarked on the journey of their calling from God without being sent any single dollar by any organization. Rather, they answered the call boldly, looking to Jesus as they left everything familiar to them behind and endeavored to preach Christ with a vision to plant churches where no church exists. They had no professional team strategizing on their behalf the way modern-day missionaries do. Instead, they simply trusted the Lord and answered His call by being on call for Him.

During the beginning of my parent's ministry, while my father was preaching in various unreached villages, my mother would sometimes travel alone or with a small team of other believers carrying large shoulder bags full of Gospel tracts and Christian books. The heavy bags would make her bend on one side as she walked miles in extremely hot temperatures. Her health suffered greatly because of this, but she continued walking door to door with the Gospel. By God's great power and mercy, they pressed on in spite of being ridiculed and often turned away.

In those days, people did not have access to Christian bookstores online or otherwise. Instead, my mother would go around selling these materials while using the opportunity to evangelize. People in India desperately wanted to learn English and loved having the chance to read. It became a blessing in disguise, because as they began reading the materials, they simultaneously read about Jesus while their purchases funded the ministry.

While outreach and sales were helpful to our ministry and allowed my mother to play a vital role in getting things off the ground, her heart was at home with her family. My siblings and I got used to being at home, waiting for my mother to return. We became accustomed to being hungry but knew that once mother was able to sell her merchandise, she would return home with bread, eggs, and plenty of food for us to eat. As children, we would patiently wait at home like baby birds in their nest as Mother was out fetching a worm for us to eat. When my brothers told their friends, we had bread and eggs for lunch and dinner, and they were very surprised. In those days, bread was not a common man's food because Hindus believed it contained eggs. What they didn't know was that it was a quick and easy fix for hungry children and any visitors in our home.

I clearly remember how God, no matter the season, sent different people our way to help meet our growing needs. It was the Lord who ultimately provided for our family day after day, and we were privileged enough to see his handiwork continually.

Years ago, Dr. P. P. Job visited Baroda for a meeting with my father, and after hearing and seeing his zeal for evangelism, he was gracious enough to send copies of some inspiring books—"Tortured for Christ" and "The Pastor's Wife" by Dr. Richard and Sabina Wurmbrand. When the shipment came, it was used to support our family and ministry. My father invited Dr. Paul Pillai to speak at one of our annual conferences in Baroda. During his visit, he saw the dedication and sacrifice of my parents and their passion for going door to door, sharing the Gospel and selling Christian literatures, and he too graciously sent us a load of his books, including "Man After God's Own Heart," "India's Search for Unknown Christ," and "God's Blueprint for the Family."

These book sales were essential to the growth and firm establishment of our ministry. It wasn't always easy; there were some days with no sales, making it hard to buy groceries. Sometimes, my mother had to wait in the shops until all the other customers had gone and quietly ask if she could take her items home on credit. As she fed us at home, she would always remind us to be thankful and that God was our Provider. For every need, our family had, prayer was our response. The truth that our family and ministry learned in those days is that Jesus will never leave nor forsake you!

PURPOSE DRIVEN MISSION
(ROMANS 10:14A)

One morning, my father was headed on one of his anonymous journeys: he himself didn't know where he was going, but he asked my sister, Lovely, if she wanted to go with him. A co-worker in the ministry, Brother James, drove them to a very remote village. My father had a letter in his pocket which he kept looking at, that told him a small bit of information. They passed many people walking, and he would inquire of them about the person he was searching for; however, people who were more interested in getting a free ride into their village, climbed into the vehicle with Papa, Lovely, and James. Because of his great love for people, Papa enjoyed their company and laughed all the way into the village. When they got there, he took his letter out, opened it, and asked for the specific person who was interested in coming to Bible school with him. Most everyone was working in the fields, so the travelers waited patiently in a little hut, while one lady prepared garlic rice with lentils for a meal. My sister observed how my father became one of the villagers. The man who is meticulous about cleanliness and his surroundings, had become one of the poor villagers. How a man from a village in Kerala became such a lover of souls in Gujarat was noteworthy in the Indian culture. My father left the ninety-nine looking for one young man who showed interest in joining the Bible College. My father pursued the passion God placed in his heart, trusted Him fully for the results, and developed a love for souls that came from the very heart of God toward the people He created.

PURPOSE DRIVEN MAN (ROMANS 10:14B)

My father routinely would travel, staying as many as two weeks away from the family, spending his time among the poorest of the poor, eating their food, and identifying with them. On one of these such trips, he had been away for a while ministering in some of the most remote villages in Gujarat, India. We were clueless about his whereabouts; given telephones were a luxury only a few could afford in India during those days. We had no idea how my father was doing on this trip. When he arrived at our house late one night, he was full of joy and exuberance. He opened his suitcase and pulled out a fairly big paper bag with all kinds of amulets, necklaces, bracelets, and rings. These were not pieces of jewelry; rather, these were items that people wore after they had made a vow to their favored deity. The bag full of the aforementioned items belonged to people from real animistic backgrounds that had accepted Jesus, followed Him in water baptism, and renounced their old way of life. This sort of Godly harvest was my father's purpose in life and the work that he was made for.

THE SECRET TO SATISFACTION
(ROMANS 10:14C)

Few people had telephones in our region of India back in the '60s and '70s, including my family. The church was still operating by the Acts chapter 2 principle that so blessed my parents. When they were in need of money or shelter, it was very common for other preachers or missionaries needing a meal or a place to stay to arrive at our home with no advance warning or notice.

As you can imagine, our resources were constantly being stretched to the max with five growing boys to feed. When people came to stay, there was even less food to go around, but we blessed what we had and shared it without complaint. Often, my mother would come to me quietly and say, "Son, be easy on this." Actually, she seldom even spoke those words out loud—I could see it in her eyes. It was the glance that reminded me, "You are the oldest. We have guests, and you know the little ones need to eat. If they don't, they will cry in the night."

In like manner, with my eyes or a slight nod, I would answer, "Okay, Mom." I would eat a small portion and then hang in the back while the others ate.

Even through the struggles of feeling like an outcast in my community, I never doubted Mother's love for me. She would come to me again later, when everyone had been fed and settled for the evening, and quietly say, "Son, I know you're hungry, but I want you to learn something. Even when you are hungry, you should not say a word about it to anyone. You are sacrificing to bless someone else, and God will reward you for that." She would wrap her arms around me and lean in as if sharing a secret: "I want you to do something. I want you to take a rope. Tie it tight around your tummy so that your stomach will not say that you are hungry. Keep quiet and do not complain or defile the name of God by saying you are hungry or that He has not provided. We are God's people. Whatever happens to us, it is His will."

Generally, my mother's principle was to never ask or share your needs with others, never to stretch your hands open before others seeking help. However, we should always be ready to help others, remembering to make our petitions and needs known to God because He knows, and He cares for us. Whenever we went through difficult times, she would talk about God's goodness, and she always reminded me never to forget all His benefits:

> *Bless the LORD, O my soul, and forget not all his benefits, who forgives all your iniquity, who heals all your diseases, who redeems your life from the pit, who crowns you with steadfast love and mercy, who satisfies you with good so that your youth is renewed like the eagle's.*
>
> **—Psalm 103:2-5**

My brothers and I would often sit, gathered around my mother's feet in the evenings, listening to her stories and words of wisdom because we loved her, and because we had no television. She would tell us stories of her experiences trusting God and share stories of how no matter how difficult things had gotten, God had always come through for her. Then she would ask things like, "Do you remember when you needed this or that, and someone came and gave it to you? Do you remember how God provided that for us? Do you remember when God sent the pigeons?" As we reflected on God's faithfulness, she would continue, "Never bad-mouth God. Do not say, 'we cannot do this' or 'we cannot afford that.' God can be trusted, and we should trust Him. God will send the ravens."

Stories from Scripture and stories from our lives and experiences trusting God were all woven together. She would read to us from the Bible, and the stories seemed to always come alive when she spoke about them in our native tongue. Moses and the Israelites, Elijah and the ravens, Abraham and Isaac and Jacob—they were all as real to us as our own flesh and blood. She would pull the strings of our hearts with them, and we cried every time Joseph's brothers sold him to the Ishmaelites; our tears flowed again when the brothers were finally reunited in Egypt.

"You need to stick together," she would tell us, wiping her own tears as we sniffled at the brothers' betrayal and forgiveness. "You are brothers, and God has given you to one another; never forget that."

SCHOOL DAZE

My mom and dad worked hard to make our time at home together feel like a safe haven. We were extremely grateful for this due to the fact that school usually felt like a battleground.

In India, school is not free like it is in America or in public schools elsewhere. Everyone is required to pay school fees, but more often than not, our family could not pay, not on time, anyway.

In our classrooms, the desks were lined up in rows, and the children sat on long benches behind the desks. Students who hadn't paid their fees on time were forced to stand on the bench so that the whole class could shame them. I was the one who was often called to stand since we never paid the tuition fees on time. Though I hated it, the teacher would call out, "B.C. Mathews, remember to bring your fees tomorrow." She said my name that way on purpose. "Did you hear me, B.C.?" I stood on the bench, my eyes on the ground, my hands clenched into fists. I could hear the other students snickering behind me.

"Don't call me B.C. My name is not B.C."

"Those are your initials, Mathews. Don't tell me they're not."

I hated that she was right. They were my initials. They were also slang for "Backward Class," a reference to the lowest caste in the system, the untouchables. My heart cried every time she called me that. Why did my parents have to name me Bennie Cherian Mathews? I would have done anything for a name like "Finny" or "Davis," like my brothers. But I was Bennie "Backward Class" Mathews all through school. It was humiliating.

I would come home and beg my parents to pay the fees. They would be busy with my brothers, or the neighbors, or the ministry, and I desperately wished they would, just one time, say, "Yes, son, don't worry, it will be taken care of tomorrow." But it was never as simple as I wished, and that desperate wish of mine always went unanswered.

"Well, son, we need to pray."

That was their answer to everything.

"We need to pray."

My mind was rarely ever on prayer. Rather, it was always on multiplication of my personal resources and figuring out how to take what little we had and turn it into more. All of us—my sister, my brothers, and I—were going to school, and no one was paying the fees on time, so we all went through the same terrible shaming.

If the school authorities did not get the fees, they sent the school messenger to our home to collect them. We called him the "School Peon," and everyone knew who he was and why he came. Whenever he walked into our neighborhood, all the neighbors would glance knowingly at one another or whisper, because he was always headed to the Mathews' house.

When he knocked on our door, my mother was ready for him. She was brave and always seemed prepared to face any challenge of any size. She would go out to meet the School Peon and would stand as tall as she could to firmly say, "We will bring the money over. Tell your Principal; we will bring it over." And she would stand there; arms crossed over her chest until he finally shrugged and walked away. My mother was a very formidable woman.

Not only did the school require tuition, but it also required us to purchase and wear uniforms. Most of the children in my school had at least two sets of uniforms consisting of two shirts and two pairs of trousers. But the Mathews children only had two changes of clothes: one school uniform and one set of church clothes. At home, we wore only T-shirts and shorts.

The other students would alternate their uniforms to ensure they were always neat and tidy. They wore one set of clothes while the second was being washed. While not exceptionally lavish, this luxury was one of my family could not afford.

We went to a Medium English school, one that uses English as the primary medium of instruction. Many of the students came from wealthy families and looked down on us because we did not have as much as they had. When they would notice that sometimes I did not bring lunch (or if I did and there was never very much of it), I would just shrug and say, "I don't want lunch." My classmates thought it was because we had no food at all, but I knew it was because I did not want to be a burden to my family and insisted that my siblings get fed first. In a strict caste system, though, being poor meant that anyone with more than us thought they were better, and they took every opportunity to rub our noses in it.

Each morning when the teacher entered the classroom, every

student was required to stand and say, "Good morning, Teacher; good morning, ma'am." The class used fountain pens, the old-fashioned kind with ink in them, and sometimes when I stood to say good morning, pranksters would squirt drops of ink on my bench. I would be very careful to avoid it, but sometimes I did not see it, and I still sat in it. They only did it to see if I would wear the same pair of trousers the next day when I came back to school. If I did, they made fun of me.

So, I would go home and wash my pants. We did not have a dryer, so I was forced to hang them outside to dry in the sun. In the summer, this worked really well but would cause my wool trousers to stay damp for days during the wintertime. We weren't able to afford an iron at that time either, so I would place coconut shells in the fire until they became very hot, carefully lay them on a steel plate, and grabbed the plate on either side with thick napkins. I would use my homemade iron on my trousers until they were dry.

It worked most of the time, but when your pants are even slightly damp in the winter, they chafe and rub. It was harrowing, and if any of my peers noticed, they would mock me mercilessly. Most of the time, I considered this to be the most painful part. "Look!" they would say, pointing and laughing over their shoulders. "He's wearing wet pants!"

In many ways, going to school was torturous for my siblings and me. I did not want to study but dreamed of going out and finding a job instead. I was tired of never having any money, of never fitting in, and of having to scrape by. Sure, God provided for us, but I wanted to help Him provide a little more. I wanted to do something—anything—to make a little money to bring home to help my father, mother, and sister, and brothers.

As the oldest, I reasoned that the same tactic my mother

had taught me with food applied to my education as well. I did not need schooling. I needed to save the extra tuition and the extra fees for the younger ones. I'd had my portion, and that was enough. Besides, it wasn't my nature to be grabbing for more. I also *hated* school and wanted nothing more than to get out into the real world and work.

My parents' job was to serve and preach, and their natural reaction to any situation was to pray. Worship was a family affair, but it did not mean much to me then. I was the son of the "crazy priest with all the children," and I was ready to be someone else. I wanted to establish my own custom for providing for our needs, and I knew that if I could make some money, life would be easier and better.

I wanted my tortured years of school to be over and just find a job.

CHAPTER 2

APPLICATION POINTS

God's faithfulness is not determined nor limited by our own faithfulness.

He is faithful, no matter how faithless we are, and His goodness is not diminished by our sinfulness. No matter what we need, God has arranged an answer as we were faithful to seek Him. Being about the Father's business came with very good benefits.

Do you ever feel like complaining about the atmosphere at home, at work, or even at church?

It probably doesn't compare to living in a house where demonic spirits would manifest. I will never forget my mother's resolve in telling the landlord that she and my father did not worry about evil spirits. They simply changed the atmosphere. You see, "They knew in whom they had believed and were persuaded that He was able to keep what they had committed to Him until the end of all days" (2 Timothy 1:12). God made that house a good place for us, and His praise was lifted up there. Whatever the circumstances, commit your way to God and trust Him to fulfill His promises.

When things do not go your way, when you have to do without so that others may prosper, is it "enough to suffer for Christ"?

My mother's principle was to never ask or share our needs with others, but to always be ready to help others and make our petitions to God because He knows, and He cares for us. When you go through difficult times, get in God's Word, talk about His goodness, and remember the times that He has come through for you before. Never forget all His benefits . . .

> *Bless the LORD, O my soul, and forget not all his benefits, who forgives all your iniquity, who heals all your diseases, who redeems your life from the pit, who crowns you with steadfast love and mercy, who satisfies you with good so that your youth is renewed like the eagle's.*
>
> **—Psalm 103:2-5**

CHAPTER 3

FIRST JOBS

When they had finished the days, as they returned, the Boy Jesus lingered behind in Jerusalem. And Joseph and His mother did not know it; but supposing Him to have been in the company, they went a day's journey, and sought Him among their relatives and acquaintances.
Luke 2:43-44

My parents were always leaps and bounds ahead of me in regards to their maturity and growth in the faith. They believed unwaveringly in God and in His promises to provide while always responding to excruciating trials through faith rather than fear. Where do we live when we have no home? Pray. How do we eat when there is no food? Pray. What do we do when there is no money for school tuition or basic necessities? Pray. It was nearly a full-time job for them.

In my mind, a full-time job should have been just that, a job. I was tired of being laughed at and sick of being poor. God did provide, but I wasn't always comfortable with how long He took. I did not see my desire for self-sufficiency as a faith issue at the time, but rather as practicality. In fact, I do not think my parents realized how far I had begun to lag behind them in my belief. They carried on in the ministry, believing God for our needs, and believing their children were walking with them. But by this time, I had determined to walk my own road, and in my thinking I was the lone hero. If no one else in my family was willing to save us from this faith-induced poverty, I would do it myself.

I was impatient and eager, so I dropped out of high school to work and make money in an effort to establish a more secure financial future for myself and my family. I knew education was important, but I did not have time to continue suffering in school, and then college, before finally receiving divine direction.

Did I mention that I was impatient?

TURNING WATER INTO WINE

The quickest way I knew to find a job was by going to a trade school and getting a certificate. Since stenography and typing were sought after in those days, I enrolled in special training, hoping my new secretarial skills would open doors to a career, or at the very least a job. The course was sponsored by a nearby Catholic Training Institute, and although I completed the training, we did not have the money to pay for my diploma or the final group photo.

I could not believe I was forced to go on without something I really needed because I lacked money, yet again. Without a diploma, I could not get a job. Without a job, I could not get 1,500 rupees. Without 1,500 rupees to pay the Catholic center, I could not get my diploma. Round and round it went.

I resentfully left the diploma behind, and every time the director of the trade school saw me, he would ask when I was coming back to retrieve it. Embarrassed, I would simply shrug my shoulders and timidly utter the word, "Soon"—all the while thinking, *If I get a job, they'll ask for the diploma, but I'll work a bit and then use the money to pay the center for the diploma.* That was my plan.

The problem with my plan was that I was barely 18, a high

school dropout, a bad typist, and my shorthand English was terrible. The fact that women were the more favorable candidates for secretarial and stenography jobs did not help either. Even though I was persistent and sought out a job everywhere I went, I could never seem to find one. I quickly became frustrated and discouraged.

According to all of my worldly logic and wisdom, this was my parents' fault. Most of my days were filled with frustration and a deep sense of regret and failure. I would come home after a day of searching for a job (and not finding one) and say to my father, "If you were not in this God-business and spending all of your time praying instead of working, we would not be in this situation." Or, "If you knew some political leaders in town, like my friends' fathers, I could get a job."

By then, I was old enough and bold enough to yell at him with the light *on*. My rants would continue for a long time until they began to border on belligerent. "You don't know anybody! What is our God doing? You say our God is real, and our God is alive, but if He is alive, why is He not providing us with a decent job? This is not good. Unless you know someone important as a reference, you don't get a job. We don't know anyone important!"

My father, with his usual sense of rationality and gentle demeanor, would calmly look at me and say, "Son, go and pray. God will make a way in His time, and what you need to do is to trust Him as you wait on Him."

That was his answer. If only he had a better response than that to help us rise above our situation. I did not like that. Pray for this. Pray for that. For everything, pray, pray, pray. I wanted action, not prayer!

My mother would come close, like she did when I was a child, and say, "Son, don't talk to your father so disrespectfully.

You know he is a man of God." She was the strong one, always protecting him. My parents were both the law and law-keepers in my life and would approach these difficult conversations with me in an almost legislative manner rather than as parents talking to their wayward child. It was like the mayor of a town setting a speed limit and the policeman enforcing it; my father laid down the law in our family, and my mother made sure we obeyed it, as written in Proverbs 1:8, "My son, hear the instruction of your father, and do not forsake the law of your mother."

When she saw that I was upset, she would share God's miracles in an effort to encourage me and remind me of God's faithfulness through difficult times. Like when we first moved to North India and she was pregnant with Finny; I cried for milk like I once cried for meat. Often, we had no milk, so she would take a glass of water, boil it, pour some sugar in it, stir it up, and pray: "God, make this better than milk in my son's body." She gave it to me by faith, and years later, she would stand with her hands on her hips and a gleam in her eye, daring me to deny the results. "Look at you," she would say, one arm gesturing from my head to my feet, "You are taller and stronger than the other Indian boys, and it's because God turned that water into milk in your body."

When she told that story I knew, to her, "Cana in Galilee" wasn't so far away. The God who once turned water into wine was still using water in miraculous ways, and she did not want me to miss it. "You have a splintered understanding," she would say. "Don't take what God has done lightly and don't talk to your father that way. The fear of the Lord is the beginning of wisdom and good understanding, and without the fear of God, no good understanding can happen. How can you have the fear of the Lord if you don't even respect your father?"

I tried to make her understand. *How could even the simplest financial concepts escape them?* Zero plus zero would always equal zero. "One of us needs a job. Prayer is not going to provide the things on the table. Somebody needs to work." I shook my head and banged my fist onto my palm. "You guys don't understand this. You have to work. You have to save money." I wasn't trying to blatantly defy God or turn from His calling, but I simply wanted my family to feel somewhat in control of our circumstances for the first time in our lives.

She would smooth her Sari (traditional dress) with her hands and say, "Son, you don't need to worry about those things. You go and study."

Any answer that wasn't "Pray," was, "Go and get an education."

I wanted education even less than I wanted to pray, and that was really saying something. I believed that if I quit school, at least my siblings would get a proper education, and I would be one less burden for my parents. I wanted to get my family out of poverty.

As my anger and frustration continued to boil over, I spent more and more time outside of the house and ended up joining a gang. I had no tolerance; I could beat up anyone. Traditionally, by the age of 12, young Indian men are given responsibility from their fathers to become the next "father." During my 12th grade year of school, my father had said, "You need to take care of them," regarding my brothers and sister. So I did just that. Only I decided to do it my way. If someone messed with one of my brothers, he would tell me, and I would take care of it.

To the community and to my brothers, I was as strict and demanding as Hitler. Whenever I was returning home, the little neighborhood children would stay out of the road because they were afraid. I created fear in them, so that they would not bully or hurt my siblings. Even my brothers were scared of me. I would spank them, take charge, and tell them what to do. They were more scared of me than they were of their own father.

I had gained a type of respect from those around me, but I still did not have the life I wanted. I wanted to go out and make money, and every time I attempted to articulate that desire to my parents, they just told me more stories of God's provision over the years. I was tired of hearing those stories! *If God provided all the time, why did He not provide me with a job? Why could He not get us out of this poor, pathetic situation?* From what I could see, my parents' way of doing things wasn't getting us anywhere.

THE BIRTH OF A CAREER

I was playing cricket in the street one day and ended up having to chase down a stray ball some ways down the road when I noticed a young woman walking along the other side. As she got closer, we recognized each other. Her name was Agnes, and we had both taken the typing course at the Catholic technical center together a couple of years prior. She walked over to me saying, "Bennie! How are you?" I replied with the typical, "Fine," and, noticing she was pregnant, added, "You got married?"

"Yes," she said, touching her belly, "I got married, and I'm working."

"Wow, congratulations!" I was jealous of her good fortune but did my best to put on a polite smile.

"Where are you working?" She asked. "You were good with typing, and you were the top steno shorthand guy in our class." She was correct; we had eight guys and 30 women in our group.

I shuffled my feet a little and looked off into the distance. "I did not get a job yet."

She looked confused as I tried to explain the difficult situation I found myself in with my family. "My father, he…he's a priest" (she was Catholic and would understand that). "I'm looking for a job because we are five brothers and one sister, and my dad and mom live by faith. They trust God to provide, and they don't have a real job; I don't know how we will survive. I have no means of finding a job, and life is miserable. If I can find a real job, I can help and provide for my family. But I do not have experience, and no one hires a person without any work experience."

She smiled very wide. "You know what, Bennie? I'll be going on maternity leave next month, and they are looking for someone to take my position at the petrochemicals company."

Now, I was smiling, too. "Great! Can you recommend me to them?" I knew I should have been more diplomatic in the way I responded and not so eager, but this seemed to be my big break, and I was beyond excited to jump at the possible job opportunity.

"Yes, of course, I'll do that." She gave me the address of the place where she worked, telling me to bring my résumé and what day and time to meet her. As we said our good-byes, I had never been so grateful for a cricket match—or a baby—in my life.

I drew up a résumé as best as I knew how and took it to her office. Soon, her manager called me. He was aware of my training, and he believed me to be a capable young man. He had no reason to doubt me, and so he said, "Agnes recommended you, and you will get the job. When she goes on maternity leave next month, we will let you know."

Finally, I had found the inspiration to pray! I prayed that God would send Agnes into labor early. When she did go into labor, they contacted me, and I started my first real job.

THE TROUBLE WITH TYPING

In those days, there were no computers, only typewriters, and white-out to cover mistakes. I was happy to have a job and especially one that wasn't overly difficult. I liked it. They paid me a good salary of roughly 1,500 rupees per month, and my mother was so happy for me. Of course, when she talked about my job, she would say, "Look! See what God did?" and I would answer her, "God did not do it, Mom, Agnes did."

I did not care about God, and no matter how many times my mom would try to remind me, "No, son, it is God who did this for you." I would set my jaw and say with anger, "No, it was Agnes, and I'm glad."

However, God was apparently not very impressed with my attitude. About a month after I started the job that I had accredited to Agnes, the manager called me into his office. He had been given a promotion at another company and would soon be moving his office to Mumbai. That meant his position would no longer exist, and the new manager was sure to come in and hire new people. My not-so-hard job had just become not-so-permanent.

"But what about Agnes?" I pleaded, hoping that I could stay in her position (and that she might stay home with her child indefinitely), but he said, "Agnes is a permanent employee of this company; she can always come back. But you are not. When I leave, you will have to as well."

I was devastated. This was not what I had expected at all. Most people would have realized at this point that it was time to run back to God and ask Him for help. When I told my mother, that is exactly what she did. She prayed and then said, "Son, God has something better for you."

No. That wasn't an answer I was willing to hear or accept.

I was angry and bitter and did not care if He had a better plan in store for me or not. In my head, this was somehow, again, my father's fault. In my eyes, I was going to lose my job, and we would not be able to eat because he wasn't acting like the father his family desperately needed him to be. It was his responsibility to get a job and feed the kids, not mine. But he did not; he was too busy praying and preaching the Gospel.

I worked my final two weeks and tried as hard as I could to make the most of it. As the end of my employment grew near, the manager called me into his office and started talking with me about plans for his going-away party. It was common to have such parties at the biggest hotel in town, the fancy ones where movie stars and rich people stayed. Normally, I would have never received the opportunity to even step foot in such a place, so I was looking forward to the party immensely. At least, I would get a free and full meal there.

My manager handed me an envelope and said, "Go and give this to the manager there. I want to make sure all the arrangements for my party are correct. There are many details to iron out, and I want everything to be just right."

I saw an opportunity and gathered all of my courage. "Could I request something from you?" I asked. I knew he liked me because we were friends.

"What is it?"

I began to recite the story I had told so many times before: "My father is a radical priest. He's crazy. All he does is stay home and pray. We are five brothers and one sister, and I am the only one with an income. My mother struggles, too, for there is no money coming in, and we are already behind on our rent." I took a deep breath. "Would you please recommend me for a job, any job, at that hotel?" The story rolled off my lips at rapid speed.

Somehow, I felt that if I could speak fast enough, he would not have the chance to question anything I was saying.

He twisted his lips a little and squinted at me. "Bennie, you're putting me in an awkward situation." Then he nodded, "But if you fill out an application, I will talk to them and give you a solid recommendation."

I was so grateful I wanted to hug him, but instead withheld the urge and simply replied, "Okay." I went to the hotel, dropped the letter off with the manager, and went directly to the Human Resources department.

"Mr. Panchal told me to ask for a job here." I held my breath, hoping the man would not ask for more information.

He barely looked at me. "All right, fill out an application and put Mr. Panchal's name down as your reference." I did what he said and returned to my office.

"I put your name as the reference," I told my manager. "If they call you, will you please say good things about me?"

He assured me and said, "Yes, that's no problem for me to do; if they ask me, I'll say what I know about you. I appreciate the work you've done here."

The hotel manager did call Mr. Panchal, my manager, and true to his word, he gave them a good reference for me. Soon, the hotel manager contacted me and requested that I come in to speak in person.

"Do you want to work here?" he asked. I wanted to shout, "YES!" but instead, I remained calm and fought back against my deep eagerness. I nodded, "Yeah!"

"I cannot pay you 1,500 rupees," he said. "Will you take 700 rupees?" That was about $30, and an amount that was still big in those days.

"I'll take it," I said.

"Good! You can start tomorrow."

My new job was in a tiny room with an older woman and an older man. One was the director's secretary, one was the assistant manager, and I was the secretary to the General Manager. I could tell from the beginning that they weren't sure what to think of me. I was young, I spoke English, and they were paranoid to the point that they feared I might say something to the manager to get them fired. They did not know that I was the one who was the most terrified in that office. I had no idea what I was doing and was positive that it appeared to be obvious.

The manager would call me to come and take dictation. I was so nervous, but I tried my best to take down exactly what he was saying. I knew the other two were watching me, and I made a lot of mistakes. Every time the manager would look at a letter I gave him, he would tell me to change this or that, and I would have to start from scratch. My wastepaper basket began filling with used letterhead, crumpled in frustration after yet another typing mistake. Letterhead was expensive, and it did not take long before the other two in my office reported me. "That Mathews guy is throwing out a lot of letterheads," they said to the manager, who soon called me into his office.

I knew it was bad when I went in. He motioned for me to sit down and rocked back in his chair. He had the look of a man who was about to give bad news.

"Bennie, you are a nice kid, but you don't know how to do your job." I hung my head, knowing he was right, but still wishing he would not say the words he was about to speak out. "I am very sorry, but I want you to leave."

"Sir, the situation at my house is dreadful," I said respectfully and leaned forward in my chair. "You see, my father is a crazy priest. All he does is stay home and pray." (The story became more dramatic every time I told it.) "We are five boys and one girl, and we are struggling. Sir, please, can you somehow…?"

He was not unkind but remained very firm. "Bennie, I do not run a charity or a community center. I cannot keep paying someone who cannot do his job properly."

I felt my chance of making any kind of money at all slipping away. Desperate, I tried again. "Sir, my mother, she worries. There are so many mouths to feed, and we are trying so hard . . ."

As I was nearing the point of begging, the door suddenly burst open and a man barged in. His face was flushed, and he threw his hands in the air.

"How do you expect me to make that restaurant succeed with no one to work there?" The hotel was so big that it had three restaurants to cater for all the important people who stayed there: an Indian restaurant, a Chinese restaurant, and the English restaurant this man managed. The steward had just undergone major surgery and was not coming back to work. All the extra responsibilities fell onto this man, and the strain was clearly beginning to get to him. He cursed and yelled for a few minutes (that seemed to last forever) and then pointed an angry finger at the manager saying, "If you want your business to survive at all, you need to start hiring some people. If you don't . . ." He let the unfinished threat hang in the air as he stormed out the door and slammed it behind him.

The manager, who had been so calm rocking back and forth in his chair when he was firing me, had gotten very still as the butler yelled. Now he placed all four legs of his chair on the ground and looked at me. I could tell what he was thinking, *This guy is tall and could look sharp dressed up.*

"You know what, Mathews," he said, cocking his head, "I think I have a job for you."

"I'll do anything!" I quickly responded. I knew a lifeline when I saw it, and this one was about as blatant as they come.

He pointed his pen at me, "I want you to go down to housekeeping. They'll give you a jacket and a suit, and I want you to put it on and stand at the door of the Bliss Restaurant. Open the door when people walk in and greet them properly: 'Good morning, sir...Good afternoon, sir . . .' and so on. Show them to a table, pull out their chair, help them sit, and then go back to the door. Don't do anything else. Are you willing to do that?"

A bit confused but also excited, I nearly shouted, "Yes!"

He said, "I'll pay you 300 rupees."

Although my salary had dropped from 1,500 to 700 to 300 in just a few weeks, a job was a job, and a job in a 5-star hotel was not to be refused. I confidently told him, "I'll do it."

He called housekeeping and told them what to give me. I thanked him as I walked out the door, grateful to be employed, happy to get out of my tiny office. I did not know at that point that something much more than my career was about to change.

OUT OF THE FRYING PAN

I went down to housekeeping, where they gave me an orange jacket and a penguin tie. I stood at the door like the manager told me, and although I felt like a clown, I knew better than to complain.

Working in such a high-end restaurant turned out to be a very educational experience for me. Plates on the tables were flanked by a multitude of spoons and forks, and guests did not even have to go to the sink to wash their hands as Indians were accustomed to doing. Instead, sharply dressed waiters brought them finger bowls and towels for their convenience and comfort.

It was the first time I saw wealthy people eating food before their actual meal. With their soup they ate breadsticks and rolls with real butter. Meals were served in five courses and were followed by dessert. It all seemed so extravagant to me.

One day, a man asked me what kind of ice cream we had. "Vadilal," I told him confidently, giving him the name of a certain brand of ice cream (like Breyer's or Ben & Jerry's).

"No, what *kind* of ice cream do you have?" he repeated, looking at me like I was an idiot. He meant what flavor, but I did not know that ice cream came in more than one flavor. In my mind, there was one ice cream, and it was white.

"Sir," I said, now a little confused. "We carry Vadilal ice cream." He became very upset and called the butler. "Does your man know what he's doing?" he asked angrily.

The butler apologized. "He's new here." He pulled me to the side and told me to stay quiet while he took care of it. He returned a few minutes later and steered me into the kitchen. He opened the big freezer and started pointing out ice cream to me, "Chocolate, mango, strawberry, butterscotch, banana..."

"Oh," I said, nodding, amazed and embarrassed at the same time; "I got it. I'm sorry."

Not only were there different courses and different flavors of food to learn but different attitudes toward foods as well. In my home, we barely had enough to eat, so our personal preference about what we were eating was irrelevant. I had learned to tighten my belt so that my stomach would not remind me of how hungry I was and my mouth would not complain. My parents thanked God for every bite we had, no matter how small, bland, or poor the quality was. At the restaurant, there was more than enough food for people to eat and the expectations for a fine dining experience were the norm. In fact, every table, it seemed, had plenty of delectable leftovers that were just thrown away and disregarded completely.

It was a high society hotel meant to serve and cater to the upper class, so nothing was ever reused. All of the uneaten food, no matter how high the price or quality, was taken to the dump. It hurt me to watch it all go to waste for no legitimately good reason. I knew what a difference that food could make for my brothers, my sister, and my parents. I often wished I could just take some of the extra food home to them. What a difference it would have made in our lives! Even though I was the new kid and the waiters barely spoke to me, I knew I could lose my job if I spoke up regarding such matters. So I just stood at the door, opening it and closing it, "Good morning, sir...Good afternoon, ma'am," and tried not to show how shocked, and at times repulsed, I was at the way people spent their money.

The hotel was a perfect picture of the Indian caste system. People of the highest castes: movie stars, cricket players, and wealthy families could come and go easily, spending what seemed like an endless supply of money and never fear the consequences of their recklessness. Middle caste people worked there as waiters or butlers or stewards, serving the elite class of guests above them and ignoring or speaking down to those in the class below, like those who cleaned the floors, washed the dishes, took out the garbage, or opened and closed doors. When you grow up in that system, you always dream of climbing to a better caste, to do something more in life, but you are completely unable to move forward. The caste system controls everything, and there is no getting around it.

DOOR OF OPPORTUNITY

As I stood outside the hotel door day after day, I would anxiously glance around, trying to be prepared for whoever might be approaching the hotel. If it was someone famous, I wanted to be able to greet him or her by name. One day, I saw a very pretty girl walking toward my restaurant and recognized her immediately. She was from my high school. I was horrified. What if she saw me? What if she recognized me and found out that I was simply a doorkeeper? My worst nightmare was the thought that she would tell everyone from school how she saw Bennie Mathews and that he was merely a lowly doorkeeper at a hotel.

The potential humiliation was too much for me, so before she could see me, I ran into the hotel and slipped into the kitchen to hide. I was hoping no one would notice, but the butler followed me in.

"What are you doing in here?" he snapped, motioning his hands toward the dining room. "There are so many people out there!"

"I—I'm not feeling well," I stammered. It wasn't a lie, after all. The thought of that girl telling everyone I was working a low caste job made me physically ill. "Please, just give me a few minutes. I need to…" Before I could finish my pleading to be left alone, the kitchen supervisor walked in and asked, *What was the matter with me?* I repeated myself with desperation in my voice, hoping to divert the conversation elsewhere.

"I'm just a bit dizzy," I said, trying to peek through the small window in the kitchen door. I saw the girl being seated for lunch and knew it would be a while before she left. "I need to rest here for a little bit.

Fortunately, the kitchen supervisor had pity on me and allowed me to stay in the back. He shooed the butler out of the kitchen and showed me to a chair. While I was being seated, he fetched me a glass of water and assured me that I was going to be just fine. I waited as long as possible, peering through the little window into the dining room every few minutes to see if she was gone. When I was sure she had finally left, I thanked the kitchen supervisor and cautiously made my way back through the dining room to return to my post at the door. I was incredibly paranoid she would come back, but I feared the consequences of overstaying my welcome in the kitchen far more.

As I continued on throughout the workday at my post, I decided it was time that God and I had a little talk. "I know You are there, God, because I've seen You work." I did, in fact, believe in Him after the lifetime of miracles I had witnessed in my family; how could I not? I just did not like the way my parents went about believing in Him. They trusted God to take care of everything, instead of taking care of anything for themselves. I figured maybe God and I could make an arrangement that benefitted both of us.

"I know this job is a miracle from You because I could have been fired from this hotel if the butler hadn't come into the manager's office when he did. But You know how I feel about being a doorkeeper. If You give me a better position here, if You change my situation in this place, I promise not to take a dime from my paycheck from this day forward. I will give the entire amount to my parents, and if they want to waste it on evangelism, so be it." I'd grown used to the fact that though you could buy a liter of milk for 60 paise, my father would spend 120 paise on a ticket to go to another town and preach the Gospel instead. His version of economics seemed like nothing but foolishness to me.

Every time he recklessly donated our small amount of income, I would say things to my mom like, "Do you understand the math here? Are you guys out of your mind? Don't you know that with 60 paise, you can buy milk for your children? For 60 paise, you can make sure your children are strong and healthy! You can give them milk that will build muscle and sustain them!" I would go on and on.

And every time I did *that*, my mother would look up at me and remind me of the sugar water and how God worked a miracle within my own body.

"Your father is a man of God," she would tell me over and over. "He is serving God, and you don't know what God has done for us. How can you say such things? God has provided for us, and He will provide again."

Standing by the door that day, I knew my parents would do foolish things with the money: they would feed strangers, help other people in need (even though we were in need ourselves), and share the Gospel without saving enough to ensure there was enough left over for milk for their own children. Disregarding the consequences of what my parents would do with the money I worked so hard for, I committed to giving it all to them—every penny.

I prayed, "God, if You change my situation here, I'll give everything to my mom."

In one month's time, I was promoted to the steward of the restaurant.

CHAPTER 3

APPLICATION POINTS

Since the Garden of Eden, the enemy has tried to convince mankind that self-sufficiency is the answer; that God doesn't truly have our best interest in mind.

Sadly, we still fall for his lies and still miss the mark. As a young man, I did not see my full-on pursuit of self-sufficiency as a faith issue. I did not see it as a pride issue. I simply saw it as practicality. When was the last time you evaluated your pursuit of success? Do you rely more on your own skills, or more on prayer, faith, and obedience?

Our best attempts at fighting God and doing things our own way will always end up in failure.

As hard as I worked, I did not recognize that I was becoming more like the prodigal son. Working in the restaurant, I saw the leftovers from the higher caste's meals being thrown away and wished there was a way I could take some of it home to eat. Without recognizing it, I was living according to the caste system of the world that surrounded me rather than living like the child of a King.

God responds to faith, even imperfect, immature, baby-steps of faith.

As soon as I committed my way to God even a little bit, things changed. I prayed, "God, if You change my situation here,

I'll give everything to my mom for the family and ministry." In one month's time, I was promoted to the steward of the restaurant. I still had a long way to go, and a lot of lessons to learn.

Do not be afraid to start moving more toward the Father's business.

Not only will He take care of what concerns you, but He will also stretch you and train you for greater and greater things.

CHAPTER 4

THE BUSINESSMAN

So when they did not find Him, they returned to Jerusalem, seeking Him. Now so it was that after three days they found Him in the temple, sitting in the midst of the teachers, both listening to them and asking them questions
Luke 2:45-46

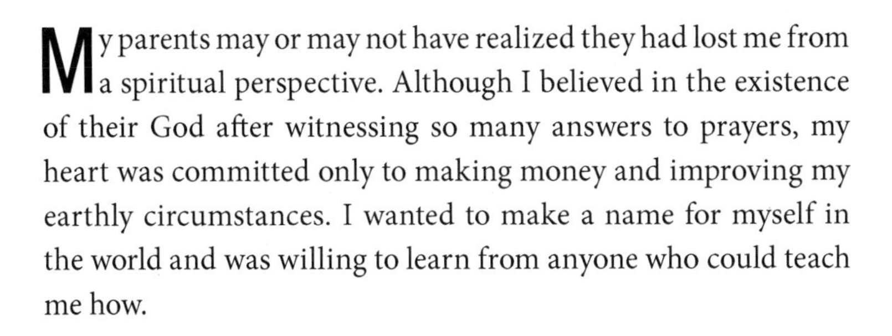

My parents may or may not have realized they had lost me from a spiritual perspective. Although I believed in the existence of their God after witnessing so many answers to prayers, my heart was committed only to making money and improving my earthly circumstances. I wanted to make a name for myself in the world and was willing to learn from anyone who could teach me how.

MOVING ON UP

After the embarrassing incident with the Vadilal ice cream, the management of the hotel knew that if I was to become the steward of the restaurant, I needed to obtain some form of formal instruction. They sent me to some special training classes for food and beverage management, along with a quick course on hotel management.

It wasn't very long until I became the manager of a very lucrative hotel restaurant.

I worked extremely hard and daily went out of my way to

build good relationships with the people who came into the restaurant. Frequently, I would receive job offers from some of the successful clientele. Relished in this new favor, I would show the offer letters I received from various companies to my manager (the same manager who was going to fire me initially), and he would say, "They're offering to pay you that much? Okay, I will pay you more." He would then tear up the employment letter and send me back to work with a bigger paycheck.

I soon became the manager of two restaurants and had much staff reporting to me. Life in that hotel was good, and I loved every second of it. Very important people continued to stay at the hotel, including famous cricket players, movie stars, and heads of major corporations. That is how I became good friends with the owner of Hindustan Motors (the Indian equivalent of General Motors in America). My friends would often ask when they could come by to see if I could get them autographs. It was rather surreal to me during this time of my life because I remembered being a kid and looking over at that hotel from across the street, never dreaming that I could one day even step inside, let alone work there or become an important employee of that place.

Finally, God had given me a position where I found His favor among people, and, as a result, life for my family was better than I had ever recalled it being. There was a steady income for them now, just as I had promised, and I continued to give my entire paycheck to my mother each month. I never withheld a dime or bought a single thing for myself.

My mother was so happy during those days. Once, she took me aside and confided by saying, "Son, I was ashamed when we went to stores to buy things because I would have to wait for people to leave, and then go and ask to buy on credit." In those days, we did not have credit cards. You would just say to the store clerk or the owner, "I can pay you sometime next week or in a few days, can I just take some things now?" After having to do that for many years, she finally had the money to simply purchase the things we needed. She smiled and laid her hand on my arm and told me, "For the first time, I felt like I was a rich person, like all other women in our community walking into a store, and I wasn't ashamed. I could just say, 'I'll take two kilos of rice and three kilos of wheat,' instead of waiting for everyone to leave." At this point, I could not help but smile with gratitude myself. Those were the words I had worked so hard for and waited so many years to hear.

GIVING UP THE GHOST

My parents' evangelism efforts had started to bear fruits by now. New believers in the village began to come and worship together with our family. That meant every Sunday, and we would take everything out of the room that served as both our living room and bedroom and put it outside in order to turn our home into a worship space.

By this time, however, the owner of our rented house began to realize there was no evil spirit haunting the house—and he wanted the house back! He and his family would yell at us when they saw us outside. The neighbor opposite our house had the same distaste for us; they did not like us, so he would join the landlord and yell to my father, "Cherian! Is this the time to pray? You are disturbing the peace of this community with your loud singing." He was angry and would threaten people who came to our house for worship. It discouraged them from coming for the services, and it made our lives difficult. But how could we move somewhere else? No one wanted to rent us space because they knew we would hold

Christian worship services wherever we lived.

The true root of the problem was that the landlord had been charging us a very low rent and now knew he could get three times what we'd been paying. So he took my family to court to make his case. He told the judge, "These people are using this house for worship. They have made it into a church! It is not a church; it is a house. They are not using the residential property for the intended purpose and are a nuisance to everyone on our entire block."

It was a painful season for my family, especially since court cases are always prolonged and tiring. The landlord had filed a case against us for praying in the house and not paying our agreed-upon amount of rent on time. He increased our rent from 90 rupees per month to 150 intentionally, knowing that my parents could not pay the inflated rate. Even though I had a good job, it remained a struggle to pay for the needs of a growing family, and by that time, we were about a year and a half behind on our rent payments.

To our surprise, our lawyer told us, "Until there is a petition and a hearing, you don't have to pay any rent. Keep the money and wait until the decision comes." That was encouraging to us, but we did not know what would happen when the court finally heard our case.

As the litigation continued to drag on, a Catholic school nearby was gracious enough to grant us access to their school hall and classrooms for our worship services, so we moved our growing church there. Even though our house was no longer used as a "church," the owner remained very angry. He began insisting that we leave altogether because he wanted to charge more rent for the house.

Both of my parents confronted this situation the way they

did every situation in prayer. However, my mother put her faith into action and did the groundwork for the trial process. She made sure to be punctual to each and every court session. When she was finally called to testify, God showed us His favor and mercy by impressing on the judge's heart to have pity on her for being harassed by a rich landlord.

"So, you have been paying 90 rupees per month for many years, and all of a sudden, you are being charged 150 rupees?"

"Yes, sir."

"How long have you been paying the increased price?"

My mother told the court how long and allowed them to calculate the time of increased payment before turning back to her.

"It appears, Mrs. Mathews, that you have overpaid," the judge began. "Pay the court 1,620 rupees to cover the 18 months' back rent, and from now on pay 90 per month in rent. Come here to the court to make the payment, and we will give it to your landlord. You do not have to deal with him yourself. Until you find a new home, no one will force you to leave. Do you understand?"

She understood the judge's instructions clearly and praised God all the way home. He had once again intervened in our time of need and worked out the details in our favor. We rejoiced as a family over the fact that we would no longer have to deal with our angry landlord, and because we no longer had to worry about being evicted. Although we owed a huge lump sum, my parents were confident that God would provide—as He always did.

GOD'S GIFTS AND HIS TIMING
(ECCLESIASTES 3:1)

In our neighborhood, I'd sometimes find my brothers sitting

outside a neighbor's window to listen to the neighbor's record player. They simply liked the music, but it made me upset, and I would grab them by their hand and send them home. On the way, I would sternly reprimand them for lurking around people's homes, because the neighbors did not like us: "You need to be in your house! If you need a record player, God will provide a record player."

Of course, finally, having a good job meant that I could provide food, necessities, and rent, as well as a few nice things we had only ever dreamed about. One day at the hotel, a guest purchased a new record player and gave me his old one for free. My brothers were so elated when I brought it home and could not believe our stroke of fortune. Before long, a German guest came to stay at my hotel. We often talked during his stay and quickly became friends. When he returned to Germany, he left me with his state-of-the-art double-deck cassette player as a gesture of friendship. It made us the only home in our entire neighborhood to own such a thing. For the first time, our street was filled with the sound of music on a regular basis.

Our humble little home was filling up with things we'd long gone without. God was showing me that He was working faithfully in our lives. I recognized God's hand in these things, and although it did not necessarily soften my heart, it widened my understanding of God's favor, power, and the way He chooses to intervene in our lives. I learned to understand His favor in my life and to not bad-mouth my lack or my needs to others. I was learning that when the path seems foggy, there is no need to worry. FOG is simply an acronym for the Favor of God.

As I walked through the restaurant one afternoon, I noticed an American man having lunch by himself. I could tell he was an American because he did not have any cigarettes in his shirt pocket, a near non-negotiable if he had been European. That was the Indian understanding of Western men...Europeans smoke, Americans do not. Since it was part of my job to talk with patrons and build relationships with them, I approached him so I could introduce myself.

"Sir, how is everything? Are you enjoying your meal?" I asked, using the most proper tone of voice I could muster.

He nodded, "Oh yeah, everything is fine, thanks."

I continued to engage in small-talk the way I was accustomed to with the guests. "I'm glad to hear it. May I ask where you are from?"

"I'm from America," he replied, but I noticed he was looking at me oddly. I did not know why, and I did not know what else to say, so I wished him a good day and moved on through the restaurant.

A little while later, I was standing near the door, surveying the room. I could sense the American man looking at me, trying to catch my attention, so I went back to his table.

"Sir, is everything all right?"

He nodded and said, "I have a question. Do you mind answering it?"

I nodded, "Please, go ahead."

"Your name tag says, Bennie Matthew. Are you a Christian?"

A bit uneasy of what he was expecting from me; I gave a slight smile and said, "Yes, sir, I am a born-again Christian."

He got so excited that he accidentally shook the table and rattled the cutlery. He jumped up and, after giving me a big hug, exclaimed, "Praise God! My name is Mack."

We sat down, and he continued, "I've been in this country for three months, and I have not seen or met a single Christian." He was there working for an oil company and began to tell me more of his story. "I am from Houston, Texas, and I attend Houston Northwest Baptist Church. My church is praying for me and my trip, and I have been deeply longing to meet with another believer. I am truly excited to meet you. How do you know Jesus?"

"My parents are in ministry full-time," I said. "I'm born-again, but I'm still half-and-half sometimes. When I find favor from God in material things, I give honor to God, but other times I depend on my own strength and understanding." I felt compelled to be honest. I was a sideline Christian who thought my life was 50% me and 50% God. Nevertheless, Mack was thrilled to find a fellow believer, and we talked for some time. He invited me up to his room later, and we sat there and talked for hours.

As I was about to leave, he called to me and said, "Bennie, wait, I want to give you something. Don't take it wrong," he said as he put some money in my hand.

I put it down, "No, I cannot possibly take this money."

He said, "No, please, I want you to keep it." He took the money and put it in my shirt pocket. By this time, I was in tears. I went to the bathroom and washed my hands and face, and went back to the restaurant, looking at the money in complete astonishment. This brother had given me about two and a half, maybe three, months' worth of my salary. I put it back in my pocket, reminding myself of my commitment that whatever I got would go straight to my mother; and not only my paycheck, but all my tips. That was the covenant I had made with God, and I intended to honor it.

Usually, when I came home from work at midnight or 1:00 a.m., I would give my mother the money I'd made that day, and she would sleepily put it under her pillow. We got milk and water deliveries in the morning and evening since we did not have a refrigerator, and she would use the change from my tips to pay the delivery man each morning. Sometimes, even though I hadn't gone to bed until late, she would wake me up at 5:00 a.m. in a panic, unable to find the money.

Most of the time, it had just slipped out of the pillowcase and fallen under the bed, it happened at least once or twice a month, but when she woke me that particular morning, she sounded more alarmed than usual.

"Son, tell me, who gave you this money?"

I was hardly awake, and I mumbled into my blankets, "Mom, the money is under the pillow, I saw you put it under the pillow."

She shook my shoulder, rigorously, "Son, I want you to get up."

"Mom, the money is there. Please don't bother me; I want to sleep."

She shifted into her firm voice, "Son, get up and tell me where you got the money." My mother was obviously alarmed with the huge amount of money under her pillow and was curious to know the details of the source. She knew it wasn't a payday, so I should not have gotten paid so much.

"Where did this money come from?" she sternly asked again.

I tried brushing off the conversation one more time. "Mom, I'll tell you the story later."

She said, "No, I want you to tell me now!"

Finally, I sat up. "Mom, an American, came to the restaurant. He is a Christian, and his name is Mack. He's been in this country for about three months and has been eagerly waiting to meet another believer. I am the first Christian he has met here, and he was ecstatic to finally be able to sit down and discuss the Lord. He's a Baptist, lives in Houston, and is working here for some oil company or something and wanted to give me the money. I tried to decline the gift, but he refused and insisted that I have it. Now it's yours."

She shook her head, "Son, you won't believe this."

"What?" I asked, partly aggravated and debating whether or not I could go back to sleep.

She said, "Today is the day that I have to pay the court the fees we owe for our house rent. I have been praying, 'God, how will I ever pay this?' I did not know if they would evict us from our home if we could not pay the money, and so I've been praying. Can you imagine the magnitude of this miracle? God sends a man from America; he roams around India for three months until he finally meets you, a day before this lady needs rent money. God spoke to him, and he gave you the exact amount we needed at just the right time."

Our God, again, proved to be an on-time God!

It reminded me of the story of the widow of Zarephath. She had no advance warning, no knowledge that Elijah was coming, but she was picking up a couple of sticks at exactly the right spot and exactly the right time to meet the prophet. How much time does it take to pick up two sticks? The prophet met her and asked her to fetch him a cup of water—during a time of drought, no less, but she was willing. As she turned to go and get the water, he said, "Oh, and can you bake me a piece of bread, too?"

She had been collecting two sticks in order to make a final meal for herself and her son before they died, and she tried explaining this to Elijah. But, she knew he was a man of God, and she chose to be obedient with the very little she had. She gave out of her nothingness, and when she did, the Lord took what she gave and did a miracle. He kept on giving right back to her.

God sent my new American friend named Mack to India at just the right time. It was no accident; it wasn't by chance, and it wasn't luck. This was a divine appointment and the favor of

God. God sent him to meet me so that, together, we could see and experience His miraculous works.

Mom finally let me go back to sleep and went off rejoicing as she finally paid the court fees. The whole experience was completely orchestrated by God. I continued to bring all the money I made to my mother and marveled as God took what I gave and kept lavishing it back on to me.

CAMERAS AND COMPATRIOTS

Settling the court issues with the landlord was a tremendous relief for my family, but we realized we needed to buy a house somewhere else very soon. The church was growing, and we needed space to worship corporately as well as a prayer hall. My mother found a property that would suit our needs, but of course, there was not enough money to buy it.

My parents did what they always did when we needed something: they prayed. I did what I always did when we needed something: I went to work.

It was during that time that a European man came to stay at the hotel. He brought with him a Nikon SLR camera with an expensive zoom lens. It was a very costly camera, worth roughly $1,400 to $1,800 in those days. I would drive him to various locations in the afternoons, give him tips that only a local could offer, advise him so that he was able to save money, and interpret for him whenever he would speak to locals. He taught me how to take pictures with that camera and then gave me the camera as a gift before he left to return home.

I was completely stunned and at a loss for words. I took it to a photographer friend of mine who owned a photo studio right next to the hotel. He, too, was shocked and said, "Who gave you this, Bennie? You are one of the first people in Baroda to own a camera like this. My friend, a fellow fine arts college graduate, is looking for one just like this and has been working with his Singapore connection to import one. I know he will pay you 20,000 rupees if you want to sell it." That was $1,600 or more in those days. My business mind started churning, and I thought, "I could buy a car for that amount and run a taxi business, or buy a property." On the other hand, I wanted to keep my job because that was a steady source of income.

I replied to my eager friend, "Oh, I don't know if I should sell it or not; maybe I should keep it." Staying true to my usual ambition and investment-focused mind, I decided I would learn to use the camera and run a professional photography business on the side. However, I did agree to meet with the man from the fine arts college who wanted a camera like it and ended up becoming good friends with him. He was a professional photographer who specialized in weddings and other formal events. I went with him on several photo shoots and learned how to use my SLR camera very quickly. He would even borrow my camera from time to time to shoot for special projects. I was grateful that he introduced me to photography and was excited to discover business opportunities to help my family finally come out of poverty.

We were a big family, and our needs were severe and urgent.

Still pursuing the property for our new home, my parents had attempted to secure a loan for a down payment but were unsuccessful. I finally decided to sell the camera in order to help with our financial situation. Though the camera alone would not bring in enough money to pay for the house, it would bring enough in for the initial down payment.

That camera was an incredible blessing from God because

it gave me the opportunity to make friends and connections with people who were artists, interior designers, and architects. In those days, scanners and imaging machines weren't available to do presentations, so cameras were used as much as possible. Spending my free afternoons with people in that field broadened my knowledge beyond just the food and beverage profession. I kept my eyes and ears open to learn, and I was generous in my dealings with people because the generosity of my parents was in my DNA, which in turn opened new doors of opportunities for me.

Opportunities to make new friends, even among influential people, came by often. Everyone thought I was becoming a highly influential person by working in this fancy, high-end hotel. However, the reality was that I was merely an ordinary man who had the favor of an extraordinary God.

I was often taken by surprise by my own words, ideas, drawings, and other creativity God allowed me to express. Even though I knew deep down, it was from Him alone, and I kept thinking it was partly God and partly myself. As I look back, I know it was the hand of God in the "glove" of my life that was directing, guiding, and helping put the spotlight on me. He was orchestrating events in my favor—His work can bring blessings out of nothing.

One afternoon, while I was spending time at my photographer friend's studio, I mentioned how we were struggling and in need of significant funds before we could buy the house. Even though he wasn't a believer, I believe God moved in his heart and persuaded him to loan me 18,000 rupees that day. That was the exact remainder of the money we needed to sign the papers for our new house. My parents were so surprised, and so were other members of our church. It was yet another example my mother could share about God's miracle-working hand.

I had to acknowledge it was God behind all of those miracles.

God's favor was so apparent in the relationships I formed at the hotel—with CEOs of companies, administrative team members, and business owners—many of them asked me to be the coordinator of all their major company events going forward.

Though a few gave false hope of a future with their organization in order to benefit from my services, most truly followed through with great offers and appointments to join their companies. As before, I would take those letters to the General Manager of my hotel, and he would match my salary to the new offer. Oswald Mills and Hindustan Motors were two companies that always asked for me when they had to deal with our hotel. They complimented my management abilities, so my manager asked me to represent them at every event. Even the family of the founding CEOs of Hindustan Motors and other key leaders trusted me enough to give me the freedom to organize their events.

One day, Mr. Kailash, the Chief Liaison Officer of Hindustan Motors and a very good friend of mine, called me at work and asked me to immediately meet him at the front desk. I was very concerned and immediately rushed to find him. I could see that Mr. Kailash was with many of his friends, so I thought he needed me to run an errand for him or fetch something he had left behind. As he saw me, he enthusiastically greeted me, and I shook his hand. He then introduced me to the man next to him, "This is the Chief Project Manager, Mr. K. K. Gopinathan, the man who will be the voice of Mr. C. K. Birla, and he is from South India just like you." I tried not to cringe. I still hated being identified as a 'South Indian' because of how it was used to tease and torment me during my school days. To my peers, South

Indians were rednecks or hillbillies. I always pretended I was from North India in order to avoid being associated with such terrible stigmas.

"This is the guy I was telling you about," Mr. Kailash said to Gopinathan, gesturing to me. "Mathews is a good friend, a hard worker, and went out of his way to help us during our launch here by taking care of our needs."

"All right," said Gopinathan. He looked at me, intently, "Can you come to my office tomorrow?"

"Yes, sir," I nervously replied.

That night, I was far too nervous to sleep well. I woke up early the next morning, got dressed in my very best, and went to his office. He made me a stunning offer and asked if I would be a supervisor and manage the Guesthouse for Hindustan Motors and assist them with the transportation department. They wanted to start a guest house with accommodations and luxury, similar to one of the five-star hotels. He explained, "Because we will have so many executives staying with us while they travel on business, we want to have our own place. As you have experience running the hotel business, we want you to make it possible. We are negotiating and are in the process of purchasing an eight-story building. We want to convert the top four floors into luxurious hotel-type housing. Money is not an issue, and I want you to work with our interior designer and make sure everything is done right. Your experience from this hotel will be a great asset to our business!"

"That's fine," I stammered. "I don't know anything about the transport business, but I will help you."

"Oh, it's easy to learn; we'll teach you, and we know you are a fast learner," Mr. Gopinathan responded.

I figured he had favored me because I was South Indian and

wanted to help a fellow southerner. He laid out the salary, travel budget, and the extra expenses they would cover for me. In the end, it was about three times the amount I was earning at the hotel. He gave me a letter of appointment on Hindustan Motors letterhead, which I deemed an incredible honor. I never dreamed of such an opportunity!

As I had done so many times before, I showed the letter to my General Manager at the hotel right away. He read the letter and sighed. He looked up at me with a sense of remorse and said, "Bennie, it is better for you to go there. I would love for you to stay here, but I think this is a good move. You will only enhance your career by going to work for them." God had used him to help my family come out of poverty, and I was very grateful for everything I had learned while working in his hotel. I had no idea the kind of things the Lord had in store when I first began as his employee and was so fortunate for my training and the many friends who helped develop my experience in design and photography.

I moved over to Hindustan Motors and was put in charge of their eight-story building. It was fully equipped for foreigners and top executives to come and stay in comfort, boasting at least a million dollars' worth of furniture, mattresses, air conditioners, and a litany of amenities—things even rich local people did not have.

Hindustan Motors' guesthouse was previously managed by a man who cost the company a lot of money. When I started, I quickly began saving money for the company just as I was used to doing for my family. The decrease in expenses made Mr. Gopinathan even happier. He could not believe we could run such a lavish place on such a tight budget.

Like Joseph, who experienced God's hand upon him because

he gave God the glory, the Lord was giving me His favor. I saw incredible things happen in that place, and I met a great number of amazing people. It was a comfortable job that I was proud to have. I felt like royalty; I could drive a car home to my parents' or be chauffeured by a car and driver from the guesthouse. I was providing for my family, and people respected me; I was finally "somebody."

My parents loved the things that God was doing in my life and would often remind me of whom to give praise to, saying, "Son, you know God is doing this." And I would reply, "Yes, I know."

It was true, I did know God was actively engaged in my life, but I still felt that learning to be self-sufficient was my most important goal. I was proud of whom I had become, and I believed my climb up the Indian corporate ladder would continue indefinitely. I was happy with my "50/50" life. I knew my parent's reminders that this was "all God" were so I could become one of "them." But I belonged in the business world.

However, one cannot stay true to their Christian convictions and survive the corruption in the Indian business world.

God had other plans.

CHAPTER 4

APPLICATION POINTS

Our Heavenly Father is willing to bless us when we leave our lives in His hands.

As I began to walk in faith, I began to "taste and see" the goodness of God in my life. He moved in our favor in small things like record players, and in large things like rent disputes. However, my heart remained committed only to making money and moving up in the world. I continued to limit Him.

- What is limiting the fullness of God from operating in your life?
- Are you relying more on your own abilities?
- Pray and ask God to show you how to fully surrender.

God can work through our faithfulness even when our understanding is limited.

Though I was reluctant to follow God the way my parents did, one thing I remained faithful about was giving the money I made to my mother. When God brought Mack from Houston into my life—and his monetary gift—I remembered my covenant to give it to my mother. I had no idea it was the full amount she needed the very next day to settle our rent dispute, but God knew, and once again proved Himself an on-time God who is intimately involved in the details of our lives.

Are you being obedient "with the little" so that God can do what He wishes with more?

I was an ordinary man who had the favor of an extraordinary God. I started as a doorman at a hotel, the lowest job there, yet God's favor opened doors for me on a regular basis. Are you grateful for the small things He has done in your life?

CHAPTER 5

THE CITY THAT NEVER SLEEPS

So when they saw Him, they were amazed; and His mother said to Him, "Son, why have You done this to us? Look, Your father and I have sought You anxiously."
Luke 2:48

Even at the young age of 12, Jesus knew that pleasing His earthly parents wasn't as important as pleasing His Heavenly Father. That alone was His most important business at hand.Doing business in what I perceived to be my father's way—giving, serving, while getting by on scraps and morsels—did not interest me at all. I knew God was big, always on time and that He faithfully provided things we needed, but I finally had a very important job and was satisfied with doing business my way: working hard to get to the top. I was content with my position running the Hindustan Motors guesthouse, and I knew that it was only a matter of time before God would provide an even better position to suit my large ambitions. I was partly right. God did, in fact, have a new position for me, but it wasn't at all where I thought it would be.

GOING TO AMERICA

After some time, my aunt Alice and several of my cousins

from my father's side of the family emigrated to America. They wanted all of us to move there together as a family, but my father wasn't interested. The ministry was growing, and he felt his place was to stay put and continue to invest everything he could in God's business. Even though I was making more money than I ever had, the financial situation at home was still very tight, with eight people living on one income.

My mother tried to reason with my father: "If you go to America and get your green card, you can bring the boys over. If they are working hard in the States, they can send money back here to India, and we will have more than enough to do God's work!"

My father finally agreed and began the process for himself, my brother Finny, and me to gain our proper documentation. We were the oldest, so we were chosen to go out of all the siblings. To file legally and wait for a visa to America is a long process, so we spent a lot of time standing in lines and being treated badly by people. It was a tough thing, and many times I thought, "Who wants to be in America? I don't."

We were thoroughly investigated before we were allowed to go. One Sunday morning, we came home to find two large, muscular FBI agents waiting at our door. They had many questions for us, including, "Are you really the Mathews family? Why do you have a Christian name? Do you really have six kids? Are you telling the truth?"

I was 22 years old when we made our trip to the United States. I remember thinking, "I work at Hindustan Motors. I have good certificates from all the jobs I have ever held and recommendation letters from people who will boast about me and my abilities. I will go to America and make millions, no problem." I was so confident that everything would happen for me quickly and easily in America that I told my brother I would buy him a high-end Royal Enfield motorcycle.

GOING OUT WITH A BANG

I left Mumbai and headed to America on the first and only Air India flight of my life. In those days, patriotism was so strong and deeply embedded into the culture that if you left India and you did not fly Air India, you were considered to be some sort of traitor. For that reason, a Pan American flight was out of the question; it had to be Air India. Only then would the immigration people not harass you with questions like, "Where are you going? Why are you going there? Show me your papers." I decided I would never fly Air India again, even if someone gave me a free ticket. That was the extent of my patriotism. But at least I was finally bound for New York!

Everything was fine for about two hours. Then the pilot's voice came over the intercom. "We are experiencing some technical difficulties," he said. "We are turning the plane around and going back to Mumbai."

The flight attendants quickly began to walk up and down the aisles, fussing over all the passengers and giving emergency landing instructions; "In case this happens, you must take this, you must do that. Everyone, please be seated and buckle up!"

Sitting next to me was a young man who looked to be in his 30s. He took out his pen and started writing his name, "Ajit," on his arm. "Man, there is something wrong with this flight," he said. "I have been flying for a long time, so I know they are not telling us the whole truth."

I could not figure him out but could feel his nervousness in almost an infectious way. I asked why he wrote on his arm, to which he replied, "I wrote my name so that if this plane crashes, they'll know who I am!"

There was fear in my heart, too. I had only flown once before, and that was a short domestic flight. This was my first international flight, and the guy next to me had written his name on his arm so the authorities could identify his body if we crashed. I could not believe this was really happening!

I knew I had the hope of salvation through Christ if we all perished, but it was obvious this man did not have that same hope. Still, I was too scared to share anything with him. In fact, I had never been bold enough to share anything about Christ with anyone up to that point. The pilot dumped fuel, and the flight attendants prepared the cabin. It was a very scary situation, and the next hour or two seemed like an eternity. Many thoughts were running through my mind, and I was starting to wonder if this USA trip was even worth it. It rattled me and made me confess my trust in God several times at 32,000 feet.

We finally landed safely, and the plane was pulled over to one side of the runway where several fire engines and emergency personnel waited in the rain to assist with whatever the problem was. The flight attendants shuffled us all off the plane, and we were led by the police to an isolated room. That is when we received news that there had been a bomb threat, which had prompted the emergency landing. It also prompted all kinds of security screenings before we could leave again.

I kept thinking, "Going to America is tough! But somehow, I have to get across the ocean to America, so my friends will know I made it too." Going to America from India, or anywhere out of India in those days, was a ticket out of poverty—almost anyone I knew would have given a kidney to move to America. Even today, Americans do not fully realize the value of living in their country. That thought gave me the courage to board another airplane after an 18-hour delay.

GETTING MY BEARINGS

I was very happy to see my father and uncle waiting for me at the airport after finally landing in New York around 8 p.m. that Saturday night. Driving home, I remember being so surprised to see that everyone seemed to be riding in a car. I could not see anyone walking on the streets at all. Cars kept whizzing back and forth, and I thought, "Does everyone drive in this country?" My father had been going back and forth to America for a few years now, so he was used to it. But for me, it was a completely enthralling revelation. There were hardly any potholes in the roads at all, no cows on the street, no one was spitting or even walking on the streets, all the roads were paved; everything was decent and in perfect order. I had never seen anything like it in my life. I really liked the logistics and efficiency!

I was going to live in the attic of my Aunt Alice's three-story house in New York. When we got there, I walked up wooden stairs and across wooden floors, wondering if they were safe or if they would break. Her house did not seem to have any concrete in it at all, like the houses in India. Even the toilets were different! But because of the excitement and enthusiasm of being in America, it did not take me very long to adjust.

I wanted to find a job and start work right away, but I knew the first thing I had to do in America was to find a church. When I left India, my mother said to me, "Son, you have to go to church. Wherever you go, be faithful to that place. Remember that your dad is a pastor and how discouraging it is when someone comes and then leaves. Your testimony should be that you are faithful to one church. Stick to one place. Wherever God leads you, be faithful to that church." For my parents, faithfulness has always been foundational to everything else in their life. They had always drilled it into me to be faithful: to God, to family, to justice, to church, and in every aspect of life. That is how I learned the importance of faithfulness.

Someone told my father there was going to be a mission conference at a church in Harlem called "Bethel Gospel Assembly." They invited us to go. For the first time, I saw a vibrant and lively worship from the believers in that congregation. Everyone was worshipping, singing with big voices, and dancing. It was not like our formal, Indian style of worship; we are more conservative, to say the least. This was something totally different and new, and I liked it. I deeply contemplated their preaching style, authentic worship, and their passionate heart for missions and was refreshed to see my faith through such a new and exciting lens. In fact, they emphasized missions and giving above almost anything else, and I really liked that system. I believed in giving and being generous, so I prayed, "Okay, God, is this the church I should attend?" I did not hear an audible response from God, but I knew He had led me there, so Bethel Gospel Assembly became my church, and I was faithful there.

Of course, my Aunt Alice believed that finding a church and a stable job was vital, but she also believed that I needed to find a wife. She began lining up Indian girls in the community to meet me soon after I arrived and seemed to be on a mission in regard to my love life. I was an eligible Indian bachelor, and since there were more girls than boys in the Indian community, everyone had decided it was time for me to get married. The week I landed, the pastor of my aunt's church came to her home to visit me, pray with me, and see if I was legitimately born-again so that they could begin introducing me to the girls in the church.

Meanwhile, I was thinking, "I'm here to work and to make money. Marriage is not my thing." I was in America to find a job, not a wife.

LOOKING FOR A JOB

Having held such a prominent position at Hindustan Motors, along with my experience in the hotel and restaurant business, I thought it would be easy to find a similar job in America. Even though I wasn't raised in a toxic caste system, that mentality had crept into my thinking, and I could not "lower myself" to work as a waiter or a server of any kind. I was a food and beverage coordinator, and I would not settle for anything less than a job in management.

One day I walked all the way from 34th Street to 49th Street. New York blocks are long, and it seemed like I had walked forever. I would stop in every restaurant I saw and ask, "Do you need a manager?" I carried a big file of all my Indian documents and recommendations, but I quickly learned that nobody cared about my Indian paperwork. They just asked if I had experience and told me to fill out a form. They all told me to start as a waiter and work my way up, but I knew I wasn't going to do that. In my mind, I had already earned my stripes in India and had no intention of going through that again.

I had searched diligently for three months when I finally got an appointment to work as a reservation agent with TWA Airlines in the World Trade Center. I settled on the position and started the training immediately, but was still looking for another job in the meantime. I received the selective service registration card in the mail, along with an offer to join the U.S. Army. The thought of joining the Army really interested me, as I did not have a real job yet. According to the Indian custom, I had to consult my elders first. I shared my idea of joining—which led to me getting all sorts of calls from my immediate family, warning me about it: "America is always at war with other countries," and "We should be in God's army." Since I was not very knowledgeable about these things, I reluctantly listened to the advice of my family and friends. I desperately needed a good job to help my family, and I was getting anxious about finding the right direction.

A few days later, my aunt told me they were looking for a dietary aide at the nursing home where she worked. I thought that a dietary aide's job was to tell people how many calories were in everything, so I believed I could do that with no problem. In fact, it did not seem different from being a food and beverage coordinator. She knew someone in the kitchen, so I went and applied for the job. I interviewed with the main dietician, a sharply dressed Chinese woman named Connie.

She asked me, "Do you even know what a dietary aide is?"

I responded confidently by saying, "Oh yeah, I worked as a food and beverage manager."

Connie said, "Okay. We'll pay you $10 an hour. Is that all right?"

The president of India did not make $10 an hour in those days. Of course, it was all right!

"That's fine," I said, trying to remain cool and not look overly eager.

"Let me show you the job then."

Connie took me to the back of the kitchen, where there were three huge tanks. All three of them had water in them, and big utensils hung on the side. She started explaining how I would take a dish, put it in one solution, clean it, take the big brush, dunk it in that solution, take it out, put it into next and clean it. Lastly, I was to use the big water sprayer to rinse it and put it on the dryer.

I was shocked. She wanted me to be a dishwasher!

"I'm sorry," I said, feeling rather offended by the new job description. "Do you know whom you're talking to?" Obviously, she did not. "I worked like you in an extravagant hotel with over 30 people under my supervision. I was the supervisor of a well-known hotel owned by a company like GM here in America."

She cocked her head and raised an eyebrow. "And where was it you said you were working?"

"In India."

"That was India. This is America. Welcome to America!" She then abruptly told me, "If you want this job, then take it. If not, don't waste my time."

"Okay, fine," I said with a somewhat confident smile and turned to leave. As I was walking out, the man who introduced me to Connie and a friend of my aunt stopped me. He said, "What are you doing, Bennie? For three months you haven't had a job. This job is a good job, man, just take it."

I tried to reason with him. "But at home, I never washed a dish. My mother never let me wash them. If people in India knew that Bennie Mathews was working as a dishwasher in America, it would be shameful. I can go back to India and be in a higher managerial position at the company where I was working. Do you know where I worked?"

"Bennie," he said with a sigh, "you don't understand. This is America. You'll be getting $10 an hour! Nobody in India will see you do this. Just work there until you get another job."

He was very convincing and made some really good points, so I turned around and went right back to Connie's office and humbly accepted the job. She gave me my instructions like a drill instructor—I had to wear white pants, a white shirt, and a special hat to wash the dishes. Moving from management level to a dishwasher's life was demeaning for me. As I started washing those dishes that the first day, tears of frustration and shame welled up in my eyes. I had to splash water on my face because I did not want anyone to see me cry. I thought, "God, why do you have me here? I hate this job." The gloves were all too large for my hands, so I could not wear them, and the chemicals in the water made my skin start to peel. I was miserable.

When I got back home, I showed my red and peeling hands to my father.

"Look at this! Is this America? This is what you called me over for? I was better off in India!"

I called my mother.

"Mom, life is terrible here. I don't like this place. Today, I was washing the dishes of people who were spitting on their plates; the chemicals are so harsh; my hands are raw and peeling..." I kept lodging one complaint after the next. My mother knows I'm a clean freak. Even in India, where generally, everything is dirty, I liked to be clean. I never walked barefoot and always had my own way of doing things so that my possessions were clean. I had even created my own room under the stairs, which led to the upstairs tenants. I wasn't going to share my bed with any of my siblings. I was a "germaphobe" living among germs.

She responded, just like a mother, and said the words I wanted to hear, "Son, you should just come back. Last week, I saw your manager from Hindustan Motors, and he asked me how you're doing. He misses you, and I think he will give you your job back. Why don't you come back?"

FATHER'S ADVICE—LISTEN, MY SON (PROVERBS 1:8)

Just then, my father walked into the room, snatched the phone out of my hand and slammed it down. "Don't you do that again," he said, pointing his finger at me. "Everyone has to grow from the bottom up. Do you know who gets to come from the top down? A gravedigger. Everything that grows does so from the bottom up, and so will you. Never complain like that to your mother again."

He was firm, but I was angry and feeling sorry for myself. I thought he did not care about me and was further convinced of my lowly situation. However, he simply knew that God was breaking me like a horse needs to be broken before it can be of any good use. God was preparing me to use me, even though I kept complaining, "Oh God, why this?"

The one thing I did know how to be was faithful, so I continued—faithfully working at the nursing home. Someone there found out I had experience working with computers one day. I had used the old green screen Macintosh computers at Hindustan Motors to maintain the inventory. I loved the computer room in India because it had incredible air conditioning.

Connie said to me, "Mathews, do you know how to use Lotus and Word? Can you help me get this menu typed?" I pretended like I did because even if I did not, I knew I could figure it out quickly.

I typed the new menu and made it look as nice as I possibly could using some fancy fonts. Connie was very impressed, and before long, she started calling me into the office to work on other typing projects for her as well. She would assign me to go on the floors and put out menus and such. Eventually, I moved up from a dishwasher to her assistant and keeping the stock room. My dishwashing team was not happy with my promotion, probably due to the poor attitude I initially started out with. Connie favored me and would listen if I recommended a potential employee.

While I was working under Connie's supervision, I was continuing my training with TWA Airlines to be a reservation agent. I would work from 6-10 a.m. at the nursing home and then go home, change clothes, and walk to the subway station to take a train to the World Trade Center for my training at TWA from 4-11 p.m. I would not get home until midnight or later, and then I would catch a little sleep until I was up again and headed to the nursing home. If Connie wasn't there, I would have to wash dishes and take trays to different floors. It was exhausting.

One of my aunt's cousins called me one day and said, "Bennie, there's a good job at Our Lady of Mercy Medical Center. They are looking for a secretary, and they pay $13 an hour. That's a good job, Bennie! You can go to college."

I responded very enthusiastically because it was, in fact, a good job. "Wow, that's nice!" I responded, but being a reservation agent at TWA Airlines seemed like a more stable and long-term position. They would only pay me $8 an hour, but if people back in India heard that I was working for an airline, they would be more impressed. As much as I wanted to make money, I also wanted to look good in the eyes of others. God was still breaking me, but I was stubborn.

My aunt tried to reason with me, explaining, "At TWA, you will make less money, plus you will have to *pay* money to take the subway to get there. And do you know what happens on the subway? People get shot on the subway. It can happen, Bennie. You had better take this job. It is very close to our home, and the commute is very short."

I told her I would think about it.

For about two more weeks, I continued my schedule of working at the nursing home in the morning and TWA in the evening. Finally, I could take it no longer and called my supervisor at TWA, explaining that I would not be continuing. He was angry, but I was tired. The next week, I started my new job as a ward secretary at Our Lady of Mercy Medical Center.

There was a slight issue with this new position, however—I absolutely hated hospitals. Some of it had to do with my phobia of germs. When my father was diagnosed with diabetes and admitted to the hospital, I would not go to visit him due to my terrible fear of contracting some fatal virus or disease. I just did not like the medical profession at all, so it was more than ironic for me to have a job in a hospital.

My aunt's cousin was the nurse recruiter and was kind enough to teach me things like how to do CPR and how to take a temperature. On my first day, the charge nurse, Susan, asked me to take a discharged patient downstairs to the front of the hospital. I struggled with this request. Not only was I a clean freak, but I did not like touching people, especially sick people in hospitals. Nobody told me that I was going to actually interact with the patients. I was hired to be a ward secretary.

I became frustrated and prideful again and said, "I have to take the patient downstairs? That's not in the job description."

Susan patiently yet firmly looked at me and said, "Bennie, you have to take the patient downstairs."

Again, adamantly, I looked at her sternly and said, "No, they did not tell me that was part of the deal." Right away, she went inside and called my aunt's cousin, Marie.

Marie came up. "What's the problem here, Bennie? This is your first day, and already they are calling me?"

I said, "She wants me to take a patient downstairs. Is that my job?"

"Yes, Bennie, that's the job, and there's nothing wrong in doing that."

I could not help thinking, "Why did I say *yes* to this job? I would have been better off at TWA. At least I would not have to do *this.*»

Reluctantly, I finally went off to the discharged patient's room, where I was able to get him into a wheelchair and push him to the elevator. That is when I remembered Our Lady of Mercy is a teaching hospital. The elevator doors opened—it was full of the young Indian medical interns. There they stood, each one training to be a doctor, and there I stood, pushing a man in a wheelchair like an orderly. I kept my head down and hoped none of them would notice me. I was so embarrassed, so full of pride.

THE BREAKING PROCESS TO MULTIPLY (MARK 6:41)

The Saint Thomas Christians are a group of Christians from the Malabar coast (now Kerala) in South India, who follow Syriac Christianity. They are the oldest Christian community on the subcontinent, with roots dating back to the First Century AD, believed to be converted from the elite Brahmin class. Growing up, I always heard we had a Syrian Christian heritage. Syrian Christians are too prideful to do mediocre jobs. The class or caste system is engraved in them. The Syrian Christians believe that they are pure descendants of the high caste Brahmin, who were the first to be converted by the disciple Thomas, missionary to India. My maternal grandfather told me when I was younger that new converts to Christianity were the lower caste. Looking back, it is so discouraging to think of how blinded I was toward my views of faith.

When I was growing up in India, my friends often compared me to other Christians in the area. I grew tired of taking the time to explain to my friends that I was different. Hindi movies portrayed Christians as low caste people who were drunkards and smokers. My family did not drink or smoke, so it was clear to my friends in this regard that we were different. If my friends or people at work offered me a cigarette, I would say no. They used to think that Christians were free to do whatever they wanted due to skewed knowledge they had of the biblical notion of grace. I would paint a horrible picture of North Indian Christians, not realizing I was doing the opposite of what God had in mind for "all who believe." This kind of racism is still prevalent among many traditionalist Kerala Christians. For a long time, my grandfather would not even enter a coffee or tea shop if the waiter or the cook was a dark-skinned Indian man, because that would mean mingling with the lowest caste.

It is because the caste system was still alive in me that I got upset when asked to push the wheelchair. God was chipping away at my pride, bit by bit. Although I would pray every night, "Please don't let there be any discharges tonight," there would always be discharges. Not only was God teaching me that humbly serving others was not a bad thing to do, but He was also preparing me for a medical ministry in my future. God doesn't need training in doing things efficiently, but most of the time, we do.

As I continued to be faithful to that job, pushing people in wheelchairs, God opened other doors, and I soon had a new job in the admitting department. I received better pay and enjoyed the work much more. Life was finally becoming comfortable. So comfortable, in fact, that I started developing a new habit: drinking. I was losing weight, but all the commercials on TV showed men with muscles drinking beer. I thought a few beers might give me some muscles, too. That idea went away one night after work. I was having a beer as I walked home down 233rd Street in the Bronx. It was drizzling, and when I crossed the street, I slipped. My feet flew out from under me, and I landed with my head on the pavement. When I came to, I was lying on the road and could hear cars whizzing past me on either side. I quickly got up and ran to the other side of the road.

All I could think was, "Oh, Lord! What would be the headlines tomorrow morning? 'Pastor Mathews' son killed in New York because he was drunk!?'" I had been living like a hypocrite for far too long, and I knew it. I would act one way in front of my family and the church and differently when I was on my own. I knew I had to make a change. Right then and there, I decided to make a drastic and very serious decision. "God," I prayed, "I will never do this again. I will be a righteous man who lives for You."

I meant it, but after a few days, I felt like I could use a beer again. I still had one foot in God's camp and one in mine.

TEST: THE BACKDROP FOR A BEAUTIFUL TESTIMONY

I had been in America for about a year and a half, and everything seemed to be going well until one day, I suddenly developed an alarmingly high fever. I was shivering and felt chronically nauseated. I went to the Emergency Room at my hospital, but all they could tell me, "It's just a virus. There's nothing we can do."

It continued on and off for a while. I started to feel a wave of paranoia sweep over me. It was around 1989, and there was so much public speculation about HIV and AIDS. Hysteria and rumors fueled even more fear in crowded major cities like New York. I began wondering if the American government was telling the truth and if AIDS was not just a sexually transmitted disease at all. Maybe it could be in the air? Who knew? As a precaution, I always carried my own small bar of soap around in a plastic bag in my pocket, so I would not have to touch any used soap in public restrooms. But I was beginning to wonder if I had contracted AIDS from someone at the nursing home or hospital.

Finally, I became so ill that my aunt took me to the hospital. I fainted between the Emergency Room doors. She brought me in on a cart, then I threw up and fainted again. The next thing I remember is waking up in an isolation room. It was one of the infectious disease isolation rooms on my floor, and I recognized it because it was yellow, and the nurses would come and go out of it in yellow gowns and yellow masks. It was where AIDS patients were kept.

I woke up very confused and feeling just as ill as ever. I was glad to see Ophelia, a friend who also happened to be a nurse on my floor, waiting in the room with me. She was wearing yellow protective clothing. I asked her, "What happened to me?"

"I don't know, Bennie," she said. "Dr. Reddy, the infectious disease specialist, sent your blood off to be tested."

"Oh no," I thought. "My fears are true. I have AIDS."

She patted my arm with her gloved hands: "Bennie, you are paranoid, don't worry."

"Don't worry? Do you know what is wrong with me?"

She shook her head, "No, I don't know."

After Ophelia was gone, I tried to read my chart, but I did not see anything except my temperature. It had been very high, but now it had started to come down. I could not tell what was wrong with me, but I knew it was time to make a sincere commitment to God. So I prayed.

"God, I have played with You all my life and now know I was wrong. Please give me one chance to get out of this place. If this is AIDS or something even worse, save me from this disease. God, heal me, and I'll live for you forever. I will never make a mistake, never do a thing to hinder Your kingdom purpose. This is my decision-making time. I'll trust you 100%—no more 50%. I'm all Yours, God."

That night, a doctor friend of mine from India who happened to be doing his fellowship at the hospital came to visit me. When he came into the room, I asked desperately, "Can you please tell me what is wrong with me?" And he said, "Not to worry, man; you have malaria."

I thought, "Oh, thank God."

Everyone else was surprised that malaria could have been dormant in my body for so long. In my mind, I knew what had happened. God wanted to wake me up and get me back on the right track. I should have been living for His purposes all along, not for worldly things.

When I got out of the hospital, I was a changed man. From that day until now, my life has been 100% God.

CHAPTER 5

APPLICATION POINTS

Satisfaction is a dead-end.

God was faithful to show Himself as an "on-time God" in so many ways, providing things I needed for myself and for my family. However, I finally had a very important job, and I was satisfied with doing business my way. I was satisfied benefitting from the goodness of God operating in my life and convinced I'd struck the perfect balance of "half me, half God."

- If you're making that mistake, ask God to change your heart and give you a hunger for His business.

- When the balance in your life is all God, not half God, you will find He is providing for all your needs.

God will tear down the fortresses of pride in your life.

I had so much pride in the position I had achieved and the way God had blessed my partial obedience. It was quite a jolt to go from corporate star to unknown dishwasher! But God was teaching me that humbly serving others is of greater value in His economy than proudly serving the heads of major corporations. He was stripping me of the "half me half Him" in which I had trusted and put my faith in for so long.

Do not ignore the things God uses to get your attention. Do not despise the things God uses to teach you His ways.

CHAPTER 6

THE BUSINESS PARTNER

And He said to them, "Why did you seek Me? Did you not know that I must be about My Father's business?"
Luke 2:49

When Jesus made it clear to His parents that doing the work of His Heavenly Father was the most important thing in His life, it marked the beginning of a lifetime of ministry. Everything that came after it was done in faithfulness and for the glory of God.

When I told the Lord He could have 100% of me, not just 50%, it was the start of a lifetime of genuinely seeing Him, and seeing Him work in me and through me for His glory. One of the first ways I allowed God's 100% in my life was to show His authority over my life by letting Him bring me a life mate. I did not want to leave such an important decision up to myself.

TRUE LOVE IS BLIND

My Aunt Alice had been suggesting one girl after the other, urging me to get married from the moment I landed in America. Even my dad began calling from India, urging the issue, saying, "Bennie, you need to get married." They just did not understand that I wanted to work and make money first and not get married immediately. Once my dad began insisting that it was time for me to get married, I finally relented, with certain conditions.

I told my father, "Okay, Dad. I will get married, but I want you to find me a wife from India. I don't want anyone from here."

He responded by saying, "Bennie, that's a bad idea. Bringing a wife to America will take a long time with the immigration and the legal processes. Don't you remember how hard that was for you? Just pick one who is already in America."

I replied, "I don't want anybody from here. I want someone from India, and I don't want to select her; I want you to go and do it." I was adamant.

He sighed, "Okay." Then he called my aunt: "Why can't you find him a girl there?"

She scoffed back, saying, "I bring him all these girls, and he is not interested! I think he is not interested in girls!" She was afraid I had given in to the American culture.

When my aunt found out that I was bent on marrying someone from India, she said, "Bennie, are you out of your mind? You know they drive on the other side of the road in India. Are you going to bring her here, teach her to drive, get her a certification to work with, and so on? I think you should marry someone from here. What about so-and-so? She has long hair, and you like long hair."

I would not yield.

My father finally accepted my decision and began putting feelers out in India, spreading the word that I was officially on the market. At pastors' meetings, he would let it be known that he was looking for a wife for his son in America. That stirred up quite a response. It did not matter what I looked like; marrying a boy in America was any girl's ticket to a better life.

People started sending my father photos and testimonies, and he would review them before forwarding them to me. I got a dozen testimonies and pictures of prospective girls to look over, and one, in particular, stood out to me. She shared how she was saved at the age of 11 and came from a Catholic background; she was very zealous about serving God. She had been praying about marrying into a family that was in ministry, a large family, and for it to be God-honoring. "I need to serve God, and I want to love God," she wrote.

I liked her passion and purpose, as well as the Scriptures she shared in her letter. I did not like the fact that she had short hair, however. My aunt was right; I liked long hair. It is an Indian thing, but such things were why I did not want to make such a decision on my own. I did not want to date because I was afraid I would approach dating like I would if I was buying a car—you find a problem with the tires, the model, the color, the mileage, and you judge it as unacceptable and move on. I knew if finding a wife was left up to me, I would fail. Although I did not pursue the input of my family on many matters in my life, this was an issue I knew I desperately wanted their advice on.

I wanted God to take care of my marriage. I truly trusted Him at that spiritual high in my life like never before. I knew He could do great things, and I had resolved to be faithful to Him.

I called my father in India, "Dad, I like the testimony of this girl, Lina. Where is she?" He gave me her background and agreed to look into the details about her and her family. He also told me to send a picture that he could share with her, so I had a friend take a side profile photo to send him. My father made copies of my one-sided photo and gave them to several people, including Lina's parents. I continued learning things about Lina and her family, like the fact that she and her sister were the first ones to get saved in a staunch Roman Catholic family with her parents following shortly after. Her sister's husband, Pastor Wilson, and his brother, Sunny, were pretty well known as Christian composers and musicians. We had hosted Sunny in our home when he had ministered at our church. I also visited Sunny's home several times. He was like another brother to me. I felt like I already knew a lot about Lina's family, and my family agreed to go forward with the proposal. My father asked me to come to India to meet Lina and her family.

"Dad," I said, "You know that I am working hard and making money. I cannot take a single day off. I am trying to save all of my vacation time so that when I come, I can stay in India for a while."

"Son, you need to come now," he said in his deep voice. I knew he was serious. We said our good-byes, and I immediately called my younger brother, "Finny, can you go check this girl out and tell me what you think?"

"You want me to do what?"

"Go, meet her family, meet with her, and tell me what she's like," I prompted.

I could almost see him rolling his eyes from a thousand miles away as he reluctantly agreed. "Okay, fine."

He knew the family, so he went to visit them. When he got back, I called him again.

"So, what do you think about the girl?"

"I think she is good for you, her testimony is amazing, and she is very passionate about serving God. If you want to know anything more, you need to come here and talk to her yourself."

"No, that's good," I said. "I'll take it from here."

By this time, I had written a letter to Lina, and she had written back to me. We had not spoken on the phone yet, only through letters, and we were both anxiously anticipating each time we would hear from one another. I wrote to her that I trusted God 100%, and even though I was living in America, nothing belonged to me. I had tasted the goodness of God, and my life belonged to Him. Ministry was my priority, and I was working hard so that I could financially support the ministry my parents were so faithfully carrying out. I put everything out there and told her, "I have dedicated my life to God."

I was looking for someone who would love God and serve God, and Lina was a woman who was on fire for Him. Her letters made it very clear. I know this is not the conventional way to find a wife, and I would never tell anyone else that they should go about it this way, but it was the way God planned it for my life. The Holy Spirit spoke to my heart and said, "This is it. She is the one you need."

So I called my father and said, "I like her. Can you arrange the engagement?"

Engagement in India is not when a boy gets down on one knee and offers a diamond ring to a girl as a romantic gesture. It is two families coming together to see how they are going to get along and invest in the future. Sometimes, if parents are forcing their daughter to marry someone she does not want, the bride-to-be won't even show up to the engagement. Her parents will leave her at home so that she doesn't make a scene.

I think my engagement was the only one where the groom-to-be was absent! I called my father to tell him that I was not coming. I knew he would not be happy when I told him, so I was nearly terrified to relay the news.

My father was perplexed, "What are you saying?"

"I cannot come. I have to save all of my vacation time for the actual wedding."

The day soon came for the families to get together, but it was not pleasant. My father called to tell me the whole story.

Lina's relatives wanted to meet the boy she was going to marry, and cultural norms meant I should have been there.

They were starting to get concerned. What was I hiding? What was wrong with me? Not showing up was a huge incentive to be suspicious. It could have turned ugly, but Lina's brother-in-law, Wilson, stood up for me and said, "I know Bennie. He looks like his brother, Finny."

The family, after much speculation and consideration, agreed to set the wedding date for February 10, 1990.

"They've agreed to the date," my father said with some excitement, "Now, you must come and meet with them."

I agreed. I was supposed to go to India toward the end of January, but I was trying my best to stay frugal, wanting to work more and save more and have more days off when I got there. So I left New York on February 2 and reached India two days later. My brother and I weren't able to make the 12-hour drive to Lina's home until February 7. We arrived at about lunchtime, but Lina's father was still at work. We had to wait until he came home to get his permission to see Lina. By the time she and I finally met face-to-face, we were both so nervous that we did not really know what to say to each other.

I finally blurted out, "You know, I want to tell you one more time that I don't have anything. Nothing belongs to me; anything that I have belongs to God. I have given my life to Him. Is that okay with you?" I knew that if this marriage were to work, she had to have a complete understanding of the covenant I had made with God.

"That's fine," she smiled. "I have made the same decision for my life. We'll talk about it later."

My brother and I drove back home a few hours later, and I was still reeling from finally being able to meet and talk with my future wife. On February 9, the day before the wedding, my family, friends, and I traveled all night by bus back to her home.

The next day at 4:30 in the afternoon, Lina and I got married.

THE GREAT ADVENTURE OF LOVE

When people in America are asked why they got married, the typical response is something like, “I was so in love with her/him,” or “It was love at first sight.” When people ask me why I got married, I tell them, “I married her so that I could fall in love with her.” As the years have gone by, my love for Lina just keeps getting stronger and keeps growing. We are much more in love now than we ever were before, and I fall in love with her daily. It has, indeed been an incredible adventure.

After the wedding, we stayed at Lina’s home with her family. Her parents had two daughters and anything the daughters wanted, the father provided. For every little issue or need, Lina’s father was there to resolve the matter quickly. It was very different in my family; we could cry and beg, but nothing happened until God would do something to help. I knew it was going to be an adjustment for her.

When I brought Lina back to my family’s home, the first morning, she asked, “Do you have a sink so I can brush my teeth?”

I was thinking about my grand plans for a honeymoon, but her question brought me right back to reality.

“No,” I said, “We don’t have a sink.”

“Then, where do you spit?”

That was easy. “Oh, we go to the back of the house and just spit against the wall.”

I could see her face starting to lose some wedded bliss as she replied, “It will splatter on my dress!”

“Then you just aim better. Go down like this,” I demonstrated, "or you can spit in the toilet."

All traces of bliss were now gone from her face, replaced by something closer to horror. I realized I was in big trouble. It had never occurred to me that our missionary-style life and our motto, "Wherever He leads me I will follow, whatever He feeds me I will swallow, I'll live as He wants me to," might take some getting used to for Lina.

I had to do something, and I had to do it quickly. When Lina came back from her first backyard tooth-brushing experience, I assured her, "I'll make some arrangements." The next morning, I went out and bought a sink. I got a plumber to come and put a tube down into the gutter trap so that the next time she brushed her teeth, she would be more comfortable.

Of course, I could see that it was going to take more than a sink to help our situation. After all, I had to return to America soon, but Lina would have to wait in India for her immigration paperwork to go through. Neither of us knew how long it would take. So I made a daring proposition: "You come from a family where everything was provided. I come from a family where we were completely accustomed to having nothing. We have to get to know each other and how this family functions." I took a deep breath, reluctant to ask my next question. "Is it okay if we postpone the honeymoon? I think it will help us both to understand each other better if we stayed with family here."

Her face did not reveal anything about how she was feeling, so I continued.

"I want to tell you something, though, Mrs. Lina Mathews. If you give this honeymoon away, God will open doors for you in the future. You will never lack time of vacation. God will give you a bigger honeymoon than this."

She was quiet for a moment, and then she nodded. "If you

think that's the best idea, let's do it." She never complained about it once. I quickly realized that the woman God had brought me was one of incredible character and virtue. I continued to praise Him for the tremendous blessing that He brought to me in Lina.

We stayed at my parents' home until I had to fly back to the United States. It was essential for us to do everything correctly in regards to immigration and to make sure we did not skip any steps. Now the long, agonizing process of waiting began before Lina could join me in America.

Those two and a half years were so painful and forced a lot of growth in both Lina and myself. I saved every one of my 20 days of vacation to make sure when I saw her, and we had substantial time to spend together. I worked Christmas, Thanksgiving, and any other day I could, so that I could take the time to go back to India and be with her. She was always in tears when I left her, making it harder each time. We would record messages to one another on cassette tapes and send them back and forth with family and friends who were traveling so that we could hear each other's voices. I would write long letters to her, and she would write long ones back to me. We would wait eagerly by the mailbox all the time, profoundly anticipating the next one. It seemed more like courtship through letters, which made our love stronger. Even though this was difficult, it was also a valuable time of relationship-building for us, and the love we did not yet have before our wedding, we indeed found then.

Finally, Lina's paperwork came through, and she was able to come to New York. It was a beautiful reunion and will forever be a fond memory of mine—one I will hold onto for eternity.

Soon after her arrival, our church was participating in a national church missions conference held in Lancaster, Pennsylvania. The Missions Director of the church called and said, "Brother Mathews, you should come to this missions conference. You would love it." He went on and on about the incredible speakers and worship that would be featured. It sounded like a great opportunity, so I agreed. He proceeded by telling me, "You don't have to worry about a thing; we will take care of your hotel and your food and all the arrangements. It will be like a honeymoon for you and your wife." Little did he know that we had been waiting for so long for an actual honeymoon.

We went to the missions conference and, as promised, everything was completely paid for. The conference lasted three days, and on the final day, so much snow fell that the entire state of Pennsylvania went on emergency alert and declared that it was no longer safe to travel. The Missions Director called to reassure us, "Brother Bennie, you stay right there. You're on your honeymoon; you two enjoy yourselves, and we will take care of all your expenses." Everyone there treated us like a king and queen.

I told my wife, "Can you imagine the blessings of following God and doing His will? Jesus said, 'If you give a cup of water in My name, you have rewards forever.' The sacrifice you were willing to make when we got married, God has honored. This is all a reward for your obedience."

God continues to honor Lina's obedience to this day. Over the years, He has given us many vacations to beautiful holiday destinations and beaches, even to places most people are never able to visit. When my daughter got married, one of our family friends provided an all-inclusive honeymoon trip to Belize as their wedding gift. I reminded my daughter how her mother had given up her honeymoon for a higher purpose and that they were reaping the benefits from that sacrifice. When my son got engaged, he asked if he would be able to go to Belize. Our friends replied yes, he could go as his older sister did. God takes the little we give and makes it into something glorious.

YEARNING FOR A CHILD

Once we were finally home together in New York, life was blissful and beautiful. Lina got a job in the same hospital where I was working, and our thoughts soon turned toward having children. We wanted many children and peaceful life and craved the normalcy that came with that. We wanted to be like other Indians we grew up with (apart from the 'lots of children' part)—we wanted to make money, retire, move somewhere South and buy a motel or start a business. That was our goal, and we were excited to pursue it.

Everything was fine in the beginning, but after the first year, Lina had not become pregnant. Then two years passed, then three, then four—still no children. People were telling me, "Bennie, you need to start having children. The clock is ticking." At every family gathering, well-intentioned relatives would probe and ask things like, "So, when is the happy news coming?"

In Indian culture, if anything is wrong regarding family or fertility, the blame always falls on the woman. It is the same in the Bible: Jacob and Rachel, Elkanah and Hannah, Zacharias and Elizabeth. Generally, no one thinks it could be the man's fault.

It was so difficult for Lina, and she was becoming increasingly frustrated and discouraged. After numerous visits to doctors and countless invasive procedures, for which she was totally unprepared, she had finally had enough and said, "Bennie, I cannot do this anymore. Why can't the Lord just give us a child?"

"God doesn't have to give us a child," I tried to reassure her. "We are fine, just the two of us. We are doing great because we have each other. Who needs more than this?"

While the sentiment was sweet, Lina was unconvinced. "No," she firmly told me. "I need a child. If God could just give me one . . ."

I told her, "We don't need one," but in my heart, I was thinking, "God, she's right." I knew I was just trying to make her feel better. The idea of going the rest of our lives without having children of our own felt nearly unbearable.

She would often sit by the window and watch the kids playing outside and wonder how God deals with the issue of unwanted pregnancies ending in abortion. She could not understand why He would withhold from her the blessing of a child. For hours she would cry out to God, as Hannah did, asking for a child.

In front of my wife, I put on a smile and would say, "We are happy together, and God is in control of everything in our lives. Let's not worry." But in my heart, I, too, was praying, "God, why can't You bless us with just one child?"

I had always been the one working hard and saving money so that it could be used for ministry purposes. I believed I had done the best I could for God and my family, so I was struggling to understand why He seemed not to answer this one prayer that my wife and I desperately ached for. I started thinking about how my mother always wanted me to serve God. Even when I was making money and taking care of the family financially, she would say, "Son, money is great, but I would rather have you serving God." I would tell her, "Mom, your God needs His money, and I am the money, man." I was the "Show Me the Money" kind of guy and was comfortable viewing life through this lens. Yet, even after I would forfeit all of my paychecks and tips to her, she would make it clear that I should be serving God. My idea of good business, and hers had always been very different; my thoughts generally involved relying more on my abilities than on God's.

I was watching television one day after church, and as I flipped through the channels, I noticed a special on the host of *Family Feud*. He was telling the story of how he had been adopted by Mormons, which led him to become a Mormon himself.

A few days later, I heard about mafia gangs "adopting" kids—taking them from the streets and forcing them to commit crimes. Similarly, I knew of children in Africa who were recruited by rebel forces and trained to fight. I started thinking to myself, "Bennie, if these guys can do these things, why not adopt some kids and bring them up in a stable and loving environment where they are taught to fear the Lord?"

So I said to Lina, "Why don't we adopt some children?"

She said, "No, I don't want to adopt now. I want God to give me one of my own. If He gives me one, I'll adopt 10. But I want one." She was adamant, and I finally was starting to see that this was an issue very close to her heart.

I let it go, but in my mind, I started thinking, *Why can't she just drop this? Let's be at peace with our situation.*

Lina was like Hannah, who came to God and prayed for a child. People made fun of Hannah, and even the priest could not understand her deep longing to have a child of her own. Like Hannah, Lina was crying out to God to bless her with a child, and she never gave up. She was persistent and unwavering.

At church one Sunday morning, Bishop William spoke on the topic, "With God, All Things Are Possible." He said we need to follow God, and we should launch out into the deep and unknown aspects of life. Matthew left everything he knew at the tax collectors table and followed Christ instead. I felt like he was asking me to leave my job and follow God, something I was used to feeling pressured about. I resisted the altar call. Bishop knew the Word of God very well and was able to articulate its messages and truths in brilliant ways. I know some of his sermons by heart because he was a great preacher, and his style was so good that a common man like me could easily understand. He frequently challenged people for the cause of missions.

Every time I went to church, and he spoke, it was like someone had lit a fire under my pew. That day especially, I could hear my mother's prayers being answered through him, the Spirit speaking to my heart, saying, "You should be serving God. Follow Him and start serving Him." The issue was that I did not personally know anything about serving God and had never really done it before. It was not what I had ever wanted to do, and at that point in my life, I had never even shared the Gospel message with anyone. My goal was to make money as a businessman. After all, I was the one supporting our ministry through my finances.

My wife and I were doing well financially and felt that we had reached a certain level of stability with our income. She was a social worker in the admitting office at the hospital where I was employed and found the work fulfilling. My goal was to eventually study and become a medical recorder to receive both a pay increase and the personal satisfaction that came from having a well-respected job. I was already a quarter of the way there, working a part-time job in the medical records office, and I hoped to one day become a radiology technician or an x-ray technician—anything professional that could bring in more money. Making more money was always my dream.

As Bishop William shared from Matthew 9—"Jesus said, 'Matthew, follow me!' and he left everything and followed"—I felt the Holy Spirit tugging at my heart, so I went forward to pray. When we got home, I said, "Lina, Mom has been bugging me to serve God to serve God. Why don't we make a decision that if God gives us one child, we will be willing to leave all these things and serve Him 100%?"

Lina mustered up as much of a smile as she could and exclaimed, "If God gives me one child, I'll do anything."

I told her, "If God gives us a baby, we will buy a piece of property in India with our own money. Our child will be dedicated not at church, but as the first child on that property. And on that land, we will build a children's home, and we will adopt many children and raise them up in fear of God."

Tears were streaming down her face. "I'll do that," she whispered. So, we prayed.

The following Tuesday evening, we went to church for a special weekday service where a man named Pastor Carlton Brown was speaking. When the altar call was given, we went forward. He prayed over us, and we dedicated our lives to serve the Lord with this new commitment.

Sometimes God brings us to a corner to get our attention and to align ourselves with His purposes. When we are stubborn and running away from His purposes, He uses circumstances to direct us back the way He wants us to go.

A year later, in 1994, God miraculously answered our prayers and blessed us with a beautiful baby girl who filled our lives with happiness, wonder, and awe. The Bible tells us repeatedly how all children are a gift from God. Psalm 127:3 says children are a heritage from the Lord—they are a reward from Him. God had heard our cries, wiped away our tears with the greatest miracle and blessing in our lives. We named her Faith-Hannah, for faith in God, for the confidence it would take to keep the commitment we had made to serve God, and the persistent prayers like Hannah, for God's answer to one who prayed earnestly for a child.

I had never taken the time to study the Bible, so preaching would not come naturally to me. I knew that. I was barely able to recite more than John 3:16, though I had encouraged people to read the four spiritual laws often. I had no idea how I was going to serve God, but I knew that God was real, God was moving, and that I was experiencing His work in my life. Lina and I dedicated our lives totally to His service and were never the same again. I was confident of one thing: that I had a testimony to share with people. And though I did not know much about the Bible, I knew one thing: I knew I could point people to Jesus, or at least say, "Look, this is what the God of the Bible is doing in my life."

Finally, after many years filled with countless journeys, both physical and spiritual, I was truly beginning to understand the importance of being about the Father's business. Nothing else mattered. As much as I had fought it, my steps were turning in the same direction as my father's, and I knew I would take up the family business of serving God. Life was to be lived for His glory, and although I could not see what God had in store for me, I was determined to be faithful.

CHAPTER 6
APPLICATION POINTS

When you choose to surrender every area of your life to God, He will faithfully point out any unknown strongholds that keep Him from having full reign in your life.

I had tasted the goodness of God, and my life belonged to Him. But as my wife and I continued to wait and pray for God to give us children, I realized He was beginning to touch the last stronghold in my life. I was still working jobs to make money for the ministry rather than letting go and being in ministry.

- God will bring you to a corner, a stopping point, to get your attention so you can align yourself to His purpose.
- When we are stubborn and running away from His purpose, He directs us back to the way He wants us to go. Aren't you glad?!

You will never find a better business partner than God!

He always makes way for His plans to come to fruition. He always makes sure those who partner with Him are taken care of. When you finally understand the importance of being about the Father's business, nothing else compares.

- Are there any areas of your life that are not 100% God's?
- Do you trust Him with every decision?

Are you sharing with others the things God has done in your life?

Your testimony of God's goodness may be just what someone else desperately needs to hear. Do not hold back.

> *Surely goodness and mercy shall follow me all the days of my life, and I will dwell in the house of the Lord forever.*
>
> **—Psalm 23:6**

A HEART-TO-HEART

Q&A

WITH BROTHER BENNIE

BREAKFAST WITH BENNIE

While speaking at a conference in Kentucky the morning session was called "Breakfast with Bennie." I had the wonderful opportunity to answer some personal questions about me and my life. I want to share some of those answers with you here.

How do you introduce yourself?

I say that I am a follower of Jesus Christ, the husband to Lina, and the father of Faith-Hannah, Laramie, Ben-Israel, Elizabeth, Joy-Ruth, and William. I tell people that the Lord brought my family together through His grace and that we are growing and joyfully serving Him with our lives.

What does every child deserve to have in life?

I believe every child deserves to have love, care, and positive affirmation. Every child is special to God, and He has a plan for each one of their lives. I believe that by showing children the love, care, and affirmation they deserve and need, we are truly serving God Himself!

What was your worst work experience?

Once while visiting a small village and an unknown people group, a little child brought me a glass of water. The water was from the local river, and I knew it was unsafe to drink. Meanwhile, the child was very dirty, and the steel cup he served it to me in was as well. His father insisted that I should drink it, and in an effort to not offend, I did.

What's something you don't want to regret when you're older?

I have no regrets, and I cannot stress this enough. The Lord has been far too gracious to me for me to consider any part of my life, no matter how it may have appeared to me at the time, to be a regret. Who I am today and the identity I have found to be true of myself is directly due to the fact that the Lord has considered me to be a partner to complete the task of His Kingdom. I am blessed beyond words can explain. Like David says in Psalm 37:25, "I have been young, and now am old; yet I have not seen the righteous forsaken, nor his descendants begging bread."

What words inspire you?

Words that inspire me are directly related to what I do every day in order to grow the Kingdom of God—"help, welcome, and goodness." I believe these are the words that stir and inspire me most.

What qualities do you find admirable in others?

I believe humility and generosity are the two qualities that particularly cause me to admire someone. Those qualities aren't inherently found in most of us in a consistent way, so to see others truly living out their lives in a humble and generous way really inspires me.

What is the saddest thing that has happened to you?

That's a difficult question . . . I would probably say the death of my third sister and the miscarriage of our fourth child.

If you could have witnessed one particular event in history, what would it be?

I would love to go back in time to witness the moment when Elijah was taken up to Heaven. Being able to see how Elisha took the cloak that had fallen from Elijah and struck the water with it in order for him to cross over is something I can't even imagine witnessing. The entire life and ministry of Elijah was nothing short of incredible.

Have you ever been genuinely afraid for your physical safety due to your work in the ministry?

Yes, in fact, this has happened on several different occasions while serving on the mission field. Once while visiting a region where Christians are severely persecuted, my team and I went to assist martyred families and those who were displaced because of the severe atrocities happening to Christians in their nation. We saw homes, churches, motor vehicles, and personal properties of thousands of Christians damaged, burned, and utterly destroyed. Believers were forced to abandon everything they knew and retreat into the surrounding jungles to hide. Over 20,000 believers were either hiding or living in underfunded refugee camps. As a team, we took relief items to help persecuted believers and would attend an old church to encourage them, including eight pastors' wives whose husbands had been murdered the previous week.

As we met together, militant leaders and mobsters barged into our meeting room and told us to leave that area or face death. The local police force stood off in the distance, watching all these things occur, and refused to help us. We were forced to leave the area while an entourage of vehicles of all shapes and sizes followed our vehicle. They yelled and threatened us as they escorted us out of the region. Even through the intensity of the situation, my team and I trusted fully in the Lord and had complete peace.

Another one of the scariest instances I can recall is when I was crossing the border of Benin into Tago, a region in West Africa. I was alone, and the immigration officers were intimidating and very hostile. He questioned me and suggested I pay him bribe money in order to get through. I told him I was a man of God and that I was there to visit a church. He didn't care and kept me in that room for some time before my driver was able to talk him into letting me through. The Lord was watching over me throughout the entire experience.

When you see peers and competitors getting things you want, how do you react?

I genuinely try to never compete and compare myself with others. I believe God gave me the best attributes I need to complete the mission and task with which He has entrusted me.

What's going to be carved on your (hypothetical) tombstone?

If it can say that "Bennie served God and has done what he could for his family and loved his people and sought to be a good and godly servant of God," I will be pleased and at peace. After all, Scripture says, "Because I live, you shall also live" (John 14:19), and

"He that does the will of God abideth forever" (John 2:17).

What most encourages you in your work?

When people accept Jesus Christ as their Lord and Savior. When my hand is in the posture of giving. When I get to help people and children in need. When people accept a challenge and complete the vision. When I can be a ladder and help others climb high in leadership.

What are you most proud of?

My parents, wife, children, biological family, and my ministry family. I am also proud of the call of God on my life.

What do you most enjoy about your work?

Helping people realize their dreams. To be a dream contractor and dream builder is something that will outlive me and make a difference for eternity.

Is this where you thought you would end up?

Never in my life did I think I would be in missions or be involved in active missionary outreach. I kept my compass away from serving God for most of my life.

What's the most out-of-character choice you've ever made?

To quit my secular job and move to Lynchburg without counting the cost and becoming a full-time student at Liberty University.

What are you starving for?

God's righteousness and a great revival across America and around the world.

What is your life verse?

John 3:30: *"He must increase, but I must decrease."*

John 13:17: *"If ye know these things, happy are ye if ye do them."*

What food do you love the most?

I would have to say Chinese food is my favorite.

PART TWO

LEARNING THE BUSINESS

Joining the family business was just the beginning of my new-found relationship and venture with God. I had learned firsthand the consequences of being in business solely for myself. I saw how easy it was to get stingy, selfish, worried, and resentful.

When I was focused on making money and living life whatever way I pleased, I never had enough. I was always working for a little more here and a little more there. But when I committed to making a drastic lifestyle change and going into my Father's business, everything I knew turned upside down as I began to learn the ropes of a very different lifestyle. Sometimes, it was terrifying, and sometimes it was mystifying, but when we worked faithfully, it was always glorifying God. Life wasn't always easy, but we learned to trust Him in all things. He provided over and above anything we could ever imagine.

Many of the blessings we received came *from* God's hand, but they came *through* God's people in His church. God brought many people into our lives who were working hard to serve Him and to bless others. Their encouragement, friendship, and fellowship greatly uplifted us in our journey of living by faith. It is a privilege to not only serve God by blessing others but to be blessed by others who are serving God; it is a wonderful partnership designed by Him. God's plan for His people is a wonderful circle of life!

As I learned, going into business with your Heavenly Father means:

1. You can no longer find excuses not to serve Him.

2. God's business becomes your business.

3. God's priorities become your priorities.

4. Whatever moves His heart moves your heart.

Thousands of books have been written on how to succeed in business. They are full of advice on the things one *must* do to be a success in the corporate world. When God wrote a book, He outlined what one *must* do to succeed in His business. Jesus mentioned those "musts" throughout His ministry, and I learned them from Him as I began this adventure.

CHAPTER 7

I MUST FOLLOW WHERE HE LEADS

When He had called the people to Himself, with His disciples also, He said to them, "Whoever desires to come after Me, let him deny himself, and take up his cross, and follow Me."
Mark 8:34

Sometimes God tears down the things we spend years building up so that He can build something better. I believe that is what God began to do in my life once I surrendered to His will and His service. For years, I had depended on myself alone to provide for my needs and for the needs of my family. Although I had seen God give us what we lacked time and time again, somehow it still seemed easier to work on my own. I had worked hard, persisted, and pushed against His will to have my own way for a long time.

THE AMERICAN EXPRESS EXPERIENCE

I remember accompanying my uncle to a hardware store in Yonkers, New York, one day in 1988. I hadn't been in America for very long and was taking every opportunity I could to get out and see my new home. Never had I been to or even witnessed such an enormous store in all my days—one single place that contained everything you could possibly need to construct a house. I was in awe of all that was for sale and was experiencing real culture shock—in the best way. We picked up what he needed and went to check out. While my uncle was paying the cashier, my gaze fell on a rack where several credit card applications had been placed. I picked up the green American Express card form and recalled the many times I had witnessed rich people use American Express cards at the hotel and restaurant where I worked, so I was immediately drawn to it.

As I picked up the application, my uncle warned me not to reach too high above my station. I asked him what he meant. "That's Amex, and you won't have a shot at getting that until you establish a solid credit score." I had to respect him, so I placed the application back on the rack. However, the idea of being a credit card holder had already taken root in my mind. As my uncle walked toward the exit, I picked up the form and discreetly tucked it into my jacket. When I got home, I went up to my attic room and read the entire application, even the fine print about APR—all of it. I was tempted to fill out the application form right then and there, especially since I did not have to purchase a stamp (it had prepaid postage). I was even fascinated by the fact that the paper itself formed the envelope. I'd never seen anything like it.

After submitting my application, I wasn't sure if they would even take it seriously enough to reply. A few weeks later, my uncle picked up the mail on his way home from work, and there was a letter from American Express addressed to me. My uncle was extremely curious. "How was it that Bennie had received a letter not from India, but American Express?" My uncle called me down and handed me the letter, asking me to read it. Equally as excited as I was anxious, I quickly ripped open the envelope.

It was a disappointing letter written in typical, gracious American fashion, thanking me for my request but informing me that I did not have enough established credit, and I was ineligible for the card. My uncle took that opportunity to teach me a lesson in Credit Card 101. I felt remorse because not only did I get denied for a credit card, I knew my uncle was going to think I had disobeyed his advice and not taken him seriously. I went up to my room with some regret, but like always, I had never been able to take 'no' for an answer from anyone. I would always quietly go round till I found a route that would get me what I wanted. Even in my stubbornness and arrogance, God protected and preserved me for a greater purpose. After a few days had passed, I resolved not to accept defeat and instead wrote a letter.

In the best handwriting, I could manage, I addressed the person who had sent me the rejection letter.

> *I come from India, and I am a new immigrant. I had a reputed position and career in India. As a new immigrant in the great United States of America, I will go through the growing pains that everyone experiences. But one day, I know my situation will change. When that happens, you will be approaching me to be a member of your services. I will not accept it, because you did not help me in the time of my need. I have a very urgent and dire need right now: my family is moving from India to come to the U.S., and I have to purchase airline tickets and also take care of several other needs. I need a credit card now because that will help me build my credit. I know God will bless you because you are helping me, and I am helping people, too.*

I attached copies of every recommendation I'd received from all of my previous employers to indicate that I was a professional and that I deserved the card. I posted the letter with the mindset that I would one day be a wealthy businessman. A few weeks passed when one day, my uncle returned from work, calling me downstairs just like before. He handed me a heavy American Express envelope. I opened it, and sure enough, it contained the green American Express credit card, complete with the logo of the man wearing a helmet in the center! I was astonished, and my uncle could not believe it either. He turned the card over to see whether it was indeed in my name, checking to see if there had been some kind of a mistake. Still refusing to accept what he saw fully, he accusingly asked me whether I had used someone else's social security number. I laughed and told him what I had done—to no avail. He remained incredulous. However, I was far too elated even to notice. I started praising God because I could use that card to buy tickets for my mother and four siblings to make the trip to America from India. It gave me the freedom to do things that were a priority and to settle my family in the States.

I still have the Amex card to this very day. It has "Member Since 1989" printed on it and often reminds me of how my life in America began. I do not use any other card in emergencies; it is always Amex because, in some kind of miraculous fluke, they helped me.

Of course, I found later that my inexperience and carelessness would come back to bite me. God had to tear down the tower I had built— and needed to rebuild on Him this time instead of my strength. Since this was of my own doing, it had to come undone at some point or the other. He began to bring me to places where depending on Him, became my only option, and He began to call me to places I would never have expected.

LYNCHBURG DOESN'T SOUND GOOD

After the birth of our baby girl in 1994, we moved into a new apartment. It had a brand-new carpet with up-to-date furnishings that we could never have been able to afford a few years prior. On the day of our housewarming party, friends and family gathered to celebrate God's blessings with us and to simply have a wonderful time of rejoicing. Later that same day, I went down to the mailbox and found an envelope with a return address from Liberty University. It was a letter from Dr. Jerry Falwell saying that if my loved ones and I moved to Lynchburg, Virginia, he would give me a full scholarship to attend Liberty Bible Institute. It just seemed too good to be true. I kept looking for the fine print or some sort of disclaimer, but it wasn't there.

I brought it up to Lina. "What is this?" she said, "Why is this university offering you a scholarship?"

I shrugged. "I don't know. I don't even know who gave them our address, but it looks legitimate."

She looked at the letter again and nodded. "Wow. That sounds really nice." She glanced up at me and added, "You could learn the Bible."

She was right, but the more I thought about it, the more mixed feelings I developed. We had just moved into our new apartment! I thought, "Are you kidding? It's in Lynchburg, Virginia." My sister went to school there, but I wasn't even sure exactly where it was. The whole idea sounded crazy, but it seemed that God had brought it to us, so we decided to pray about it.

After a while, we felt like God was leading us to Lynchburg. If I was going to serve Him, knowing the Bible was probably a good first step. Since most of my brothers had moved to the U.S. by that time, I called them with the exciting news.

I said, "You know, guys, God is leading us to move to Lynchburg, Virginia."

"Where?"

"Lynch-burg." The name alone sounded a little foreboding for a foreigner.

"That doesn't sound good," they said.

With growing confidence, I replied, "But that is where God is leading us."

"Are you out of your mind? Don't do it!" They tried to convince us otherwise, but I knew I had to follow where I felt God was leading my little family. There were a million reasons not to go, but obedience doesn't always make sense.

In those days, there were no online realtors to help you find a place to live. We called the university to see if they could help, and they were gracious enough to give us some phone numbers of local apartment complexes and real estate agents. We found a small apartment for $250 per month and were able to sign a six-month lease. Of course, neither of us had jobs yet, and since we were living on our savings, we needed someplace inexpensive. We thought we could start there and perhaps find something else as time went on. I knew God could bring us to just the right home. I had seen Him do it before, in India and New York, and I knew He could do it again.

My aunt had lived in a lovely apartment in New York before moving into a house. When she left the apartment, she asked the man who was taking it to call her if he ever planned to leave. I had been in America for about two years before my brothers started planning to come. My apartment was the right size for one man, but not four. Just as I was getting concerned about where I was going to put them all, the man who had taken my aunt's large apartment called her to inform her that he was moving to Texas.

My aunt and I went to talk with him, and he said he would make it available for me. He also said that it would cost too much to bring all of his furniture with him; it was easier to sell it in New York and to buy new things in Texas.

My aunt looked at me. "Why don't you buy it?" she asked.

The apartment was fully furnished with beds, bedroom suites, a microwave, stereo, television, sofas, pull-out couches—everything four single immigrant brothers would possibly need. But I had just paid for a van in India to help with the ministry, and most of my savings was in there as well. All I could offer him at the time was $3,000.

He sized me up. "$3,000?" He knew I was the son of a missionary. He nodded. "I'll take it."

So I called up my brothers. Three days later, they were in America and moving into our new apartment. I knew that the same God who worked everything out in that situation would work things out in Lynchburg, too. It had only been a few years now I could forget His goodness so quickly?

NEW LIFE AND NEW VAN

The apartment we found in Lynchburg was a semi-basement studio apartment. Our landlady lived upstairs and went to work around 5:00 each morning. But our daughter, Faith, was still an infant and would sometimes cry in the night. The floors were so thin that every time she cried, our landlady would bang on the floor with a broom and yell, "Stop it! Put your kid to bed!" The next day, she would come down and lecture me. "Mathews, I have to wake up and get to work early. I can't sleep when your kid is crying all night long. You need to do something." She complained quite frequently.

Since Lina was pregnant with our second child by then, when Faith cried in the night, I would get up and take her out to the car until she was quiet. Once she was sleeping, I would bring her back in and try to get some sleep myself. Most of the time, I did not sleep. It was a challenging time in our lives, and we were very stressed.

On top of that, one day, I went to buy a church history book for class when the unthinkable happened. While I was making a U-turn to turn into the bookstore, a truck seemed to come out of nowhere and rammed into the side of my car. My sister was sitting in the passenger seat, and she was thrown out of her seat and onto me. I wasn't hurt, but she was very bruised. The door was completely bent in half, and both windows were shattered. The police came and wrote me a ticket and told me that my car was so severely damaged and I was not allowed to drive it anymore. They did permit me to move it, so I took the car home. I put plastic over the windows and taped it in place. It did not look too bad. I did not know how I was going to get to school or take care of my family. I still drove it to a couple of places and just hoped the police would only pass me on the car's good side. When I drove to church, I would park the car in such a way that people could only see the undamaged side, and whenever I was on the road, I was always scared and anxious about being pulled over by the police.

So, I was a student, our landlord was giving us a hard time, Lina was pregnant, we did not have jobs, and now we did not have a vehicle. It was January—it was cold—and I was so frustrated. In the midst of it all, I kept thinking, "God, You did great things for my parents. I know You can do great things for us, even in this situation."

We surrendered our lives, our needs, and our circumstances to God and prayed.

While I was praying one morning—thinking, "God, why can't You do something here?"—the phone rang. It was Frank, a friend of mine from West Virginia.

He said, "Bennie, I've been praying for you and your family. God laid it on my heart that I need to buy you a van because you have a second child on the way, and I know how difficult things have been for you with the move and all. My pastor is selling his van, and I'd like to buy it for you and bless you with it."

I could barely get the words out, "Frank, I don't know what to tell you. An accident destroys my car, and I cannot even open it from one side. The police told me I must not drive it. I don't know who told you, but I am in desperate need of a new car."

He said, "I've been praying, and God pressed this on my heart. But I guess if that's what has been going on, you can't come here to pick the van up now, can you?"

"No, I'm afraid I can't."

"I'm going to call my pastor," Frank said, "and then I'll call you right back." When he called back, it was to tell me that he and his pastor planned to drive to Lynchburg in two separate vehicles so that they could leave the van with me and then drive back to West Virginia together.

A couple of days later, that was exactly what they did. They parked the van in front of my house and came in for a short visit. I signed Frank's $4,000 check over to his pastor, and they handed me the keys and the title to the van, as well as some money for registration. When they left to drive back to West Virginia, Lina and I praised the Lord for His goodness to us.

Again, God proved to be an on-time God. I had remembered my mother's teaching from childhood: "Don't tell anyone you need anything. Don't badmouth God by saying, 'I need this, or I don't have that.'" If one of us said, "We cannot afford this," she would say, "There is no *can't*, for I can do all things through Christ, so it is not just me. If God wants me to have it, He will give it to me, so why do you say, 'We cannot afford it?' It has nothing to do with affording or not affording —if you do not have it now, it is not required now. With our strength, we can do nothing, but through God's strength, we can do everything."

Those words were always ringing in my ears, and that is the reason I had not called anyone up to say, "I need a car, can you help me?" The Lord knew our situation and provided exactly what we needed, precisely when we needed it. It brought some relief to our troubles and was a very important reminder of His work in our lives because our housing situation was getting worse and worse.

HOMELESS & MOTORHOME

We had only lived in our basement apartment for two months when our landlady asked us to leave. I said, "I have a lease for six months—you can't do that."

"I don't care," she said, "I'm going to get the law involved and get you out of here."

When I broke the news to Lina, she said, "We are Christians, and she is not. We must be Christ-like. We want her to feel like we did the right thing. Let's give her a week and then we will find another place to stay. We can leave. Who cares about our lease papers?"

She was right. I started looking for another apartment, but it was difficult. Every housing application wanted me to sign a form stating I made at least $270 per week. The problem was that I did not make $270 per week. I did not make anything per week. We were living on our savings and by faith. Most people who own apartment complexes do not understand that.

With our one-week deadline creeping closer but no leads on a new place to live, we made the difficult decision to send Lina and Faith back to India until I could get things sorted out for us in Lynchburg. In the meantime, my friend Marty offered the use of a storage unit for all of our belongings. Another friend, Tony, said I could stay with him and his wife at their place near Liberty University until I found one of my own.

I missed my wife and daughter tremendously, but Lina was safe and back in India with her family, and I was grateful to have a place to stay. I have back problems, so I would drive to the storage unit every afternoon to sleep on my mattress for a while. After my nap, I would drive to the local library to pick up a newspaper and look for apartments. Over and over, it was the same problem at every housing complex: I did not have a job, so no one would rent to me. It was frustrating, and I found myself praying and talking to God as if He did not understand the urgency of my situation.

That week, the Lord introduced me to Debbie, a Christian woman who was a realtor and a member of Thomas Road Baptist Church. After she heard my story, she said, "Bennie, no one will rent to you because you don't have a regular income. You need to think about buying a house. That's the only thing that will work." She suggested asking one of my brothers to help, but my younger brother had just gotten a job, so I knew I could not ask him to do that. I kept trying my best to find an apartment instead.

Tony and his wife lived in a one-bedroom apartment, and I slept on a pullout couch in the living room. When I arrived at

Tony's house one evening, he and his wife were waiting up for me on that couch.

"Hey guys," I said, "is everything okay?"

Tony looked embarrassed as he started, "Bennie, our landlady called, she said that you have to leave. She is living on a limited budget and having too many tenants is impacting her utilities. She said her water bill is too high now, and she thinks that you are the reason." He sighed, "She said that either you leave or we have to leave."

I was tired, and that was not good news, but I was grateful for the hospitality they had offered me, and I wasn't going to argue or hold a grudge. "Okay," I said, "I'll pack my things and leave in the morning."

Tony shook his head. "I'm sorry, Bennie, you have to leave now. I promised her you would go tonight."

I had no idea where I would go, but I got up and quickly packed my things, and I thanked them for all they had done to help me. I drove around for a while, confused and tense. I headed toward Madison Heights, about 20-30 minutes from the Liberty campus. When I reached the small shopping center there, I parked my van in the Kmart parking lot. I was thinking, "God, what is this? Is it Your will that I should be here that I should be homeless?" I slept in the van that night.

The next morning, I put my toothbrush in one pocket, my shaving kit in another, and I went into Kmart. I walked around a bit to stretch my body, then slipped into the restroom to brush my teeth and shave quickly, and then went to class. For the next couple of days, I got ready in the Kmart restroom in the mornings and slept on my mattress at the storage unit in the afternoons. I would buy a combo lunch at a Chinese restaurant near the university to drink the hot soup for lunch and save the rest for dinner. Since Kmart and the storage facility were several miles from school, the van's engine would be warm by the time I arrived, so I would lay my Chinese food container on it and heat it up. Needless to say, after several days of that routine, I was only 'dry cleaned,' using wipes and whatever I could find in the Kmart bathroom, and I started being late to class.

I was doing *everything* I could to save money while I continued looking for an apartment. In those days, no one had cell phones, and every time I called Debbie the realtor, it would cost me 10 cents. If she did not answer and I had to leave a voicemail, the dime was wasted. Although 10 cents might not seem like much, I was counting every single penny. I kept thinking, "What am I going to do? Has God forsaken me? Is Lynchburg not God's will?" Even though He had just shown me His provision with the van a few months earlier, my circumstances were making me doubt His calling upon my life. I continued praying that God will make a way and give me an apartment somewhere soon.

On certain days, free coffee and bread were available to those who arrived early at David's Place, the location where Liberty Bible Institute held its classes. I skipped getting ready at Kmart on free breakfast days, so that I was sure I made it to class on time. One of those days, I was brushing my teeth in the school restroom when my friend Ron walked in.

"Bennie," he said. "I heard you're not at Tony's place anymore. Where are you staying?"

Trying to be funny, I said, "I'm in a mobile home." And although I wanted to laugh, my heart suddenly broke, and I was immediately in tears.

"What's the matter, buddy?" I knew Ron was genuinely concerned.

I said, "Man, I cannot find an apartment. The truth is, I'm

sleeping in my van."

"You knucklehead, you should have told me." He went straight away and called his wife. "This boy, he's so hardheaded. He's been sleeping in his van and did not even tell anyone." I could not help it; my mother's words were hard to forget, and I had made my pleas before God. Ron said to me, "My wife says you're a knucklehead for not letting us know. Come on over and stay with us." I went to his home that day, grateful again for God's provision. They took excellent care of me.

In the meantime, Debbie kept telling me, "Bennie, unless you buy a place, you will not find something easily."

"Show me something cheap to buy, and maybe I can try it." I was open to anything at that point.

She said, "I have a townhome. My husband and I own it, and we want to sell it. Do you want to look at it?"

"Sure." We went and looked at it, and I liked it, so we started discussing finances.

"Debbie, I know you want to sell this townhome for $50,000, but the bank won't loan me money because I don't have a job. I cannot burden my brothers with my problems because I don't think it is the right thing to do. I do have a proposition to make for your consideration. How much did your husband rent this for before?"

She said, "$450 per month."

"What if I give you the whole year's rent?" I wasn't sure where it would come from, but God had brought pigeons to my mother when I wanted meat and a van from West Virginia when I had no car. I could not even count the many miracles in between, and I knew God could do anything. "Will you give me this apartment if I give you one year's rent money upfront so you won't have to worry about me not paying you?"

I could see her rolling the idea around in her head. "Hmmm... I will discuss it with my husband."

I was planning to go to Raleigh, North Carolina, to visit my brother over the weekend to give Ron and his wife a little space, so I asked Debbie, "Do you think you could let me know by Monday?"

She said she needed to talk to her husband, and we left it at that. I drove down to North Carolina to visit my brother, Finny, who was going to seminary there. While I was there, I got a call from Mike, a friend of mine in Texas.

He said, "Bennie, where are you, man? I called New York, and your brother said you were in Virginia at Tony's place. Tony said you are at Ron's place. Ron said you are in Raleigh. What's happening?"

I said, "Foxes have holes, birds have nests, but I have no place to lay my head. I'm trying to sort things out."

"Where's Lina?"

"She's in India," I replied.

He said, "Oh, Bennie. Let me call you back."

A few minutes later, he did. "Bennie, I'm starting a new business and praying about different ventures. God laid it on my heart that I should give you money—not Alpha Ministries—I should give *you* money. I'm sending you a check by FedEx. It's a cashier's check so you can go to any bank and show your I.D. and get the money." I did not know what to say. He kept talking: "I want you to get this money and use it for yourself. Maybe you can spread it all out on your bed and smell the American dollars. Did you know American dollars smell good?"

I did not. "I've never had the chance to do that."

He said, "Well, you should. Now go and cash this money."

Just like he said, he sent me a check. It was there on Monday when I returned. I had promised Debbie that if she and her husband agreed to my proposition (paying for a year's rent at once), I would give her $4,800. The check from Texas was for $5,000. God even gave me enough money to tithe on it.

Debbie called me that Monday and said, "Bennie, my husband agreed to your proposition. Are you able to do it?"

"Yes, I am!"

My on-time God had added another miracle to the list. Although for a time, it had felt like He was only taking things from me—my car, my family, my home, my dignity—He was actually teaching me to rely on Him and not on myself.

When I was willing to serve Him and hold tight to Him in the midst of those difficulties, He restored each one to me, providing over and above anything I could imagine. When I let Him lead me, He took me to places I would never have—*could never have*—gone on my own.

I sent Debbie a check for $4,800, and then I called Lina in India to tell her she could come home. I could not wait to see her and my sweet daughter, Faith, again. A couple of days later, we moved into our new townhome. That was the beginning of our life in Lynchburg.

THE ARRIVAL OF OUR SON

When Lina was finally able to come back from India, she was already in her third trimester. We called several health clinics in the area, but they declined to take her as a patient because she hadn't been under a doctor's prenatal care. Finally, a clinic accepted her soon to find out there could be complications and that the baby was breached. The doctor suggested amniocentesis to examine for genetic abnormalities, but we declined. We came home and prayed for the next few days, and Lina was on bed rest. Our tears poured out freely as we prayed for a miracle. Lina faced the risk of the RH factor, and the doctor suggested induced labor a month early.

The baby was at high risk for hemolytic anemia, where red blood cells are destroyed faster than the body can replace them. The doctors said that the baby would need a blood transfusion at birth and be prepared for other health concerns.

Our last ultrasound revealed that the baby had miraculously turned from its breached position, and we praised God for the confirmation that He was in control. On the morning of the medically induced labor, God gave us Joshua 10:13b -14 ". . . So the sun stood still in the midst of heaven, and did not hasten to go down for about a whole day. And there has been no day like that, before it or after it, that the Lord heeded the voice of a man; for the Lord fought for Israel."

The doctor said that they were ready for the blood transfusion and told us not to worry, but we were praying and believing for our miracle. On the day he was born, the sun did standstill. He arrived in this world perfectly beautiful and healthy. He was indeed the miracle we'd been praying for. The doctor said the baby wouldn't need the transfusion after all. To God, be the glory! We named him Ben-Israel: son of God's triumph! Ben means Son of my right hand. Israel means: Triumphant with God/may God prevail. Every single day since he was born, he has added something amazing to our lives. He has grown into a remarkable person, so full of love and care. He graduated with honors from college with a degree in healthcare management debt-free and is happily married to Elizabeth.

CHAPTER 7

APPLICATION POINTS

Are you ready for "on the job training"?

When I was focused on making money and living life my way, I never had enough. I was always working for a little more, a little more. When I determined to make a lifestyle change and go into my Father's business, everything I knew turned upside down, and I began to learn the ropes of a very different way of living.

Sometimes God tears down the things we spend years building up so that He can build something better than we could ever imagine.

I went to Lynchburg, Virginia, to attend Liberty University because God had provided a scholarship. During that time, I lost my vehicle...lost my home, and my wife had to take my daughter back to India for a season just to get by. Yet our on-time God provided through a chain of events that I could never have imagined.

God will bring you to places where, depending on Him, becomes your only option.

Although for a time, it felt like God was only taking things away from me, He was actually teaching me to trust Him and not myself.

Are you willing to hold on to your faith, even when things get hard?

When I remained willing to serve God and held tight to His promises in the midst of those difficulties, He restored each thing to me, providing over and above anything I could have imagined. When I let Him lead me, He took me to places I could never have gone on my own.

> *Therefore do not cast away your confidence, which has great reward. For you have need of endurance, so that after you have done the will of God, you may receive the promise . . .*
>
> **—Hebrews 10:35-36**

CHAPTER 8

"I MUST DO THE WORKS OF HIM WHO SENT ME"

"I must work the works of Him who sent Me while it is day; the night is coming when no one can work. As long as I am in the world, I am the light of the world."
John 9:4-5

As I grew in my understanding of what it meant to be about the "Father's business," I learned that missionaries and people who lived on the edge of faith as my parents did were not the only people doing the work of the Heavenly Father. I remained involved in helping my parents sustain their ministry in India, and in America, precious brothers and sisters in Christ came alongside Lina and me to support us. We became their ministry. It was a beautiful picture of the Body of Christ in action—a living organism moving and breathing and doing the works of the One who had sent us to Lynchburg, Virginia.

We found a church when we moved to Madison Heights, and just like in New York, I had committed that we would be faithful to it. I never asked if they could take us on as missionaries or if they could support us. In fact, during our first couple of years there, most people did not even know we had a ministry. I did not feel like we should promote ourselves or make a plea on our own behalf. If we needed something, we knew that God would take care of it.

LANDLOCKED

Many exciting things were going on in India through my father's ministry, Alpha Ministries, and I was the Alpha Ministries representative in America. I was the man behind the scenes taking care of everyday administrative work, like handling tax exemptions, booking churches for my father and brother, and driving them around when they visited. From time to time, I would go by myself to share the work of Alpha Ministries in churches, and God would always open doors or new opportunities. For the first ten years that we lived in Lynchburg, I did not take any salary from the ministry at all. Lina and I lived on faith and the generosity of others who designated specific gifts to us. Lina never complained or questioned, and she knew we are in this together, and she is always willing and ready to pay the price and fulfill the vision.

We had enjoyed Debbie's townhome, but we were expecting our third child and were outgrowing the space. We used one bedroom as the Alpha office, the other as the bedroom, and then we had the living room. With two children and one on the way, things were tight. Plus, Debbie was ready to sell the property.

One of our friends lived in an apartment complex in Madison Heights that was owned by a Christian businessman who was a member of the church. My friend worked maintenance at the complex, and he informed me there were several three-bedroom apartments available. He gave me the owner's number, so I called and shared my need. The owner had me fill out an application—but then never called me. When I checked back, the owner informed me that they did not have a three-bedroom apartment available at the time. No one would rent to a family who was technically unemployed.

A friend of Lina's gave us the name of another realtor, but her suggestion was one we'd heard so many times before: "Tell your husband you should try and buy a house rather than renting." However, we were in the same situation we were in before when we moved into Debbie's townhome. I still did not have a "regular" job, and I would not be able to take a dime from the ministry. But this realtor had a new idea. She said, "Talk to your brothers. If one of them will buy a property, you can pay the rent to him. It will be a win-win situation."

So I called my brother Jimmy and explained the situation to him. I said, "I'm not asking for a favor. If you are interested in buying a house, this is an idea."

He replied, "You know what? I do have some money. Do you have any that you can contribute as well?"

I was able to come up with minimal funds toward the purchase; it was something, nevertheless, so it was a deal. Jimmy would buy the house, and I would rent it from him.

We looked around and found a nice property in Madison Heights that had been on the market for about a year. The house was in excellent condition with a split foyer, three bedrooms, and an acre of land. Lina and I prayed about it, and it seemed to be the place where the Lord was leading us. I spoke with the owner, and we agreed on a price. The day we came to sign the contract, the owner and his realtor asked if we wanted to check out the house one more time. When I walked around it, I noticed that there was now a "For Sale" sign on one half of the acre of land I thought belonged to the house.

I asked the realtor, "Doesn't that property belong to this house?"

She shook her head, "Oh no, I did not tell you? That wasn't your property."

I did not know what to think. This was bad and had taken me entirely by surprise! They should have told us we were only getting a half-acre of land for the price we agreed upon.

I called Jimmy and told him about the situation. I felt like the owners were trying to "cheat a foreigner," and I was frustrated. Jimmy thought very carefully and finally advised me not to sign the contract.

"No, I can't do that. If they are trying to cheat us, God will take care of that. But if we don't take it, I will be homeless. We need a place to live in." I felt stuck between a rock and a hard place.

He said, "Do whatever you want then. It's more for you than for me, so pick the place that will serve your purpose best. Do what you think is right."

I told Jimmy, "Whatever loss you suffer, I'll pay you back, but right now, we need to take this place."

With that, I went back in to sign the contract and told the seller's realtor, "What you did today was not right. You let me believe this house came with the full acre of land. You should have told me upfront that it did not. If I had known, I would have done things differently."

She apologized, and since I did not want to make a big issue over it, I just kept quiet, signed the papers, and left the place. When I got home and told Lina, she was upset. She said, "You should have talked to them more, that land belongs to this property."

I knew God would take care of these things, so I told her not to worry.

My growing family moved into the home with the half-acre of land. It was a smooth transition because we did not have much that belonged to us. We did not even own a vacuum cleaner. We had several friends from the young married group at church who were all excited when they heard we had purchased a house. They not only helped us move in, but they also took care of us while we were there. One lady would come with her vacuum cleaner and vacuum our house. A couple of guys would come over and help me work on our van, which was having a little mechanical trouble at that time. Another friend would bring his lawnmower and mow our grass when he had the chance. I'm sure the neighbors wondered about the "Indian diplomat" living in their neighborhood who had all these white people coming over to work for him! My family and I found it very amusing.

All the while, the original owner of the property came every week to mow the grass or otherwise maintain his remaining half acre. One day as I returned home from school, I noticed a man putting wooden stakes and orange tape around the half acre. He appeared to be measuring to build a house. As I watched through the window, I sighed. I could feel trouble coming. I said to Lina, "The good view you have will soon be gone. Now there will be a house there."

Women are historical (not hysterical—historical). They remember everything. She gave me that "I-told-you-so" look and said, "Bennie, you should not have signed those papers."

There was nothing I could do about it at that point. "You know what? Don't even worry about that," I said. "Don't even mention it. God knew that this is what we needed, and that's fine. We could handle a less than desirable view if it meant having a roof over our heads."

The next afternoon, the original owner came knocking on my door.

"Hey, how are you?" I asked. Even though I felt he had cheated us, I was determined to show him God's love. "Would you like to come in?"

He said, "No, that's fine. I came to tell you that my lawyer messed up. Apparently, the half-acre does belong to you as part of this property. It's in your name, and I'm going to file with the court to try and get it back."

I said, "You can do whatever you want," trying to seem as though I was fine either way. As the man left, I hurriedly called Jimmy to tell him what was going on.

He said, "Great! He cannot do anything. The lawyer was correct. The property was never divided like that. The whole acre was under one name, but the guy tried to cheat you out of what was rightfully yours because he wanted to sell it separately and make more money." Jimmy was happy that the man who tried to cheat us would get nothing after all.

I knew that legally Jimmy was correct, but in my heart, I was thinking, "This is not right. The Bible says if someone asks you to go one mile, go with him two miles."

I walked over to the half-acre with the stakes and orange tape and said to the man, "Listen, I don't want you to get upset over this. To be frank with you, you shouldn't have the property because you knew all along it was ours. You assumed an ignorant foreigner was getting cheated by a smart guy, but you forgot that there is a God over us all, who in His time will take care of all things."

He mumbled some sort of answer and didn't look very happy.

I continued, "You and I both know you tried to cheat us, but I want to tell you something; my brother says that even if you go to court, you will not get anything. However, I know your heart is set on this. You took care of this property for a year, hoping you would get some money for it, and I don't want you ever to feel that there was a Christian family here who tried to rob you. I will do my best to get you some money out of the kindness of my heart, even though I owe you nothing.

He said, "What can you give me? I was expecting to get $25,000 for this property."

I said, "Friend, that's not at all what I meant. I'll try to get you some money, so you are not disheartened."

I walked back to the house and called Jimmy again. Of course, Jimmy is much more American than I am and is a very educated guy and knows the business. When I explained to him what I wanted to do, he exclaimed, "You should not give that guy a dime!" He did not get what I was trying to say.

"No," I explained, "I must do this because that man's blood, sweat, and tears have soaked that property for a long time. I don't want to cause him pain and anguish over this." Even so, Jimmy would have no part of giving the man more money.

The market value in those days was $4,000 for that half-acre of land. I gathered some money on my own and called to have the previous owner come and see us on a specific day. I handed him a check, and I said, "No one else in America would do this, but I want you to know that we are Christians, and we do the right thing. I want you to have this check and be blessed. The next time you get a chance, be a blessing to someone else."

Even though my friends and family completely disagreed on giving that man money, we did not owe him, and I knew in my heart that it was the right thing to do. I could have used that money to buy a lawnmower, a vacuum cleaner, or to use it to fix our van, but I did not need to worry about those things. I wanted to teach the man a lesson of grace and mercy so that he would never do such a dishonest thing again to anyone else. He and his realtor tried to play a trick on the new homeowners, but they did not know that we served a God who would protect us and provide for our needs. I wanted this to be known to his wife and his children. And I wanted my children to know that we will be faithful to God, even when it feels like others are unfaithful to us.

No one ever built a house on that half-acre of land. It belonged to us, and the house there became a comfortable home for my family.

JOY UNSPEAKABLE

Amidst all the chaos and the sickness, we learned that Lina was pregnant with our third child. We were beyond happy and so excited about the blessing God was bringing in our lives. At the very first doctor's appointment, we were told to be very careful because it was going to be a high-risk pregnancy. The RH factor was again a significant issue of concern, and the doctor recommended periodic assessment to monitor and control the levels of protein in the blood, implying that the condition was life-threatening for the baby.

Lina and I prayed for the health of the baby unceasingly. Every day of the nine months, we cried out to God and prayed for a miracle. We prayed according to Psalms 139:13-14, "For You formed my inward parts; You covered me in my mother's womb. I will praise You, for I am fearfully and wonderfully made; Marvelous are Your works, And that my soul knows very well." We fully trusted that God was forming every detail of the baby in the womb, and we were not worried.

As the day of delivery came closer, I had to leave for India because of an emergency, but my sister flew down from New York to be with Lina. When the baby was overdue, my sister had to go back. Lina was assured by her friends with prayers and comfort.

There was a severe thunderstorm that night with lightning

that lit the sky occasionally. Lina prayed for strength to make it through that night with the other two kids asleep in the room, unaware of the distress she was feeling. Psalms 4:7 "You have put more joy in my heart…", was her only assurance. That night she was rushed to the hospital, she made sure to put Faith & Ben in a friend's care. Lina was confident that God would see her through this, and sure enough, the baby arrived in just an hour. Despite undergoing a life-threatening condition, Joy-ruth entered the world as beautiful and healthy as can be. We named her Joy because it stands for Jesus first, others next, and yourself last. Ruth stands for loyalty, beauty, and companionship.

Joy-Ruth is hardworking, motivated, focused, and the joy of our lives. She continues to diligently use her God-given abilities and talents to serve others and glorify God through worship throughout high school and college, leading thousands into the presence of God. She cares deeply about people and is very sensitive to meeting their needs to the best of her abilities. Joy graduated debt-free with high honors and will be working as an ICU nurse. God has been so faithful to us and our children in our walk of faith.

COLLEGE LIFE AND EVERYDAY MIRACLES

The Dodge Grand Caravan that Frank from West Virginia bought for us continued to be a blessing. When my father came to visit, I became his chauffeur. I drove him to different churches all over so he could speak and share what was going on in India. When my brother visited, I did the same. As the ministry grew, my driving responsibilities with them grew as well.

After a year or so, Lina began driving too, but we still had just one vehicle. If my father or brother and I were traveling a long distance for the ministry, Lina was left with no transportation back at home. It was always difficult to figure out how she could get to work or take care of the baby or run errands if she needed something. I hated to leave her like that, so I always tried to borrow someone's car when I traveled.

The Lord provided a young lady named Priscilla, a student at Liberty University and a friend of my sister's, to solve this problem. Someone had previously given her a Pontiac Grand Am, but it was a stick shift, and she did not know how to drive it. She wasn't interested in learning how to either, so the car often just sat in the parking lot. Anytime I needed it, she was gracious enough to let me take it and use it. It was a timely blessing and great help.

God knew our needs, down to what might seem like the most insignificant detail. He never failed to provide what we needed right when we needed it. As others around us committed to doing the works God had called them to do, we were richly blessed through it.

SATURDAY NIGHT FELLOWSHIP

On Saturday nights, my wife and I often made it a point to invite students over to our townhome for a casual get-together for fellowship and growing together as a community. We would worship the Lord together and talk about what He was doing in our lives. One Saturday afternoon before one of these get-togethers, Lina came downstairs.

"We don't have any toilet paper, Bennie."

Sometimes I was tired of never having anything. "Well, we

don't have any money either," I sighed. "What should we do?"

"If someone uses the toilet, it is going to be very difficult for them." She was always gentle and wise, thinking like a woman. I was a guy and often struggled to think in such diplomatic terms.

"Okay, that's fine. If need be, tomorrow morning, I'll go and buy some with the credit card." The credit card was always our last resort and used only in the most urgent of circumstances. "It'll be fine."

She sighed and went back to preparing dinner for the evening. I think she must have been praying, too.

Before long, our friends started to arrive, and, by faith, Lina played the gracious hostess, offering them food and drinks. Suddenly, my friend Tony walked through the door. He was carrying a huge multi-pack of toilet paper.

"Bennie, my wife has gone crazy with toilet paper. She found it on sale and bought a mountain of it. We've stashed it under the bed and in the side tables and under the sinks, and we've run out of space. We thought maybe you guys could use some." He handed it to me, and I could not tell if I was about to burst out laughing or crying tears of gratitude.

"You're not going to believe this, Tony. When I asked the Lord to give us this day our daily bread, this is exactly what I was hoping He would give. We had just run out of toilet paper and did not have any way of getting more before our guests arrived." Lina testified to this truth.

"Well, now, you do!" Tony's smile took over his entire face.

It was a perfect example of how God provided us with things that might not seem relevant to the rest of the world but met the exact needs of our hearts. That night, toilet paper was a tender expression of God's love and provision for us. It was confirmation that He was orchestrating and directing our lives. Psalm 37:23

says, "The steps of a good man are ordered by the Lord, and He delights in his way." How does God delight in us? By seeing us rejoice in Him and by seeing His work lived out in our lives. Someone said, "God is bigger than big and closer than close. God's promises are bigger than anything we can imagine or hope for. God's promises exist in categories we don't even have." The way He fulfills them is in the most personal and intimate way possible. When we set our course for God, He will always be there to direct our paths. "I will instruct you and teach you in the way you should go; I will guide you with My eye" (Psalm 32:8).

We rejoiced when God provided our first and second vehicle for us, and we rejoiced when He brought toilet paper "out of the blue." It became more and more apparent every day how God was not only interested in the details of our lives, but actively intervening on our behalf.

Many of our friends were students, too, and together, we formed a small community. We enjoyed having them over to visit, and although we never asked any of them for help, they were always willing to step in and lend us a hand. I do not know if they wanted to bless us with laughter as well as with financial gifts, but many times when our friends left our home, we would find $20 bills rolled up in places. They knew we would not accept money if they gave it to us, so they would do things like unroll the toilet paper, put the $20 bill in, and roll it back up. Imagine going to the bathroom, and $20 just drops from the toilet paper roll. God revealed Himself not only as of the God who provides but as One with a sense of humor; our lives seemed to be characterized by toilet paper miracles.

As our friends were determined to serve us, we were also determined to be about our Father's business, serving others.

BLESSINGS FROM STRANGERS AND FRIENDS

One day, after dropping off our daughter at kindergarten, we were passing a local muffler shop when we saw a couple with some suitcases standing by the side of the road. The man was holding a sign that read, "Stranded. Need help. Need money."

When I saw the sign, I said to my wife, "Man, that's so sad. I hope God will provide."

She paused. "So do I."

By now, I knew what her pauses meant. "Do you think we should make a U-turn?" I asked.

"Let's do it."

We made a U-turn and came back. I pulled up in front of them and asked, "Hey man, what's going on? How can I help you?"

The man spoke up and told us they were from Vermont. They were stranded and wanted to get back home, but needed money for a ticket and other things.

While he was talking, I was thinking, "We don't have anything either. We're students, and our situation is bad. We're not even stable financially to be giving our money away to others." I knew exactly how he was feeling. I looked around in my car and found a tract called, "You are Special." I handed it to him and told him to take it and pray. Then I asked Lina how much money she had. I already knew I did not have any.

She said, "I only have this $20 bill, nothing more."

I said, "You know what? At least we have a home." I gave the bill to the couple, and I said, "I don't have any more money—this is our last $20."

The man's eyes got big, and he refused to accept it, "I can't take your last bit of money!"

I explained, "No, I want you to take it. I'm not telling you it's the last of our money because I want you to have pity on us; I'm telling you so that you don't think I'm holding out on you. I wish I had more. If I did, I would give it to you. This is all the money I have to give, but let me offer you one other thing: Trust God. Life is short. James 4:14 says life is 'a vapor that appears for a little time and then vanishes away.' Anything can happen anytime, so you should do your very best in anything that you do for God. Trust in Him. With God, all things are possible. Believe me, it's true. I wish you could see how we are experiencing that in our lives. Please just read the tract."

As we drove away, I thought about how the Lord saw Hagar in her pain and confusion, and He blessed her with the promise that she would be the mother of many descendants. After the encounter, Hagar called the Lord "El Roi," which means, "the God who sees me" (Genesis 16:13). He is "El Roi," and He sees, guides, and cares for us just as He did Hagar. We may feel ignored or rejected by friends and family, but we know that our Father sees not only the face we present to the world but all of our secret feelings and fears.

This encounter happened on a Friday—at the end of a week that had also been exceptionally frustrating for me. I had called several people and several churches, asking only for the opportunity to share what God was doing in India. Hundreds of pastors were being trained, children's homes were caring for orphans, churches were being planted, and the Holy Spirit was working in incredible ways. The church in India was exploding, and my enthusiasm to share all that God had allowed to take place in my life was unquenchable. When I called and spoke to the secretary of a prominent church in Lynchburg, she told me that her pastor did not take appointments. If I wanted to meet him, I should come to the Wednesday night service and wait in line to see him like everyone else. I felt wounded and angry. Did anyone even care about what God was doing?

On Sunday morning, we went to our church, and the associate pastor, Clarkson, was preaching while our pastor was away for the week. He started, "You know, God gives all of us opportunities to serve one another. We, as a church, are in desperate need."

I was thinking, "God, I am in desperate need. Do You see? Our last $20 is gone, and we don't have anything. We have gas, and we can use the credit card, but the interest rate is so high it is detrimental. Oh God, please do something here." My prayers were a jumbled mess, and my desperation seemed so severe that I wasn't even sure how to articulate my needs anymore.

The pastor continued, "God gives us opportunities all the time to glorify His name. This weekend, I met a couple from Vermont that had become stranded here, so I stopped and shared the Word of God with them. I took them to a motel and put them up for the night. Do you know that this couple received Jesus Christ? The next morning, I made arrangements for them to go back to Vermont and was able to see their enthusiasm as new believers in the faith firsthand. Keep your eyes open because unless we look and have the eyes to perceive the opportunity, we cannot have the opportunity."

As I was sitting there, I felt like someone was tapping on my shoulder. The Holy Spirit whispered to my heart, "See, Bennie? I provided for them. I can take care of your needs, too. Just take it easy. Trust in Me. Hang on."

I came out of that service and said to Lina, "Can you imagine that we got to be a part of that blessing. Even though we did not have much, we did what we could, and God performed that miracle."

She agreed. "Yes, it is amazing!"

God had blessed us in ways we could not even hope for through our interaction with the couple from Vermont. I went back home that afternoon, renewed with hope and thankful for a God who gives as much *through* us as He gives *to* us. It was a privilege to be about His business.

Sunday evening, we did not make the trip back to church. Even though gas prices were much lower in those days, it was still expensive for us to drive our cars too often. We stayed home but invited our friend Martin and his family over to visit. Before they arrived, Lina called me upstairs while she was changing our son to say how we were almost out of diapers and wipes.

I sighed, "Yeah, we'll have to go to the store. Tonight, though, Martin and his family are coming, so we will wait until tomorrow to get some."

With resolve, she agreed, saying, "I'll make do with what I have for now, but I just don't have much."

"I know, Lina. Let's just make it through tonight, and then we'll figure something out. For now, I want to focus on encouraging Martin and his family. We'll sort it out later."

Lina was resourceful, and I knew I could count on her to make the most out of what God had provided for us. She finished taking care of our children and prepared for Martin's family to come. They had about five or six kids of their own at the time (now I believe they have 11). When they arrived, all the children ran around together for a bit, as kids do, but we sat with Martin and his wife and had a good visit. It was a refreshing time of fellowship, and we loved every minute of it. After they left that night, we sat down as a family, talked about a few things, prayed, and then went to bed.

THE TREASURE HUNT CLUES

The next morning, I had some dealings with India that needed attention early in the morning, so I got up before everyone else and went to the office. When I came back home, it was around 8:00 a.m. Lina was upstairs with the children, and I settled into my chair to spend time speaking to God in prayer and to read the Scriptures.

I opened my Bible and could barely believe my eyes. Right there, in the middle of the Psalms, was a $100 bill. I just simply stared at it for a minute, trying to figure out what it was doing there. Still unable to tear my eyes away, I called upstairs, "Lina, did Tony come here last night or this morning?"

"No, why?"

I said, "There's a $100 bill right here!" I barely got the words out before she was running down the stairs.

She took it right out of my Bible. "Awesome! Do you remember we need diapers? God sees our needs, and He has provided for us once again."

I was so puzzled. "Who could have possibly done this?" I was still trying to figure out the mystery, and she already had her coat on to buy what we needed.

She was so excited that she nearly forgot to grab her purse. "Can you take care of the baby? I'm going to get diapers and wipes. Thanks, love you. Bye!" Out the door she went, ecstatic over the incredible blessing God had once again given us.

And off she went to Kmart. She got what she needed and was waiting in line to pay. When it was nearly her turn, she started digging through her purse for the money and saw that the $100 bill was about to fall. "Oh no!" she thought. "Did I not put it away properly?" But when she opened her wallet, inside was another

$100. She looked from one bill to the other, her eyes getting bigger and bigger.

She paid for the diapers and wipes and nearly flew home to tell me. "You won't believe it! I found a $100 bill in my purse!" As she told me the story, she got more and more excited. I could hardly believe it either.

"That's amazing!" I said. While I was still pondering it all, she went upstairs to change our son and put a new diaper on him. As she laid him on the changing table, she lifted the last of the wipes, and underneath was a wet $100 bill.

I heard her squeal, and I ran up the steps. She was holding the baby on the table with one hand and holding up $100 with the other. "I don't believe this! There is a $100 bill right here!" We both thought it at the same time, but she said it first: "It must be Martin!" The entire scenario seemed too good to be true.

I called Martin and said, "Martin, did you put the money here?"

"Bennie," he said, "You know that I won't tell you." I could almost see the twinkle in his eye through the phone. "But I want to ask you, where did you find the first money?"

"I found it in my Bible."

"Well then, if you found the first bill in the Bible, God will tell you where the rest of it is."

I persisted, "Can you please tell me how much you left?

He said, "Bennie, I'm not telling you. God will tell you how much you need."

That started the best treasure hunt in the history of our home. The night before, Martin's kids had fun hiding money all over the house under the ironing board, on the side tables, everywhere. On the first day, we found $800. The following day, we found the rest. It was about $1,200 total, scattered all over in different places. They hid the money because they knew we were in need. That was a timely provision of God for us as a family.

It was as if God said to us, "You need this money? I'm providing it to you. Do you need a van? A home? A second car? Toilet paper? Trust Me to know the things you need, and I will take care of you."

We were not living out any sort of "name it and claim it" kind of faith you might see on TV. This was a real, authentic, adventurous, challenging, wonderful, amazing faith that could be tangibly felt and experienced. God was showing us that when you're in His business, He gives you L.I.F.E.: **Lessons In Faith Every day**.

Our parents were living by faith, doing the work of the Father who had sent them, and we were all learning that God's way of getting things done is always more effective than our own. My parents in India, my brothers around the United States, Lina, and I in Lynchburg—all of us were blessed with opportunities to do the works of our Heavenly Father, and many around the world were blessed as a result.

CHAPTER 8

APPLICATION POINTS

"I must do the works of Him who sent me..."

When you take the work of the Father's business seriously, you will be used by God in timely ways to meet the needs of others and further His purposes here on earth.

As I grew in my understanding of what it meant to be about the "Father's business," I learned that missionaries and people who lived on the edge of faith like my parents were not the only people doing the work of the Heavenly Father. As I remained involved in helping my parents sustain their ministry in India, and in America, precious brothers and sisters in Christ answered the call of God and came alongside Lina and me to sustain us. We became their ministry. It was a beautiful picture of the Body of Christ in action; a living organism moving and breathing and doing the works of God.

Psalm 37:23 says, "The steps of a good man are ordered by the Lord, and He delights in his way."

How does God delight in us? By seeing us rejoice in Him and by seeing His work lived out in our lives. When you set your course for God, He will always be there to direct your path.

Remember . . .

As you focus on the Father's business, you might feel ignored or rejected by friends or family, but take confidence in knowing that your Father sees not only the face you present to the world but all of your secret feelings and fears as well.

As you learn about the "musts" of God, He will take care of the "musts" of your life.

After all, when we needed it, God even provided the toilet paper!

CHAPTER 9

I MUST WORSHIP HIM IN SPIRIT AND IN TRUTH

"But the hour is coming, and now is, when the true worshippers will worship the Father in spirit and truth; for the Father is seeking such to worship Him. God is Spirit, and those who worship Him must worship in spirit and truth."
John 4:23-24

My parents were true worshippers of the Father. They set an example of worship for me my entire life. Worshipping in spirit was having a heart that loved and trusted God; worshipping in truth was putting legs on that faith and living it out so that God's response was anticipated and expected in every circumstance.

This faith was deeply put to the test when my brother, Davis, was diagnosed with polio at a very young age. Over time, his physical health began to deteriorate drastically. One of the ways the doctors in India treated him was by having him lie down on a hospital bed with weights placed on his arms and legs to keep them from bending. This primal view of medicine and the human body was very common in India in those days. They told my parents the grave news that Davis would never walk again.

My mother cried harder than I realized was even possible and adamantly poured her heart out to God, "If my child has such a condition, how can I ever pray for others?"

Davis saw her during her time of lamenting and held out his hands to her. "Mummy, please hold my hand and help me sit up," he requested. He had been in bed for three months, and his limbs were thin and frail. The doctors had been clear about keeping the weights on his arms and legs at all times, but my mother had seen God work miracles before. She slowly removed the weights one by one and helped Davis to sit.

After a while, he said, "Mummy, hold my hand, and help me to walk." Davis did not have the strength in his legs to stand, but my mother spoke with his doctors, who prescribed braces and crutches for him to try and walk. The special boots for his legs went up to his hips and were very expensive. My parents had to borrow money to purchase them, but the doctors assured my parents that Davis had no hope of walking without the braces. Davis continued with his physical therapy and practiced learning to walk with the braces.

I came home from school one day, and I saw the expensive boots, braces, and crutches propped at the back of our house. In my immaturity, I told my mother it was careless that we did not have money to eat, yet she bought expensive "exercises" for her son. I told her that she needed to put them on him, and he would need them for the rest of his life. My mom was angry and told me I should not talk that way. I did not understand how her heart ached to see her son in that condition. In those days, I was very focused on daily survival alone. The idea of looking past the present circumstances was not something I could comprehend in the slightest.

My mother knew this and decided to tell me a story: "Today I was buying vegetables, and I was sharing with people around me about God's goodness. One lady asked me why my son was crippled if my God was so great. I was so broken by her question because the heathen woman was defiling the name of our God. With a heavy heart, I came home and prayed: 'It is You who called us to ministry, Lord. Your name is being defiled in this heathen land. Either You heal my son or take my son.'"

She was utterly serious about God's purpose for our lives and knew that ultimately our fate lay in His hands, not our own.

Then I watched her take my brother's tiny hands in hers. He swung his legs over the side of the bed. He pushed himself off the mattress and carefully stood to his feet. As she held his hand, the same child that doctors sentenced to a future of never walking again walked. The same Jesus who healed the lame, the crippled, and the paralytic healed my brother that day. We witnessed one of the greatest miracles of our lives—we were all awestruck at the healing God gave to him. Our family understood the power of truly worshipping God in spirit and in truth and continued to be amazed at how He hears and answers the cries of His broken people.

Today, Davis is the pastor of the largest evangelical church in Gujarat and Vice President of Alpha Bible Churches of India. We have seen and experienced God's faithfulness in our lives over and over again. Our parents' lives are testimonials to the amazing ways He led them.

THE UNIVERSITY OF VIRGINIA

During my time at Liberty University, the Lord provided so many things for my family that I got in the habit of simply trusting Him rather than worrying. Faith is active, like a muscle, and sometimes it needs to be stretched in order to get stronger. As so many of our immediate needs were being met, I began having some mysterious health issues and could not quite pinpoint what was happening. I started losing weight rather rapidly and became very weak. I could not go to school because I had a high fever and could not stop shivering. No one could figure out what was wrong with me. It felt like what happened to me in New York all over again. The story of my brother Davis came to mind many times during my illness, and the numerous times' God had proved Himself to be an on-time God...so we prayed earnestly.

One of my friends suggested going to the University of Virginia (UVA) in Charlottesville, more than an hour from Lynchburg because they have a research and teaching hospital. I decided to take his advice and went to UVA to have them run some tests, evaluate my symptoms, and see if they could finally get to the bottom of whatever was happening. Since I was also having terrible headaches, they thought maybe I had sinusitis. They gave me some medicine and sent me home. It did not work.

Lina tried to make me as comfortable as possible at home caring for me, but I kept losing weight and could not keep anything in my stomach. Lina and the kids gathered around me every day to pray for me. Their presence was a great encouragement and blessing. However, my health kept deteriorating, so I went back to the hospital. The doctors thought maybe it was a vision problem, so they did a vision test. The test showed my vision was fine. Every time they tried a new test or exam, the bills mounted up. Before long, I owed the hospital over $3,000 and had no idea how I was going to pay the bill. On top of it all, the money seemed to be wasted—no answers came of it.

Finally, the doctors stopped with exams and tests and told me that there was nothing more they could do. I prayed, "Lord, I need you to intervene. Somehow, You need to do a miracle here."

I wasn't giving up. I went back to UVA to express my growing concerns because I wasn't feeling any better, so one of the chief doctors agreed to come and speak to me. He asked a lot of questions, making sure all of the tests and treatment options available had been exercised. The other doctors seemed confused. "We have done all these tests, and they are negative," they insisted. "Bennie comes here over and over, but we can't figure out what's wrong with him." The chief doctor looked me over again.

"Stretch your hands out," he said to me. I did, and my hands were shaking. He laid a pencil across the back of it and took some measurements. "Have you checked his thyroid?" he asked, without looking up. The other doctors shook their heads and murmured, "No." He straightened up and handed the measurements to them. "Run a test for his thyroid function." When they did, they discovered I had hyperthyroidism. A radioactive treatment later and all my symptoms were gone. Though it was a season of intense trials as a family, God helped us persevere.

That terrible season finally ended with a hospital bill of more than $4,000. I began receiving collection notices and letters asking me to pay immediately. I was an unemployed college student without adequate medical insurance I had back in New York. I was at a loss for what I was going to do. It was very important to me to have a good testimony, and I knew I had to be faithful in paying what I owed.

I went back to UVA and asked to meet with someone about my bill. I explained, "I want to pay my bill and protect my credit, but this amount is too much. I need some help." As if I was the hundredth person to make that request to them that day, they sent me to the finance department.

I went to the finance department and repeated my story. The lady was obviously used to this request as well and seemed impatient, to say the least. She barely glanced up at me as she studied my paperwork. "What do you do?" she asked, uninterestedly. I could tell she asked that question a thousand times a day.

"I am a student at Liberty University," I began. "I need some help because I don't have a job. I want to pay this bill, though." I took a deep breath. "I can only afford to give you $5 per month."

Finally, I had her attention. She took her glasses off so she could get a better look at me. "Are you kidding me? Do you want to be stuck with this bill for the rest of your life?" She shook her head, amazed at my naïveté. "Can you imagine how long you are going to pay at $5 per month? You should have come up with a better figure." She put her glasses on again and leaned forward. "Can you do any better than that? Like $100 per month?"

"No, I cannot," I said. "That's too much money for me right now. Once I get a job, I can."

She squinted at my paperwork again. "You said you were in ministry. So the ministry doesn't pay you?"

"No, my commitment is that I will not take a dime from the ministry for salary until the ministry is established."

She had obviously never heard that response before. I could see that her heart had softened some, and she asked me gently, "Do you have an audit for the ministry?"

"Yes."

"Can you prove that you are a student at Liberty?" She started looking on her desk for some other forms.

"Yes, of course."

She handed me a new set of forms and told me what to do with them. I left, and after I gathered all the necessary information she requested, I mailed the package to UVA.

About a week later, I received a letter from her. It read, "Mr. Mathews, you owe $0 to UVA. From now on, if you obtain your medication from the UVA medical clinic, your cost will be $3. Everything else will be completely covered." Apparently, I was covered by some sort of special grant, and UVA actually provided medical insurance for me. I could go there anytime, and all my medical checkups and treatments were completely free. I was in awe!

God just kept sending miracle after miracle, and every time a new burden would arise, Lina and I prayed, and God made a way. His provision is incredible! No man can see it coming! He is El Roi, He sees us, and we will never be abandoned. God sees your heart and your life. He sees you in the dark, in the crowd, when you are alone. He sees you everywhere, and He sees you always. Why does He see us? Because He is a God full of goodness and mercy, He loves us; He cares for us because we are His children.

GOD IS BIGGER THAN YOUR PROBLEM

More churches allowed me to come and share the mission of Alpha Ministries, friends from our church supported us through our never-ending endeavors, and even Debbie (our first realtor) became a monthly supporter. We felt settled, and everything seemed fine.

My sister's friend Priscilla was still letting me borrow her Grand Am when I traveled for work, which allowed a lot of freedom of mind when making plans to travel. On my way to speak at a church in West Virginia one day, the car suddenly stalled. As I pulled over to the side of the road somewhere near Covington, Virginia, and took a look under the hood, I prayed earnestly, "Lord, what is happening? I don't want to be stranded." The car would start, but it would not move; the clutch wasn't working.

Just when I began to become really discouraged, a family in a maroon van pulled up behind me. The man got out and came over to help. He started asking a lot of questions, including whether I knew someone who could come and tow the car. There weren't any cell phones in those days, so I had no way of contacting anyone.

"I tell you what," he said in a thick Virginia accent, "Why don't you leave the car here and hop into my van. I'll drop you off at the next exit, and maybe you can find a tow truck or something."

I was grateful for his offer, but I was still concerned about my trip. "Tomorrow, I have to be in West Virginia speaking at a church, and now, I don't know what to do." I fiddled with the car one more time, praying for it to move.

"You're going to West Virginia?" he asked, "Well, maybe you can catch a bus or something in the next town." It was a good idea, and by then, I was convinced the Grand Am wasn't going anywhere.

"You're right," I said, pulling the keys from the ignition. "Thank you, that would be great."

He was glad to help me and made it a point to keep me from feeling as if I was a burden.

While we were driving, I told him and his family the story of who I was and what I was doing in Virginia. They did not say much but were kind enough to drop me off at the local car dealership in Covington. I told them how much I appreciated the ride and went inside.

The place had a tow truck, so we went to get the Grand-Am and bring it back to discuss the repair with the mechanic. He leaned back on his chair and looked at me.

"Are you one of Jerry's kids?"

I was really confused. I was nervous already because the car was broken and it did not belong to me. I knew getting it fixed would cost a lot of money that I did not have at the time and had no way of getting to the bus station in town. "Jerry's kids?" I could not figure out what he meant by that.

He asked me again. "Are you one of Jerry's kids?"

"What do you mean?" I just wanted to get the car fixed and was in no mood to be given a hard time.

"Are you from Liberty University?"

Suddenly a wave of relief washed over me, and I replied, "Yes, I'm a student there!"

He laughed. "That's what I mean—you're one of Jerry Falwell's kids."

Finally, I could laugh, too. "Oh, okay. Yes, yes, I am one of Jerry Falwell's kids."

He got up, wiped his hands with an already dirty rag, and asked, "How can I help you?"

I showed him the car and told him about the clutch. He looked at me, probably trying to figure out what an Indian man was doing in the middle of Virginia, and asked, "What do you do?"

I gave him a short answer. "I am a missionary, and I have to speak at a church in West Virginia tomorrow."

"Oh, good," he grinned at me, and then he leaned in and spoke softly: "Let me tell you something. This is a very expensive place to get anything done." He called it highway robbery. "I can tell my boss to let you leave your car here—just don't get it fixed here. Tell someone to come and pick it up and get it fixed somewhere else. Dealerships are always expensive. You are missionary, and a student at Liberty, and one of Jerry's kids; I understand your situation. I'm only telling you this to help you out."

I was so grateful that God had brought an honest man to me. "Thank you. I really appreciate it. Can you show me how to get a Greyhound bus or something? I need to get to West Virginia."

He said, "Let's go inside and see if someone can drop you at the bus stop nearby."

We went inside, and while he was talking to someone, I noticed the same maroon van that had dropped me off earlier was still parked along the curb. The man who was driving it saw me and walked inside.

"You know what?" he said. "My wife and I were talking. We are going to Kansas, and we will be driving through West Virginia. We can drop you off on our way if you like."

"Oh, that's great!" I hurried back to tell the mechanic that I had found a ride.

"Praise the Lord!" he said, "That's amazing!" God's faithfulness seemed to be everywhere, even in the midst of this frustrating situation.

I said good-bye to him and got back into the maroon van. It did not take long before I began to get concerned, though. In those days, there was an ad on television where a Jeep was going down the road. A man was riding a bicycle, and when the Jeep drove past him, it splashed mud and dirt all over him. A little further down the road, the Jeep broke down and got stranded. The guy on the bike came by and stopped to help the man in the Jeep. It was an ad for the Church of Jesus Christ of Latter-Day Saints.

I started thinking, "Maybe this family is Mormon, and I have to tell them who Jesus is." So, I started sharing all the stories of what God had done in my life.

When at first I had called my friend Frank (in West Virginia) from a payphone in Covington to tell him what had happened and that I would be taking a bus to get there, he told me to call him when the bus got to West Virginia and he would pick me up. But when we stopped for gas on the way, the man in the maroon van called Frank to ask for directions to his house. They wanted to take me all the way there!

Over the course of the entire drive, I got to share the Gospel with the man and his family. I went through it multiple times before finally reaching West Virginia. They were gracious and just let me talk and talk.

When we got to Charleston, West Virginia, the man paused to look at me and said, "Bennie, I am a born-again Christian, and so is my wife. We have really enjoyed hearing your testimony about God's faithfulness in your life."

I was so relieved. When my captive audience dropped me off at Frank's house, they took some brochures about Alpha Ministries . . . and have continued to be faithful supporters of our ministry ever since.

It is amazing how God brings people into your life!

Frank is the same friend who purchased his pastor's van for me, and it was his church in West Virginia, where I was scheduled to speak. When his pastor, Phil, heard my story about the Grand Am, he rented a car trailer from U-Haul and went down to Covington, Virginia, to retrieve the car. He likes to fix cars, so he just fixed it and drove it all the way back to Lynchburg with his son to drop it off—as good as new—at my house.

I asked, "How much do I owe you?" I could only imagine how expensive that car would be to fix it.

He smiled and replied, "Bennie, it's all taken care of. You don't have to worry about a thing." I tried to protest, but he laughed and shook his finger at me. "Don't rob me of my blessing!" How could I? I was so grateful! We prayed together and thanked God.

MAGNIFY AND DE-MAGNIFY

Having a growing family while attending school with a limited income came with a lot of restrictions on how we could spend money. One of the ways Lina and I budgeted was by cutting down on the amount of driving we did so that we did not have to waste gas. On weekends, the safest and coolest place to take our kids was Toys-R-Us. I would stay with the children as they played with display toys at the store while Lina would buy diapers and other things we needed. After a couple of hours of fun and games, it was time to leave the store and the toys behind. My oldest daughter did so without complaining, but my son, Ben, would often have a really difficult time parting with the new toys he had found. He had big hands that would hold on so tightly to whatever toy he had grown attached to that it was hard for us to make him put it down.

I would feel guilty about taking the toy from him because his crying made my heart melt. The happy, joyful family that went inside the Toys-R-Us store would come out in tears. "I want my Buzz Lightyear!" It was not a very happy ending to our outing.

And Lina would tell me, "We are torturing our children."

I would try to comfort her and calm my son. "Dad cannot get this toy right now, but God will provide a Buzz Lightyear one day. Just pray." It was something very hard for a two-year-old to understand. Every evening during our family prayer time, I would make Ben pray after me. Ben would put his little hands together, tightly keeping his eyes shut, and would repeat after me, "God, please give me a Buzz Lightyear." I did that sincerely because I had such great faith in my heart. When the children's birthdays or Christmas came, and friends or relatives would ask what they could get for the children, we would tell them some of the things the children wanted. When I was asked about Ben, of course, I would say, "Ben is praying for a Buzz Lightyear." I was not trying to create a miracle; instead, I wanted the children to experience what I have experienced in my life. When it was the appropriate time, I would remind them who gave them the gift, but I wanted my children to learn to have a heart of gratitude that would take them to a new altitude of faith. They would say, "Jesus worked through my aunt or uncle." That gave us the time to praise the Lord for His provision because it is the Lord who does things in our lives.

Once, after I returned from a trip to India, Ben became very sick. Lina had to pick up the other children from school and make a few other stops, so she left Ben in my care while she was out. When I noticed his temperature getting higher, I called the nearest clinic and drove him there.

When I walked in with my son, the lady behind the desk asked me what insurance I had, to which I replied that I did not have any. She then said that they did not take new walk-in patients and suggested I take him to a clinic in the next town over. I made the decision to quickly drive to the next clinic—about 30 minutes away. As I was driving, I could hear Ben breathing heavily from the back seat, growing increasingly ill. When we reached the clinic, it was totally packed. The lady at the counter said, "We don't have any room. Please take him to the Forest Clinic; they will be able to help you." I came out with a heavy heart, buckled my son in the back seat once again, and proceeded to drive to Forest, about 20 minutes further down the road. I threw a quick glance in the back to see Ben almost passed out. I totally freaked out and implored God to intervene.

There was a Chick-fil-A restaurant across the street from the Lynchburg clinic, so I rushed in to get a cup of chicken noodle soup for Ben. I quickly revived him and was so relieved when he opened his eyes. Placing a blanket over his lap, I told him, "When I was sick, my mother would pray and feed me or give me something to drink. I am going to pray over this soup for healing, and as you drink it, I will drive us to the Forest Clinic." Ben was weak and could barely respond, but he did what I asked him to do. About 20 minutes later, as I was driving, I heard my son call me from the back seat. At first, it was a weak sound, but the second time he called out to me, it was a strong voice. He said, "Dad, I'm feeling better. I want to go home and see Mama. I don't want to go to the clinic." I looked at him through my rearview mirror and could see that he was sitting up, and his countenance was improved.

I asked, "Are you sure? The clinic is so close." He responded, "I just want to go home and be with my Mom." So I turned around and headed home. By the time we reached home, he was completely healed. God heard my cries of desperation that day and healed my son.

That same evening, we all had a big celebration during our family prayer time, praising and thanking God for His faithfulness. I would often repeat the stories to remind my children of His goodness because I never want them to forget Him and His miraculous ways.

Years later, when Ben started playing basketball in high school, he did not have good basketball shoes. He had such a rapid growth spurt that we could hardly keep up with the extra clothing expenses. Worst of all, the severe growth caused him to develop a serious case of Tendinitis in his knees. He desperately needed a knee brace. Nonetheless, he loved playing basketball. His coach would often look at him and say, "Ben Mathews, you need to get some basketball shoes," and he would come home and share that with us.

Unfortunately, we had so many needs at the time that we had to repeatedly put his shoes on the "back burner." I would tell him, "Maybe next month we can get the shoes, son."

Ben, along with some of his friends from the basketball team, went shoe shopping one day. He came home and told us that his friends recommended Nike shoes because they have good cushioning to help his knees. So I went on the internet and looked into Nike basketball shoes. When I saw the price, I said, "Ben $140 is way too much money." I needed some time to budget our resources and make a responsible purchase we could handle. Ben left my room disappointed.

I said, "Ben, do you understand that the Lord can work miracles?" He answered, "Yeah," but it was clear at that point that he did not want to hear anything more about praying. I knew he needed to get his attention off the problem, off the lack, and onto God. I quickly printed the ad for the shoes he wanted and said, "Ben, will you stick this shoe ad on your bathroom mirror and pray over it?" Ben never disobeyed, and sure enough, he went and placed that ad on his mirror and started praying daily for his need to be met.

A few weeks later, a gentleman walked up to Lina after church and placed $100 in her hands. With a smile, he said, "This money is the first installment for your son's basketball shoes."

I was very surprised and asked him how he knew about this need and the prayer of our family. He replied, "Some time ago, you shared how Ben was praying for a pair of basketball shoes and how you wanted your children to learn to rely on God for their needs. That day, God impressed upon my heart to do this."

Lina came home and shared the news with Ben and the rest of our family, and we again rejoiced in God's faithfulness. When you magnify God, problems become smaller!

THERE IS NOTHING TOO HARD FOR GOD

When Faith needed a car to drive herself back and forth to attend an internship, Lina and I began to pray. I also shared the need with my mother and asked her to join us in prayer. She told me to call a friend of hers, name Philip, with a car dealership in Florida. I had never met him before, so I was reluctant, but my mother insisted. So I got Philip's phone number from my brother and called him.

Philip answered the phone, "Bennie, it's amazing! I was with your dad last month, and we were talking about you. We have never met, but I have always wanted to meet you. What's up? How can I help you?"

"I do have a favor to ask," I said. "My daughter needs a car."

He said, "I have over a hundred cars out here. Get on a plane and come get one."

I took the next flight to Orlando, and Philip's son picked me up and took me to the huge dealership. I met Philip there, and he showed me one car after another. We finally pointed to one with very low mileage, and he asked, "How about this one?"

"It's nice—how much do you want for it?"

"Bennie," he said. "Don't worry about the money."

"You don't understand," I said. "This is not for the ministry; this is for my personal use."

"No, Bennie," he answered. "It's you who doesn't understand. I am alive today because of your mother and your grandmother. You see, about 50 years ago, my family was suffering from smallpox. Many people died from it that year because it was so contagious. Even our relatives were too afraid to come to our home."

He went on to tell me how his family had been in need and were rejected by everyone they knew. But my mother and grandmother went to their home, picked up Philip and his brothers, and brought them out of the disease-afflicted house. They did not have a tarp to lay them on, so they put banana leaves on the floor. They placed the boys on the banana leaves, took coconut brushes to clean their wounds, and poured water over them.

Philip said, "Bennie, I am alive today because of your grandmother and your mother. To help the granddaughter of that woman of great faith and service is a blessing for me, so do not try to rob me of the blessing."

As I had so many times before, I was witnessing, once again, God's great provision for me through the faithful heritage of my parents. With the Psalmist, I can say, "Oh, magnify the Lord with me, and let us exalt His name together" (Psalm 34:3). When David says, "Oh, magnify the Lord with me," he does not mean, "let us make a small God look bigger than He is." He means, "I will make a big God begin to look as big as He needs to be."

You cannot magnify what you haven't seen or what you quickly forget. The magnifying glass does not change the actual image, but rather, it makes it clearer to us. We must share the details of His working in our lives with others. As we see the intricate details of His amazing ways, we are compelled to magnify Him daily in and through our lives.

My wife and I have taught our children to trust God, to magnify the Lord with us, and to live a life with an open heart and hand for God and His people. Every time we faced a challenge and only focused on that particular problem, the issue looked overpowering and overwhelming. But when you move your focus from that problem to God, He is magnified, and the problem seems to de-magnify. The problem shrinks when you know He is the solution, and you learn to trust Him regardless.

DIRECTING OUR PATHS

We have tried to instill the fear of the Lord in our children from a very young age. As a result, it wasn't very difficult for us to teach them that God has a plan for everyone and will direct the paths of those who seek Him. The most important thing I wanted them to learn is that everything belongs to God. We are merely stewards of His goodness and grace, and we need to be willing to give our all when He requires it of us. It is important to always give our first fruits to the Lord and honor Him first in everything we do. Even the little things matter. For example, when our kids were in school, we encouraged them to take extra snacks with them to share with the other children. They have grown up knowing that thinking of others is very important and should be at the forefront of their minds. We always pointed, paused, and praised God for His provision and thanked Him for His blessings.

The car Philip gave us for Faith allowed her to accept an internship with Areva, an international company in nuclear and renewable energy. It was a prestigious job that hundreds of other high school students had applied for, and Faith was one of the 12 selected from the entire central Virginia region. When she got her first paycheck, I asked her to give her first fruits to the Lord. Afterward, I asked her to divide the rest of her paycheck among my parents, brothers, and a few people who played very important roles in our life and ministry.

Faith was young and somewhat confused at this, just as any other teenager would have been. However, her obedience overrode any questioning thoughts she may have had. Even though my request seemed strange and was unheard of among her peers, she heeded her father's instruction. I imagine that was the same response Isaac had when Abraham asked him to lay on the altar. He never questioned or tried to reason with his father; he just obeyed. Faith obeyed and did what we asked her to do. I cannot tell you what a blessing it was for her and for us. The Lord gave her great favor in her lifetime for honoring Him and obeying her parents.

During Faith's senior year of high school, one of her teachers, Mr. Bouldin, wanted his students to be equipped for life in a very practical way. He assigned an essay for his class with the theme, "How are you going to pay for your college?" I was in India at the time, so Faith called and asked, "Dad, Mr. Bouldin wants to know how I am going to pay for college. Do you have a fund or plan to pay for my tuition?"

I answered, "Faith, just write, 'God will provide.'"

Of course, she exclaimed, "Dad, I cannot write that as my answer! We need to come up with some funds or ways that we can pay for my college."

I replied, "Faith, I do not have a plan or a savings account, God will provide. If you have a hard time writing that, just draw a finger pointing toward Heaven."

Faith laughed and wrote in her essay, "God will provide."

The next morning when she discussed her essay in class, her classmates laughed at her. Faith came home that day and shared how other people had plans, and they could not believe her answer. Mr. Bouldin had even asked her, "Seriously? Your parents have no plans?"

She explained to him, "My Dad told me that God would provide. I wish I had something more to write down, but that is all we have." When she shared that with me, I could hear the concern in her voice. I told Faith, "Let not your heart be troubled. Everything will be fine." She obediently took that advice and continued with her college application process.

When she graduated from high school as a salutatorian, it was one of the proudest moments of my life. We were living a legacy of obeying God's call in seeking Him and His righteousness. I was experiencing again what the Scripture says, ". . . and all these things shall be added unto you" (Matthew 6:33). I know I was busy with His Kingdom call, but He was faithful to my family and me. I have always invested in others, and it gave me joy to see His miracles working in our lives. It was a very special moment because His promises were being fulfilled in my family.

When Faith decided to go to college, I encouraged her to go to Liberty University because Dr. Ron Godwin, who was Provost at the time, was a good friend of our ministry and had often asked me when my eldest would start attending there. I would jokingly reply, "As soon as you give her a full scholarship." It turned out that Faith was offered a 75% tuition discount at Liberty because she had attended and excelled at a local Christian school. Since she hadn't decided where she wanted to go to college yet, she turned it down so that others in her class could receive it. Faith later ended up applying to Liberty after all and received a full academic scholarship.

I was not planning on taking her to check out different colleges since she already had a full ride to Liberty, but Faith felt God calling her to Cedarville University. I wondered how we could possibly send her to Ohio. We did not know anyone there, and I knew nothing about the college itself. However, I kept my concerns to myself. I wanted her to do as the Lord led her and knew that His hand would make way for her.

We were finally able to find time in my schedule to visit Cedarville. When we arrived, I was praying and asking if this is what God wanted her to do. As her admissions counselor was giving us a tour, the lady was so impressed with Faith that she offered her a job as her personal assistant at the admissions office during her freshman year if she chose to attend Cedarville University. We were taken by surprise by God's wonderful work in our lives. We saw Him working and directing her steps at the college in many ways. In the meantime, the Lord brought Dr. Thomas White to Cedarville as the new President of the university. Upon meeting him, Faith was awarded a Presidential Leadership Scholarship, which also helped us a lot financially. She really knew how to make a strong first impression. She always had the favor of God and people wherever she went.

We had no idea Ohio had so many more job opportunities than the small town where we lived in Virginia. The Lord opened doors for Faith to work at J.P. Morgan Chase and Plante Moran during her summers while studying at Cedarville. Her work in Columbus, Ohio, opened an opportunity to partner with a new young church there. This opportunity was instrumental in helping our frontline messengers with 60 much-needed motorcycles. The Lord used Pastor Chad greatly on the front lines to help equip our frontline messengers. In the last two years of our partnership, the church has supported over 60 needy children and five frontline messengers in South Asia. As time went on and everything was being unveiled, I saw His hand in the glove of history directing us. I thank the Lord for giving us the peace that passes all understanding to say "yes" when Faith decided to go to Ohio.

When Faith opened her first checking account, she did not receive her checkbook right away. I called her that Sunday and asked if she went to church and if she gave her tithe. She said, "Dad, the checkbook did not come in yet." I asked the following Sunday again, and she said she still hadn't received it. She called me the following Sunday very excited and said, "Dad, I went to church, and I gave my tithe!" I was going to bring it up casually, but she was reporting on what I asked her to do. Faith received better and better job offers every summer, and my only request remained that she always honor God with her first fruits.

Later on, Faith had a desire to go to Oxford University because she had been accepted into their study abroad program. We prayed, and the Lord worked it out for her to go. He provided the finances and took care of every little detail during her time there. We found out that one of our friends from India was living in the Oxford area, and they were able to help Faith with her move to England. She was a great testimony for His glory even while she was there. I was excited when I received a call to attend a conference in Oxford. The host did not know my daughter was in school there. When Faith came to visit me at the conference, everyone thought I came because Faith was there. I know that was a small factor, but I was genuinely answering the call of God. I had the greatest privilege to follow her around and see the entire Oxford campus. I could only praise the Lord for His faithfulness. Faith came home from Oxford with a 4.0. We have seen the Lord give her favor and grace because she honored Him and magnified the Lord with us.

I was so moved and overwhelmed with thanksgiving on the day she was finishing school. I got to see her graduate with high honors, debt-free, and with enough savings to have a nice wedding later on. Not only that, but she was offered jobs from four major companies, and ultimately accepted an offer from Ernst & Young. The night before her graduation, I was in tears magnifying the Lord and giving thanks to His holy name. I remembered the time when, shortly after she moved to Ohio and started her new job, I received a check from her in the mail with her entire first month's wages. She wrote, "You taught me when I got my first job to give my first fruits to God and to honor those who have blessed and influenced my life. No one has been a greater influence or motivator than you and Mom. Thank you for everything. I would not be here today without you." As a father, it is such a blessing to see that the lessons we taught her as a child stayed with her into adulthood.

I remember reading this in an issue of *Our Daily Bread* about the widow's giving: It made no sense for a widow to donate her last few coins to a corrupt institution in Jerusalem, where scribes who were dependent on those gifts "devour[ed] widows' houses" (Mark 12:40). But in that woman's act, Jesus saw a moving display of the proper attitude toward money (vv.41-44).

Gordon Cosby, while serving as pastor of the Church of the Savior in Washington, DC, tells of a widow whose income was barely adequate to feed and clothe her six children. Yet every week, she faithfully placed $4 in the offering plate. A deacon suggested that Cosby go to her and assure her that she could use the money instead for her family's benefit.

Cosby followed the deacon's advice—to his regret. "You are trying to take away the last thing that gives me dignity and meaning," she said. She had learned a key to giving: it can benefit the giver more than the receiver. Yes, those in poverty need financial help. But the need to give may be as important as the need to receive.

The act of giving reminds us that we live by the grace of God—

like the birds and the flowers. Those creations do not worry about their future; neither should we. Giving offers us a way to express our confidence that God will care for us just as He cares for the sparrow and lily (Matt. 6:25-34).*

Someone once said that every challenge in our way is also in God's way when we are in God's direction. I often remind my children that our middle name is "generosity." As children of God, we should have willing hearts, open hands, and always be ready to help others. When we do, we see the hand of God blessing, guiding, leading, and helping us. God's Word is true, "It is more blessed to give than to receive" (Acts 20:35).

Over and over, God has shown me that when I worship Him in spirit and in truth, doing the right things for His glory, He provides over and above anything I could think to ask of Him . . .

* **Source**: https://odb.org/2013/11/08/the-blessing-of-giving/

CHAPTER 9

APPLICATION POINTS

"I must worship Him in spirit and in truth."

Do you worship God in spirit and in truth?

Worshipping in spirit means having a heart that loves and trusts God; worshipping in truth means putting legs to your faith and living so that God's response to that faith is anticipated and expected in every circumstance.

- You cannot worship God only during the music at church on Sunday and not walk out your worship of Him in day-to-day life through the week.
- You worship "in truth" by doing what is right even when someone has done you wrong, even when no one is looking, even in the thoughts of your heart.
- Following His "musts" goes down to the very fine details of daily life.

God's ways are incredible!

He is El Roi! He sees you, and you will never be abandoned. He sees you in the dark, in the crowd, when you are alone. He sees you everywhere, and He sees you always. Why? Because He is a God full of goodness and mercy, He loves you, and He cares for you because you are His child.

Develop the habit of simply trusting Him.

Life will give you multiple opportunities to act in the flesh rather than in faith. Walking by faith is a habit. It must be practiced. You must keep your "eyes set on things above" more than on the circumstances around you. My parents modeled this for my siblings and me every single day.

- Who is watching you?
- Who is learning from your habit of trusting the Lord?

CHAPTER 10

I MUST PREACH THE GOSPEL

Now when it was day, He departed and went into a deserted place. And the crowd sought Him and came to Him, and tried to keep Him from leaving them; but He said to them, "I must preach the kingdom of God to the other cities also, because for this purpose I have been sent."

Luke 4:42-43

The faithfulness of my parents had been producing abundant fruit in India for a long time. My father's burden to proclaim the Good News of the Kingdom to the lost souls of North India had resulted in the birth of Baroda Bible Church in 1966. Within ten years, over a dozen daughter churches in the surrounding areas had been planted, and my parents' discipleship ministry had grown into a Bible school operated out of their home.

God continued to bless my father's commitment to preaching the Gospel, and in 1986 some new and amazing doors opened. Dr. Billy Graham had, for many years, been organizing conferences around the world to train and equip pastors and frontline messengers. In 1983, the Billy Graham Evangelistic Association (BGEA) held its first convention specifically for native missionaries. It was called The International Congress of Itinerant Evangelists (ICIE). In 1986, the second ICIE event was held in Amsterdam, and my mother was a part of the Alpha Ministries delegation that was privileged to attend.

These conferences were historic in that they sought out and cared for native missionaries. In those days, no one was focused on indigenous ministers. Converts reaching out to those in their own lands were often struggling just to financially support their own families and ministries. They could not even dream of affording the luxury of a plane ticket or a pastors' conference.

The BGEA changed all that. The native missionaries and pastors who were invited to attend (75% of whom were from emerging nations) were fully funded to fly to the Netherlands, stay in a hotel in Amsterdam, and attend a 10-day conference filled with valuable training sessions on evangelism.

It was the opportunity of a lifetime. It was the first time many of our frontline evangelists, preachers, and leaders in India had been treated with such respect and given the priceless opportunity to rest and be refreshed. Returning home, they did all they could to share with others what they had received in Amsterdam: tips, training, and tableware. When our people staying at the big training center saw the disposable plates, cups, and spoons being thrown out, they pulled the sturdy items out of the garbage and washed them, packed them in their suitcases, and brought them back to India. I used to visit people's homes, and they would bring out a cup or a dish from Amsterdam. "Oh," they would say, "this is the plate that the pastor gave us from Amsterdam, Holland." Everyone was blessed by the 1986 ICIE conference, even those who did not attend!

Ultimately, the BGEA gave Alpha Ministries more than just plates, cups, and tips on evangelism. Dr. Graham's vision for church-planting spread throughout the Indian delegates. They quickly began to teach and implement the various changes the conference addressed. Conference attendees began to be invited to speak in more churches, and God began to bless my father's ministry with a new vision.

Before long, my father invited several pastors to Baroda for Alpha Ministries' first pastors' conference. Everyone attending had a burden to develop effective leaders in their own churches. The conferences continued year after year, with attendance steadily increasing. In 1990, the ministry launched IMPACT (Indian Missionaries and Pastors Access Cross-cultural Training), its first large-scale pastors' conference.

I was still living in New York at the time, and though I had not yet been called into ministry myself, I was committed to helping my father serve those who had been called. I wanted to see the Good News spread throughout India, even if I did not yet feel called to do it myself. Since I was still "the moneymaker" at the time, God allowed me to play that role. I began to work two full-time jobs: one during the day and one at night, at two different hospitals in New York. The income from one job supported my family and me in New York, and the other, in its entirety, supported the huge financial undertaking of IMPACT.

I believed in my father's vision, and I believed that frontline leaders should be equipped to share the Gospel. What started as a leap of faith in 1990 and included strategies, training in church-planting, and encouragement for 300 pastors has since produced more than 26,000 alumni and an estimated 30,000 new house church plants. The IMPACT Frontline Messengers Conference has changed countless lives and continues to affect countless more for God's glory and His kingdom.

Ten years after the first IMPACT conference, I was living in Lynchburg and attending Liberty Bible Institute under the leadership of Dr. Harold Wilmington. By then, I felt called to more than just making money. I began to think about what I was learning and how it could be translated into ministry in India. Pastors and frontline messengers were being trained for ministry, but what about other believers? Shouldn't everyone have the opportunity to know, love, and understand the Word of God?

I called the leadership in India together and laid out my idea before them: What if every church became a Bible institute as well? Every pastor would spend a year training five believers in the New Testament, Old Testament, and Theology. After that year, those five would train five others, and the multiplication process would continue until everyone in the church had a solid understanding of the Scriptures.

The others in Alpha Ministries agreed on the idea, and Alpha's Church-Based Bible Institute (CBBI) was born. Dr. Ed Hindson's book *The King is Coming*, and other materials helped us develop a syllabus that became a big hit. The goal was for every believer to have at least two years of intense training (two-year learning with trade school skills and practical internship), and would be equipped as a "tent-maker," proclaiming the Good News no matter what profession he or she might have.

THE BEST PLACE IN TOWN

While still a student at Liberty, I had been blessed with the opportunity to attend Dr. Billy Graham's School of Evangelism in 1994 and was always keeping my finger on the pulse of the ministry. I deeply respected their sincere efforts to invest in native pastors. When I heard that they would be hosting another conference in Amsterdam like the ICIE conference my mother had attended, my heart burned with a desire to go. Finally, being part of the ministry myself at this point, I wanted to learn all I could from the people who had given such a vision to my parents.

I wasn't sure who to write to regarding the Amsterdam 2000 conference, so I wrote directly to the Billy Graham Association. I told them about my mother's experience at the ICIE conference in Amsterdam in 1986, and how we were all blessed by it. I explained that thanks to what she and the other delegates learned there, Alpha Ministries began conducting pastors' and frontline messengers' training in India. I told them what I felt God was doing through my life and how much I wished to attend the conference.

Soon after, they sent me an attendance form with all sorts of questions, including where I would like to stay. I wasn't picky. I wrote back that I needed a scholarship, that I was a Liberty student, and an evangelist, too. I explained that I did not have any money; I did not want to be a bother to anyone, so if someone had a sofa for me to sleep on, that would be fine. I just wanted to learn more about sharing the Gospel with people. The BGEA accepted my application, and it wasn't long before I was on an airplane, headed to Amsterdam 2000!

When I landed, I saw that my friends from India, along with many important and prominent Indian leaders, were in attendance. Several men who had attended in '86 were there as well, and now they led big ministries. I was just the American arm of a small ministry my dad started. I felt like the new kid.

As we went through the registration process, I stood around, trying to keep my distance while still being respectful to those who had attended before. They kept telling me where to go and what to do. "Bennie, you need to stand here and wait in this line." I stood in that line, but when I got to the front of it, the registration staff looked at my card and told me to stand in a different line on the other side of the room. A big-shot Indian preacher looked at me and told everyone that since I lived in America, I probably sent money to get into that "special line."

"No!" I shook my head in disbelief. "I did not pay for anything."

"You are Indian," he said. "You should stand right here with all the Indians and Africans in this line."

I walked over to where he was pointing.

When I got to the front, I was sent back to what he referred to as the "special line." It turned out that I had been assigned to stay in a classy hotel. All of our other people were assigned to the convention center, staying in temporary rooms in areas designed to accommodate thousands of people. Out of the entire group, I was the only one selected to stay at a fancy hotel in Amsterdam.

After I checked in, I went back to the convention center to hang around with the other Indian guys. I wanted to get to know them and learn from them, but they kept asking me if I had paid a lot of money to stay in the hotel. I was coming from America, after all. I reassured them over and over again, "No man, I filled out the same form you did, and I sent it in, and they gave me this place to stay." What else could I say?

When my brother landed, I went to meet him and asked him where he was staying. "Oh," he said, "I am in Yarbers (near the convention center) with everyone else. Why, where are you staying, Bennie?" I told him about the hotel, and he could not believe it either.

I could not explain it. The only answer I knew was that it was God's grace and favor. I hadn't asked for anything, and yet I was getting the best place in town. It was an amazing miracle for me. Friends have jokingly referred to me as God's "Forrest Gump" because of seemingly random things like that happening in my life. All I can say is, I work for an amazing "Boss."

PURPLE TAGS AND PERSPIRATION

On one of the first days of the conference, I was walking down the street and ran into Dr. Elmer Towns, the co-founder of Liberty University, and one of my professors. When I greeted him on the street in Amsterdam, he was surprised.

"Bennie, what are you doing here?" he said, shaking my hand.

"I'm attending the conference."

"Oh, good," he said, and he introduced me to the men he was with. They were looking for task team leaders to work on a special project collecting different ideas about evangelism so a book could be written. I knew a little bit about the project because many of the Indian leaders were already on it—each of them had an extra purple tag that read "Task Team Leader" hanging below their nametags.

Dr. Towns' friend knew I was a student at Liberty, so he asked me what else I was doing in ministry. I told him about my father, and Alpha Ministries, and how we were training about 300 native pastors to carry the Gospel throughout northern India and beyond.

"Well, you should be on the leadership team, then," he said. "We need guys like you on the Task Team." He took my existing name tag and added the special purple tag to it. Suddenly, I was a part of something I hadn't expected!

No one else expected it either. When I met my brother later that day, he pointed to my tag and asked, "Where did you get that?"

I tried to explain to him about how I had run into Dr. Towns, but I could tell by his somewhat skeptical expression that he was thinking, "Why are all of these good things happening to him?" He wasn't the only one.

I attended the special task team meetings made up of delegates from all different denominations and run by the Archbishop of Canterbury. Many of the prominent Indian mission leaders and pastors were there, too, and I felt like an insignificant little boy in the room. The leaders divided everyone into teams: 10 people to a table, and one person appointed to be the scribe. Somehow, they selected me, the guy who could not write without making mistakes.

Each table was tasked with coming up with ideas about evangelism, writing them down, and then sharing them with the group. We worked diligently on our assignment, and as the other people at my table were talking, I was writing down everything they said. When our turn came, the Archbishop of Canterbury pointed to me and said, "You, come up and share."

I was horrified. There were other very important Indian ministers at my table, and I could feel them staring at me. I began to stammer like Moses and pointed to another man at the table who was a famed preacher and Bible teacher from India…"No, please, let him do it."

The Archbishop shook his head and motioned to me to come to the front of the room. "No, you're doing it. Come on up, right here."

I had no choice. I walked to the front of the room. I could feel giant beads of sweat forming all over my body, and I was just certain everyone in the room could hear it hitting the ground with loud plops like a drippy faucet. The experience was a million times worse than having to speak in front of my teacher and classmates when I was a student at Liberty. I was so nervous, but somehow I opened my mouth and began to speak.

To this day, I do not know what I said. I do not know if people were listening or if they were making fun of me. The only thing running through my mind at the time was God's voice saying, "I am the God who gives beauty for ashes and strength for fear, I can make something out of nothing. By My word, all things are created. I can take this man who is the least in the room and put him in front of all those who are the greatest."

When I finished, I was exhilarated, even though I could not remember a single word that had come out of my mouth. It had been amazing and terrifying all at the same time. When the session was over, I wanted the other leaders at my table to know that I hadn't expected to be given such an honor, nor did I feel worthy of it. I tried to explain this to the man I had hoped would speak in my place.

"You know, uncle," (that is what Indians call men older than us when we wish to show them respect) . . ."I did not ask to speak. The archbishop did this on his own."

He said, "Oh no, that's all right. You did a very good job! I appreciate you." I tried to express my gratitude for his encouragement. I was quite humbled by what God had done.

STORMING THE GATES

I was on a kind of spiritual high coming out of that experience. Not ready to go back to my hotel, I decided to ride the tram around Amsterdam for a bit and ponder everything that had just happened. We had special passes for the convention that allowed us to ride public transportation for free. When I finally circled back to my hotel, I noticed a couple of guys that I often saw in the breakfast area speaking to some tall Dutchmen and taking out their wallets. Something from my years living in the Bronx, New York, triggered me, and I realized what was happening... they were being robbed!

Without thinking, I ran into my hotel and tossed my computer and my handbag to the man behind the desk. "Hold onto this," I said breathlessly, and then shouted loudly for everyone in the lobby to hear: "Those who are here from the Billy Graham Conference, we need your help! Our brothers are being robbed out on the street, and we need to help them!"

I turned and ran out the door with an entire group of delegates running behind me. I'm sure we looked like a scene from the movie *Independence Day.* Men from every nation running out into the street to help our brothers. The thought that I wasn't strong enough to fight the tall Dutchmen never once even crossed my mind as I charged toward them. As soon as the robbers saw the crowd heading their way, they fled.

The men being robbed, Pastors Jonathan and Joshua, were so happy to see us. "Oh thank you guys, thank you for coming to our rescue," they said over and over again. Everyone wanted to know my name and said I was a hero. I did not feel like one, though. When I went to bed that night, I kept thinking, *What if these guys had guns and hurt us? I could have been in big trouble.*

My Heavenly Father had protected me and was using the experience to expand relationships that would develop into lasting friendships later on. I went to dinner with Jonathan and Joshua, and they joked, "Bennie, we have to travel everywhere with you now since you are our protector." So, they did. We developed a system of traveling back and forth to the hotel together, and as we did, we got to know each other better. God knit our hearts together, and we became very good friends.

Jonathan and Josh were Anglicans from Singapore. Jonathan's father was the canon of Singapore Anglican Church, and Josh was a convert who was pastoring at a church. Jonathan also introduced me to a friend from Thailand, who was attending the conference.

Jonathan's Thai friend asked me about my vision for the organization, so I shared with him what we were doing through Alpha Ministries. I told him about our passion for strengthening pastors and frontline messengers, and for motivating, mobilizing, and supporting the national evangelists and pastors to reach the least-reached for Jesus Christ in all of Asia.

"Bennie," he responded, "you must come to Thailand and share some of your ideas with us. Teach us how we can do things." I was open to anything God might be doing and committed to pray about it. We all exchanged addresses at the end of the conference and promised to stay in touch.

Some months after I returned to the States, I received a call from Jonathan. He and several others were holding a follow-up conference after Amsterdam 2000, in Singapore. "Bennie," he said, "I want you to be there. Anne Graham Lotz is traveling in to speak, and it would be great for you to be a part of everything. Will you come?"

I agreed to go and was amazed at the way God was opening doors. While I was in Singapore, I met up again with Jonathan's friend from Thailand, and he introduced me to a friend of his from Myanmar (Burma). Since I was staying at Jonathan's house, we spent many hours together talking and dreaming about the ministry God could do through us in our respective countries.

NO "CHANCE" MEETINGS

I eventually returned to Singapore later with my brother Finny and an American friend named Dale to conduct pastors' training. One morning, Finny and Dale (who are more into exercise than I am), went out for a walk. I stayed in the hotel room, praying for a while, overwhelmed by the way God was working things out. "God, you are the reason I am here in Singapore," I prayed. "My heart is always thankful." Soon, I felt the need to stretch for a bit, so I walked out into the hallway.

I saw a man at the other end walking toward me. He seemed very determined, and when he got closer, he said, "Pastor?" In Asia, it's very common for people to call you "Pastor," so I answered, "Yes?"

"Praise the Lord!" he exclaimed, throwing his hands up.

"Yeah, praise the Lord," I nodded and smiled.

He went on, "I was sitting on the other side of the hotel, and I was praying. God told me that there is a man here and that I must go meet him and invite him to come to Indonesia and Myanmar because we need his help."

There was an awkward silence for a moment as I tried to wrap my mind around what he was telling me. Puzzled, I said, "Come again?" I needed him to repeat himself, partially because of his thick accent and partially because it seemed too amazing to be true. He went through his story again. It turns out; I had understood him correctly the first time.

"Will you come to Indonesia and Myanmar? We need your help."

"Come inside," I said, opening the door to my room. "Can you explain your ministry to me?" As he shared more details about how God was working in his land, tears were streaming from his eyes. Soon, I was in tears, too, blown away at how God had orchestrated such a meeting. I had been called from America to Holland, received a call in Holland to go to Singapore, and now in Singapore—at just the right time—I was receiving a call to go to Myanmar. What a great God we serve!

My father was an intercessor, and he always prayed faithfully that God would enlarge their territories, His name would be glorified through their people, and I was witnessing it right before my eyes.

Dale and Finny walked in, and I tried to explain what was going on through my excitement over what God was doing. It was a miraculous thing.

Not only did Alpha Ministries receive the opportunity to go to Indonesia and Myanmar through this "chance" meeting, but we also established a Burmese Bible school and several children's homes to the glory of God. To this day, the Good News of the Kingdom is being preached to the Burmese people through leaders developed in that country.

An invitation to Thailand came the following year through Jonathan's Thai friend. I went with some others to do the training. In our limited vision, we thought we were simply encouraging pastors and frontline messengers the way we had in many other areas. However, God was using our time there to lay a solid foundation.

In 2004, after the tsunami hit Thailand and many lives were lost, I received a call: "Bennie, we need some help here. People are suffering."

God used Alpha Ministries to bring aid to many in Thailand, and a new way of preaching the Gospel was opened to us—providing humanitarian relief. Since then, we have seen the Good News preached to the people of Sri Lanka, Nepal, and Myanmar. We have been fortunate enough to be meeting not only spiritual needs but physical needs as well.

Truly, no eye has seen, and no ear has heard what God has prepared for those who love Him! As my parents were willing to follow God where He called them, and Lina and I did the same, we prayed with one heart that God would enlarge the territory of

His ministry for His glory. From one end of the globe to another, we saw Him opening doors I could never have imagined on my own. The Good News was going places, and I was privileged to be going with it.

CHAPTER 10

APPLICATION POINTS

The favor of God has Kingdom purpose beyond opening doors and miraculous means of the provision in your personal life.

God's favor has far-reaching impact for spreading the Gospel. I'm frequently blown away, by the way, He orchestrates encounters in my life, like being called from America to Holland, then to Singapore, and then to Myanmar, and ultimately to Thailand. What a great God we serve!

To whom are you called?

If you do not know yet, it is OK. Just pray for God to use you at every opportunity. My parents prayed faithfully that God would enlarge their territories so His name would be glorified through their people. I continue to witness their prayers being answered through my life, the lives of my siblings, and the lives of my children.

Whether you stand behind a pulpit speaking to hundreds or sit on a subway speaking to one, be faithful to share His goodness.

Opportunities to share the Gospel surround us each and every day. Many times, God has prepared a single heart to hear a single word of encouragement that you might have to offer. Do not hesitate. The Good News is going places will you go with it?

> *"For Christ did not send me to baptize, but to preach the Gospel, not with wisdom of words, lest the cross of Christ should be made of no effect."*
>
> **—1 Corinthians 1:17**

CHAPTER 11

I MUST DECREASE

John answered and said, "A man can receive nothing unless it has been given to him from heaven. You yourselves bear me witness, that I said, 'I am not the Christ,' but, 'I have been sent before Him.' He who has the bride is the bridegroom; but the friend of the bridegroom, who stands and hears him, rejoices greatly because of the bridegroom's voice. Therefore this joy of mine is fulfilled. He must increase, but I must decrease.

John 3:27-30

Going with God's work meant going with God's miracles. From India to Amsterdam, to Singapore, to Myanmar, to Thailand, and Lynchburg, I was continually reminded that whether I felt qualified or not, my Heavenly Father delighted in showing me His goodness. He was doing works I could never have imagined in places I would never have dreamed of going, even in the highest offices of our land.

Life in Lynchburg was going well. When a missionary friend from India came to visit the United States, we knew he would need transportation. He was going to minister all around the country, and though he had a driver's license, he had no vehicle. Lina and I owned two vehicles by then, and when we looked at how often we used them in light of our friend's need, we knew what we had to do. I called to tell him, "If you want to use our Grand Am while you are in the country, it's all yours, man."

He was so grateful. He drove that car all over the place, and, after a while, the clutch went out again. Unfortunately, we were in a place where the repairs would have been too much for us. While I was thankful for Priscilla's gift to us, it was time to pass it on to someone else.

We decided to let him have it, so I told him, "If you can fix it and use it, go ahead. I'll just send you the title, and you can keep it." I have never traded a vehicle or sold one. The Lord freely gave to us, so we freely gave to others. It was hard for us to sell something that we received as a blessing from God. We usually found a way to pass on the blessing to others, and the Lord always gave us opportunities to do so.

Though it had been a great joy to serve our friend, having only one vehicle again was a bit difficult for our family. Lina needed to take the children to school every morning, so if I was gone over the weekend for ministry, I always had to be home by Sunday evening. It was a struggle.

Right about that time, my friend Marty called and asked to meet with me at church. As I drove up, I saw a huge bluish-black Cutlass Caprice parked out front, and Marty was standing next to it. By this time, the church members knew that Lina and I would never ask for anything, even if it was something we really needed.

"Hey, Bennie," Marty said as I walked up. He gestured to the car and asked, "What do you think?"

"It's a nice car." I nodded, looking it over. It looked like an unmarked police car.

"Well, it was donated to the Christian school (affiliated with our church) by an older gentleman who wanted to thank them for his daughter's education. Since we know that you require a vehicle, the pastor would like to give the car to you. It's yours, Bennie!"

I did not know what to say. "No, no—that's OK," I stammered, shocked that they would consider me for such an expensive gift.

He shook his head and held up his hand. "No, I insist." And then he told me the story behind it. The previous owner had never bought a new car until the age of 80. When he turned 80, he decided it was time. He went to the car dealership, picked out a car, made sure it had all the bells and whistles that he wanted, and then drove it home. He used it occasionally for about four years before he passed away. When the family saw what a big asset it was, they gave it to the church, and when the church found out about our need, they gave it to us. God, once again, proved that He was an on-time God, providing whatever we needed as we worked for Him.

When I drove it around, friends from our small group would tease me, saying, "Bennie, it looks like you're driving a police car." Others would tell me it looked like an immigration officer's car.

I knew they were only joking, so I responded with humor myself. "No," I would tell them, drawing them in before I told them the truth with a wink—"It is a President's car, only the President drives a car like this."

SPEAKING OF PRESIDENTS

> *"The king's heart is in the hand of the LORD, as the rivers of water: he turneth it whithersoever he will."*
>
> **—Proverbs 22:1**

That was about the time I started writing letters to the then-Governor George W. Bush in Texas. I got up one morning, and

God spoke to my heart that I needed to pray for Governor Bush. He seemed like a man who could lead very well. I wasn't following him on the news or anything like that, but I knew he was a great guy. What if he became President?

After praying about it, I wrote a letter to him mentioning how God had impressed upon me to lift him up in prayer. In December that year, I received a beautiful Christmas card from the Governor's mansion with a letter of appreciation from him, and Mrs. Bush thanking me for my prayers.

It wasn't long before Governor Bush was indeed running for President of the United States. I felt very strongly that he was the man to lead our country, and that God had given me a responsibility to pray earnestly for him. I prayed diligently and wrote him notes of encouragement throughout the election. When it was over, he had become the 40th President of the United States!

I got teased even more about driving a "President's car."

"Don't make fun," I would kid right back. "God is watching you. He will take care of you guys." We all laughed about it.

One evening in January, a couple of months after the election, I received a strange phone call. The man on the other end told me he was from the President's Inaugural Ball Committee.

"Mr. Mathews," he said, "May I have your social security and driver's license numbers?"

I was confused, "Who is this?"

He repeated himself. "This is Mr. (So-and-So) calling from the President's Inaugural Ball Committee."

I knew it had to be a joke. Someone was taking the jokes about my car a little too seriously and had decided to take it to the next level. Ready to dismiss the phone call altogether, I replied, "You're kidding."

"No, Mr. Mathews," he said. "I'm quite serious."

Lina came up while I was talking and began to ask me who I was on the phone with. It must have been evident on my face that the phone call was shocking, to say the least.

"Just a minute," I said to the man on the phone and held the receiver to my chest. "It's someone saying they are from the President's Inaugural Ball Committee. He wants my social security number and driver's license number." I was starting to think it might be a scam.

"Give it to them," she said. "You don't have anything to worry about. What are they going to do, rob you? We don't have anything worth stealing!"

I still wasn't convinced. "No, it's not right to give that information over the phone."

"Oh, just give it to them," she said. "Talk to them." Lina always spoke life and gave me confidence but I was still fearful.

"Could I call you back?" I asked the man.

"Of course." I wrote down the man's phone number and extension and hung up the phone. Even though I was sure none of it was real, I called back anyway. The person answered, "Inaugural Ball Committee, how may I help you?" It wasn't a joke, after all. The President's Inaugural Ball Committee wanted me to attend and help with the event. After being speechless for a moment, I gave them the information they wanted. All I could think was, "Wow!"

I still had a hard time believing everything, but a few days later, they called back to let me know they would be sending a packet of information. When the packet arrived, they called again.

"Mr. Mathews, we're calling to confirm that you received your packet and to let you know that this will be a black-tie dinner."

"A black-tie dinner," I repeated, a little confused. I was

thinking, "Why a black tie? Why not blue or red?" Not really sure what it meant, I decided to run it by Marty.

"Marty, what's a black-tie dinner?"

He laughed, a little surprised. "Bennie, where are you going for a black-tie dinner?"

"I got an invitation to the Inaugural Ball."

"What?!" He was as doubtful as I had been. "You're kidding!"

"No, the President's Inaugural Ball committee has called me a couple of times and sent me a packet. They said I have to wear a black tie to dinner."

"Man, that's amazing!" He sounded really excited. "Wow! Don't worry; we'll help you take care of everything. This is such a privilege. Wow!" He just kept saying, "This is amazing!" He was so excited I had to remind him why I had called in the first place.

"OK, a black-tie dinner is one where all the men wear tuxedos, and the women wear fancy gowns. I imagine you don't own a tuxedo, but don't worry. We have a church member who works at a tuxedo store, and I'm sure she will be more than happy to help you. As the church, we'll get you all taken care of."

The next thing I knew, the whole church got involved to help me. I had called Marty on Wednesday, and by Sunday, everyone knew what was going on. The pastor even announced it from the pulpit.

"Our country has a new President. In Washington, D.C., there will be many celebrations, including the Inaugural Ball. We cannot go, but someone from our congregation has been invited, so we are going to take up an offering to send him on our behalf."

Funny enough, I felt like I was living out the story of Cinderella. I was going to a grand ball and nothing I was wearing or using belonged to me. I kept thinking, "Who am I, God, that I am considered to go to an event such as this?"

The woman from church who owned a formal wear business took care of my tuxedo, and a pastor friend in northern Virginia, Pastor Fridley, let me stay at his home for free. He did not drive a pumpkin carriage, but he did drive me to the convention center where the Inaugural Ball was being held.

"You know, Bennie," he said. "I have worked at the Pentagon and lived in the D.C. area for the last 30 or 40 years, and I have never been invited to anything like this. This is a big deal."

I had never even been to Washington, D.C., before, and the city with all of its monuments looked very majestic. Even the cold, barren trees of January looked beautiful against the landscape. I still felt like the whole thing was a dream and felt extremely unworthy to be invited.

"Are you kidding?" he said. "This is amazing! Even though I'll never get to go, I can at least know someone who has."

He dropped me off at the convention center, and I was beyond excited about the evening. Since I was among the first ones there, I was asked to help direct some of the famous people and was free to enjoy the event. Soon the guests began to arrive, and each one was a big shot of some kind. There were senators, governors, actors, and entertainers. I got pictures with Michael W. Smith, Chuck Norris, and several others. When I saw Florida governor, Jeb Bush, in the crowd, I went over to speak with him.

"I am so privileged to be here," I said. "I prayed for your brother and am very happy for him."

"Well, pray for me, too!" he exclaimed, patting me on the shoulder as we smiled for our picture.

An inaugural ball is not like what many people would imagine. We did not wait for the President before people ate, drank, and met together. There was a live band, and everyone was eating, drinking, dancing, and having a good time long before the guest of honor arrived. Dick Cheney and his wife came and danced, and then we waited for the President and First Lady to make their grand appearance. They would arrive last, as is customary. I was paying attention to the Secret Service because I knew that when the President was about to arrive, they would be the first to know. I went out front to see what they were doing and watched them walking around.

As I was watching, I saw a guest come through the metal detectors. As soon as she did, her face went expressionless, and she collapsed. The secret service moved quickly, pulled out some tablecloths to hold up as a makeshift screen while someone gave her CPR. "Oh no," I thought. "This could be very bad." Other people were trying to call an ambulance, but the ambulance could not come through because the President was almost there. They were still working on the woman, and I began to pray when I heard the presidential music begin to play.

I went back into the ballroom. President Bush and the First Lady greeted the crowd and thanked us all for our support. Mrs. Bush was beautiful in a red gown, and the President kept smiling at her as they danced. After a few minutes, they left, and I went back to check on the woman who had fallen.

The Secret Service members were waiting outside for the ambulance. After it arrived and they loaded her in, I asked one of the men what he thought had happened to her.

"We don't know."

I knew it could blow out of proportion in the media the next day, and I was concerned it would negatively affect the President. I asked, "Will she make it?"

"No, I don't think so, she is not breathing."

I was at the Inaugural Ball because God led me to pray for George Bush long before. Suddenly, I realized I had been called there to continue praying. I went to a back corner, knelt down, and began to pray for the woman who had collapsed. "God, don't let this blow out of proportion, let Your glory come through this situation. Do a God-sized miracle for this woman." While I was praying, a different woman I had not seen before walked up to me and asked me what I was doing. I got worried. Was I not allowed to pray in this place? I told her what had happened and all of my concerns. Instead of reprimanding me, she nodded and asked if she could join me for prayer. We both knelt down and prayed for the situation together.

Afterward, Pastor Fridley came and picked me up. He had arranged for me to speak at his church the next day. I could see how it seemed important to his congregation to hear from a guy who had just stood 20 feet away from the President.

I knew to pray for that woman had been of great importance, though, and the real reason God had placed me there after all. I shared the following with the church that Sunday:

I knew the President did not even know who I was. Maybe one of his staff members just picked out my name and said, "It will be interesting for this guy to have this life experience." I do not know how this happened, but it was a dream come true for a guy like me. When I was young, our Indian neighbors would come over and point out to my mother that she had six children (as if she hadn't noticed). It was culturally accepted in those days to have only two children. So, such a large family was shameful in our community, and people used to say things like, "You will never be able to feed this many kids" or "You will never be able to educate them."

But my mother would stand up as tall as she could and answer them with dignity and pride, "These children are not my children, they are God's. God gave them to us, and they are going to be champions for Christ. They will be brave-hearts." She would say it all the time, and when the neighbors tried to offend her, she always reminded them, "Don't ever think my children are going to do menial jobs here. Oh, no. They are going to serve the living God across the nations, proclaiming the Good News of Jesus to others around the world. You will see."

Her words came true. My siblings and I have had opportunities that most people could never dream of, and so going to the Inaugural Ball was not only a wonderful experience for me, but also for my mom. She called everyone related to us in India and told them to watch the TV in case I came on. I knew they did not televise it, but she was so excited.

And for me, a guy born into that situation and ridiculed by neighbors and other children, to be sent to a grand event like this was something only God could do. I never imagined such a thing could happen to me. I did not write to the President, asking if I could come to the party. I did not send him contributions or gifts to get invited. For me, the whole experience was a display of God's faithfulness.

Do you think this party, the Inaugural Ball, is a big thing? No, there is a more magnificent party in Heaven, and that one will be the most significant privilege to attend. To have your name in the Lamb's Book of Life and to be with Him in His presence…no party on earth can compare. What we think is essential is really nothing. What God has in store for us is beyond imagination.

I did my best to encourage the congregation with these words and about the woman I had the opportunity to pray for. After the service, the pastor and many people came up and congratulated me. We had a great time together, and a friendship with that church near Washington, D.C., began right then. It developed over time into a very strong relationship and would be one to last for years to come.

A few days after I got home, I received a letter from Pastor Fridley. He wrote to tell me that there had been an article in the *Washington Post* about the woman who collapsed at the Inaugural Ball. It turns out; she was the sister of Senator Voinovich from Ohio. The article reported she had suffered a massive heart attack, but that the use of portable defibrillators saved her life.

When I saw that, it upset me. I called the Senate office and asked for Sen. Voinovich's address. I wrote him a letter to explain to him that while a portable defibrillator helped save his sister's life, there were two people on their knees, pleading and crying out to a living God for her sake. His sister was alive because of Jesus Christ, and her survival was to proclaim His glory. Sen. Voinovich never wrote back, but in my heart, I felt I was supposed to do that to give glory back to God. After the letter was sent, I finally felt peace about the situation.

A week or so after I returned home, the men's fellowship at church had a gathering because everyone wanted to hear about my experience. One of my friends asked me an interesting question that night. "Bennie," he said. "I'm a Republican. Whenever the Republican Party sends me a letter, I support them. In fact, I send them a lot of money. But they have never invited me to volunteer at the Inaugural Ball. What's the secret to your contribution?"

I wondered how to answer his question.

"You know, I can tell you only one thing," I said, "It was prayer. I prayed for that man, nothing more, nothing less, and God opened the door for me to be a testimony to him." All the glory had to be given to God—where else could it go? The Lord has continued to provide me with opportunities to meet great leaders and pray for them.

HE TRANSFORMS YOUR TEST INTO A TESTIMONY

> "There is not a square inch in the whole domain of our human existence over which Christ, who is Sovereign over all, does not cry, Mine!"
>
> **—Abraham Kuyper**

Rising persecution in northern India prompted us to assist my parents in moving the ministry base to the South. We made several trips to Bangalore to put everything in motion. My friend Rajan assisted with the formal registration, initial setup, and operation of the office, which we temporarily ran from Rajan's home. We had no access to storage facilities as we do in America, so it was paramount that we found a building as soon as possible.

My father-in-law, Mr. P. J. Augustine, was about to retire from a multinational company and showed immediate interest in our plans to move to Bangalore. His help was an answer to prayer because we needed someone to oversee the operation of the new mission office. In Indian culture, each relative has a unique title specific just to them. In Hindi, maternal grandparents are called *Nana* and *Nani*, and paternal grandparents are called *Dada* and *Dadi*. Our children took to calling Lina's father "Nana," and soon that became how we all addressed him. Mr. Augustine was similar in many ways to my own Nana, my mother's father, which made it even more personal to call him by that name.

We searched for a building that had room for an office, housing for Nana and Nani, and room for us to host visiting missionaries as well. As we prayed and looked, I received an urgent call from Nana. He informed me he would have to vacate his company quarters in Udaipur, which gave him one week to pack up and move to Bangalore. Unfortunately, everything we found either exceeded our budget or did not meet our space requirements. I soon received another call from Nana saying that the moving company had come, everything had been packed and loaded into the trucks and was on its way to Bangalore. Nana and Nani were to arrive by train in four days! Nana warned me that their belongings might arrive ahead of them. I could hear the sense of worry in his voice as he spoke.

I woke up early the next morning, was unable to fall back to sleep, and decided to go for a walk. I thought I would go have a cup of coffee without bothering Rajan. I couldn't find a coffee shop, so I asked a lady passing by if she knew of one. She said she did not, but I picked up from her accent that she was from Kerala, the birthplace of my parents.

I asked, "Are you a Malayali?" (the people group of Kerala).

She replied delightedly, "Why yes, I am!" She asked where I was from and what I was doing in town. We talked for a few minutes, and as we were parting, I asked her whether she knew of any houses nearby available for rent. I told her I was in urgent need because my in-laws were going to reach Bangalore in a few days, and their furniture had been shipped ahead of them. She told me her husband had recently found a new job in Hyderabad, and they were getting ready to move out in two weeks. "You should talk to my husband this evening," she said. "He can discuss our housing situation with you. I'm leaving for Kerala tonight, so if you come this evening, we can try and sort this out."

I went back to the house, prayed, and shared news of this meeting with Rajan. That evening, we were on the lady's doorstep, ready to speak with her husband. She invited us in and graciously introduced us to him. It was immediately apparent that he had just come home from work and was far too busy to chat because his wife was leaving town that night. As she explained our situation to her husband, he seemed to be a bit frustrated and interrupted by saying, "My wife is leaving, but I will have to hang around in Bangalore for another two weeks, so we are not interested." We apologized for inconveniencing him and left.

As Rajan and I were walking back, he realized that his friend Suresh lived directly behind the house we had just visited. Rajan suggested we visit, explaining that, though Suresh is not a believer, his wife, Lata, had recently become a Christian. He thought we could ask them about rental homes in the area and possibly find a place. Suresh and Lata received us with great joy, offered us some snacks, and asked me to share my testimony. We were discussing missions and my father-in-law's move when we heard a car pull up in their driveway. It was the same man we had met next door. He came over to give Suresh his house keys since he was going to drop his wife off at the bus station and was leaving town on business. Lata introduced us to him, saying, "Bennie, this is Vijay, our next-door neighbor." A very surprised Vijay replied, "We've met, they were just at my house."

"Do you know each other?" Lata inquired. Vijay explained he did not; it was his wife who had introduced us. Lata asked, "Vijay, why don't you give your house to them? Bennie's father and mother-in-law need a place to live. They're an elderly couple."

Vijay, who had been abrupt earlier, transformed into a different person. He immediately suggested we meet the next evening to talk. I was sure the Lord had directed us all to Lata's home that night—how else could the timing have been so perfect? The Lord delights in our steps. He knows what is best for us. Rajan and I returned to his house, rejoicing and marveling at the way God had made a way.

The next day, Vijay explained that he was going to Hyderabad for a business trip and would not return for several weeks. He casually handed me his house keys and said, "When your in-laws' furniture arrives, move all my things to the spare room and lock it. I will be arranging for a moving company in a week's time. Until their things arrive, they are free to use everything in our home."

I was shocked. No one in India would make such a generous offer to a total stranger. Furthermore, he trusted me to speak with his lawyer to arrange a lease for the house. It was so amazing that we knew it could only be the Lord.

Though the moving truck should have arrived before Nana and Nani, it did not arrive until eight days after their arrival. During that time, the use of Vijay's furnishings saved the day. When he returned one final time to move his things out, he gave me a bag full of high-end clothing and said, "I bet you can help me give this to someone in need." I've never had an experience like that in India, but it was the Lord's way of showing me that He is large and in charge!

After that season, the ministry had to move the office location several times due to shifting contract agreements. Nana suggested it would be better to find a piece of land on which to build an office and house of our own rather than borrow someone else's. In a metropolis like Bangalore, people spend most of their time stuck in traffic and travel. It would be better to have everything in close range so we could be more efficient with our time and resources. With Nana's persistence and hard work, we considered several properties in different locations. Finally, the one we did find that fit our budget was outside the city limits.

I was in Texas at the time but prayed about the choice with Nana. As I shared the Bangalore story with my long-time friend Mike, he got very excited. Mike was in the software business and suggested that I buy land, start a software business in Bangalore, and become self-supportive. Bangalore is the epicenter of technological innovation in India and is often known as India's "Silicon Valley." I was surprised to learn that Mike actually knew more about Bangalore than I did, and as always, he did not just give advice but helped with the cause. The day I was due to leave Texas, he gave me personal "seed money" and urged, once more, that I do what he suggested. He was looking forward to opening a Bangalore branch of his company. With that seed funding and other resources I had obtained, we finally purchased the land to build a home and a few small offices.

When the word went out about the land purchase, people started introducing us to builders, contractors, and architects. When I met Brother Joseph, a local builder, and contractor, our hearts were knit together almost instantly. He is a great man of God who loves the Lord, His people, and radiates joy in all circumstances. Joseph introduced me to Shirley, an architect and member of the same church we attended in Bangalore. We spent time praying and discussing several issues that led him to start funding special projects in North India.

As we planned to build, Joseph suggested that I have a small room built to house a family on the site to keep drifters from encroaching on the land. He also suggested installing a proper gate at the entrance for added security. We did not have any funds for that yet, but Nana offered to help: "I have my retirement funds and other money in Kerala. I can bring that to Bangalore and help you with construction." I wanted very much for Nana to be able to live in a house of his own. Nana was the youngest in his family, and in Indian tradition, the youngest is supposed to receive the family home. However, his father told him that because he had defiled the family name in the community by becoming a Christian and leaving the Catholic Church, Nana could no longer live in that house or ever even have one of his own. Nana had worked hard his entire life and owned several properties at different times, but never got the chance to build a home for himself.

We discussed the details, and Nana told me to repay him when I could. With this agreement, I gave what I had to Joseph to start the construction. We were very excited to see how God was working out the details.

Nana reached Kerala, and after visiting the bank, returned to his relatives' home to spend the night. Over the next few days, he stayed with different relatives and took the opportunity to share what the Lord was doing in his life. Nana was a man of great faith, conviction, and testimony. He always had a burden for his Catholic siblings and relatives. One night around dinnertime, Nana was sharing his salvation experience and explaining to his family why they should follow Jesus Christ. Suddenly, he started losing speech, and his face was beginning to droop—a severe stroke. His family rushed him to the emergency room, but by morning, Nana had gone to be with the Lord. It came as a heartbreaking shock to us all.

Nana had finished his race, and his absence left a hole in our minds and hearts that will not be filled again until we see him in Heaven. The man who never worried about earthly possessions now had a mansion in Heaven. As days went by, we knew we had to continue the vision and the construction of our ministry office. He would never want us to stop the work we were doing for the Lord.

Lina and I met with Joseph after we returned to Bangalore to tell him we had to stop the construction due to a lack of funds. About that time, I learned that my friend Mike was going through a difficult business situation while battling cancer. Circumstances seemed to be against us, so there was no option but to put the project on hold. Joseph said he would have to call his laborers off the site if they weren't going to build, and we would have to hire someone to look after the property. Joseph told me to pray and see how the Lord would work.

Several months went by, and one day I received a call from Joseph. He asked me when I was coming back to Bangalore. When I told him it would not be anytime soon, he replied, "My new friend is a bank manager, and you ought to meet him."

I ended up meeting Joseph's friend on my next trip and shared the details of our situation. He agreed to give us a loan to construct the building. I was hesitant but prayed, and the Lord gave me peace. When the bank manager saw our plans and our heart for people, he was willing to loan out whatever amount I asked of him. We took just enough to finish the first phase to build housing and the offices, and Joseph made sure the construction wrapped up quickly. It was amazing to have a place like that in Bangalore.

COURAGE'S MISSION TO GHANA

> "God, send me anywhere, only go with me. Lay any burden on me, only sustain me. And sever any tie in my heart except the tie that binds my heart to Yours."
>
> **—David Livingstone**

One day I received a call from a young family friend named Courage from Ghana, Africa. He asked me to be part of his upcoming wedding celebration and wanted to discuss a potential opportunity for a partnership in ministry there. Courage hoped to replicate in Ghana what Alpha Ministries had developed in India.

One of the largest universities in Asia was located in my hometown in India, and many African countries sent government exchange students to study there. Courage just so happened to have been one of those students. When he came to our city, he wanted to connect with my father and learn about his ministry. However, circumstances prevented him from having that opportunity. Once the matter was resolved, though, my father brought Courage home to live there, and the young man was soon a permanent fixture. Every time I visited India, Courage was there. He became like one of the family and loved what the Lord was doing in India. Every time he saw me, he would say, "Bennie, when I go back, I want to start a ministry in Ghana, too."

When Courage made his wedding plans, he called me: "Bennie, I want you to come help with the wedding and see what the Lord is doing. I want you to help me set up an Alpha branch in Ghana." Even though we did not have a vision for Africa, I promised to go.

I've always been interested in breaking ground in areas where there is "less traffic"—regions where very few people want to go. I am drawn to difficult, impenetrable, and the unreached regions that can be transformed by God. I believed God was about to open new doors of opportunities for His glory in Africa.

I had a ministry appointment in India before the wedding, so I flew to Ghana straight from home. I boarded my flight in Bombay and landed in Nairobi. From Nairobi, I had a flight that went to Freetown, Sierra Leone, via Ghana. I hadn't the faintest idea about the flight path, but just as I was about to board, the agent informed me that I had been upgraded to business class. The news made my day and provided an incredible first experience flying into a new country!

I was all ready to enjoy the comfort and ample legroom of my new seating assignment. Getting on a flight at early dawn is very tiring, so much comfort is a rare privilege to be enjoyed. Such surprises usually set the stage for me to share with the person next to me about how God provides for and encourages me. Unfortunately, the person sitting next to me did not want to have any eye contact or conversation. He was busy getting settled, and then the flight attendant started serving beverages. He seemed very serious, and his clothes suggested he was a distinguished African businessman or perhaps a United Nations representative from Africa.

Finally, before landing in Accra, Ghana, the crew was serving snacks and talking about landing procedures. They said those going to Freetown should remain seated and keep their boarding passes for security check. Those getting off in Accra should show their boarding pass at the gate. I had a difficult time deciphering the announcements because of the static from the PA system and the announcer's thick accent. I asked the man seated next to me: "What are they saying about Freetown? Does this not go to Accra?" For the first time in hours, he turned to me with a smile and asked about my destination.

I told him I was going to Accra, and he explained that the plane would land there to refuel and then fly another two hours into Freetown. He explained that Sierra Leone had been in civil war for years, and airline businesses had just started there. I was surprised to hear of the war and of the horrid atrocities carried out in that region. Living in America, we do not really hear much about the rest of the world. It is sadly ironic that we live in a land with hundreds of channels on cable television, several devoted solely to news, yet we still manage to hear only a fraction of happenings worldwide.

I asked him why he was traveling to a war-torn area like that. He replied, "I am the mayor of Freetown." He gave me his business card and said, "We need people like you to come and help rebuild our nation." As we exchanged cards, the plane landed. I disembarked, astounded by the way the Lord directs our steps. He is large and in charge of every situation in our lives!

PRAYING FOR THE NEXT PRESIDENT OF GHANA

> "Prayer is not getting man's will done in heaven, but getting God's will done on earth. It is not overcoming God's reluctance but laying hold of God's willingness."
>
> **—Richard C. Trench**

Courage was delighted to see me and took me to visit his ancestral birthplace in the Volta region of Ghana. While there, I was asked to speak at an open-air event the next day. I accepted, and I found out afterward that a local Member of Parliament was at the meetings. He introduced himself and asked us to visit his home. He was very hospitable and kind as we visited. He asked me, "Bennie, you have so great a faith; why don't you pray for our party candidate for President, Professor John Atta Mills?" I did not know what to say but humbly agreed, and we arranged for a meeting with Professor Mills in Accra on the day I was to return to India.

When I reached Accra, I received a call from Professor Mills that he was stuck in a campaign event and would not be able to meet until later that evening. Since my flight was scheduled to take off that afternoon, I suggested we pray over the phone. After we prayed, he gave me his personal contact number. I was so thrilled to be able to pray for another country's presidential candidate! Over the next several weeks, I called him many times to pray.

When the results of the first round of the presidential elections were declared, neither candidate, Nana Akufo-Addo nor John Atta Mills, received more than the 50% needed to avoid a run-off. I was asked to pray for the next run-off to be held later that month. We all prayed and eagerly waited for the results to be declared. Professor Mills won by the slightest of margins. I was delighted to receive a call from newly elected President Mills, and together, we thanked God for His faithfulness.

When I got back home, I was disappointed to find that I had somehow misplaced the business card from the mayor of Freetown, Sierra Leone. By now, you can probably guess that God did something amazing. The following year, I got a call from an old friend, Pastor Henry. He told me how the Lord had impressed upon His heart that I should accompany him to Sierra Leone to preach at a crusade. I jokingly said, "Man, you have the wrong person. I don't preach in crusades. Maybe you've got another friend named Bennie?"

Pastor Henry laughed, "Bennie, I'm getting the tickets, and you are coming."

To be polite, I told him I needed to consult with my wife before I made such a decision. But Lina could overhear us and immediately said, "Bennie, I have said this over and over again: you don't have to bring me into these ministerial decisions. I will never say no to you answering God's call. Whatever the Lord says, do it."

With that, I told Pastor Henry I would go, but this crusade business meant I would have to fast and pray. He assured me, "You'll be fine, you've observed your father. Do what he does. The Lord will be with you." Pastor Henry emailed copies of my tickets a few days later.

So in 2010, I went with Pastor Henry to Sierra Leone for my first real visit. When we landed in Freetown, my conversation with the mayor of Freetown came to mind. I could not recall his name, but I had a vague memory of what he looked like. We rested that first day, and the next morning, we had a pastors and leaders meeting. I shared what the Lord was doing on the front line. It is always exciting to speak in African churches. They are very responsive, and it boosts your spirit.

I was then told I was going to speak at Idonkare village. In their language, it literally means "I don't care." As we left Freetown, the sun was setting, and the sky grew very dark. By the time we reached Idonkcare, it was pitch black outside, and you could see every star in the sky. The vehicle stopped in front of a mosque, and we saw dim lamps shining in people's homes. I could hear a P.A. system and singing from a long way off, but as we drew closer to the mosque, I realized the meeting was behind the mosque itself. The music grew louder, and I saw more lights, and then a whole area filled with people. It was beautiful to see all of them dancing and praising God adjacent to the mosque. As I was led to the stage, I felt like David. "*Who am I, Sovereign Lord, and what is my family, that you have brought me this far and counted me worthy to stand and proclaim Your name among the multitudes.*" It was humbling to receive such great honor and to be on the receiving end. I was in tears.

As I shared, the Lord brought to mind the incident of meeting the mayor on a flight to Ghana. When I told that story, some of the people were whispering and giggling, though I knew it wasn't just a funny line. I went on with my testimony, what the Lord had done in my life, and ended by asking the people to give their lives to Jesus. That evening, over 60 men and women came to the altar to receive Him as their personal Lord and Savior. I was in tears and sobbing like a child, incapable of speech as I bore witness to God's saving grace.

I went back to my seat, and a few ladies approached me to ask for the mayor's name. I told them I could not remember but thought that his first name was William. They started dancing and rejoicing. One of the women pointed to the far end of the grounds, to the only lit home—"That is the home of Mayor William," she said. Other than the crusade ground and the mayor's home, the entire village was without electricity. The village pastor got excited and told me I absolutely had to meet with the mayor. People started praising God. They knew the mayor was not in town at the time, but he was due to return in two days. Unfortunately, we were scheduled to travel to the Kono District to conduct more crusades.

The Kono District is a diamond-rich area in the eastern region of Sierra Leone. The presence of diamonds there was, in several ways, the main reason for the country's civil war. Diamonds are supposed to be symbols of love, commitment, and joyful new beginnings, but for many people in diamond-rich countries, those sparkling stones are considered to be more of a curse than a blessing.

Over 120,000 people were killed and two million displaced during the civil war. It was one that was marked by brutal atrocities, the use of enslaved child soldiers, and amputation as a weapon of terror. The signature terror tactic of the rebels was physical. Some 20,000 civilians suffered amputations with machetes and axes. More than a decade of fighting, fueled by the use of "blood diamonds" to fund insurgents, only ended after Tony Blair sent British troops into the country.

The roads to Kono contained knee-deep holes and divots to slow the army down when they entered the region. Between the dark night and a vehicle that overheated every few miles, it was one of the scariest drives of my life. By the grace of God, we arrived safely late at night and went straight to bed. The next morning, we held the pastors and leaders conference, followed by a great crusade in the evening.

Soon after, we received a call from Mayor William's office saying he wanted to meet with me. We were still in Kono and would return to Freetown on Sunday evening. On Monday morning, we had a special prayer meeting scheduled with the President of Sierra Leone, Earnest Bai Koroma. He was a believer who invited pastors to come and pray with him at the beginning of each week. I was asked to be part of that meeting and had a flight to return to the States the following Tuesday. Pastor Henry assured me we could meet with Mayor William Tuesday morning and then head straight to the airport. I was speechless at how the Lord had orchestrated all these things. I could not wait to share these amazing stories with Lina and my parents. I was keenly aware that so many of these events were also the answer to the prayers of my father.

Tuesday morning, a delegation of people came with me to meet the Mayor. We greeted him, and I shared the story of how we met. He remembered me and was delighted to meet again. It was a great reconnection, and as we were leaving, I asked him if I could pray for him. He said he would love that and asked that I pray for his flight to America that evening. It turns out; we were to be on the very same BMI airline flight via London. Pastor Henry joked, "There you go again, flying together."

I arrived at the airport later that day knowing I had two disadvantages: 1) I was an Indian, and 2) I was traveling out of a diamond-rich country. Most Indians visiting Sierra Leone were diamond merchants and owned several mines. They were required to go through specialized security checks. When my turn came, the officer looked at me very seriously and instructed me to open my luggage. I had two bags because we take things for people when making missions trips, which means we sometimes return with an empty suitcase. Suspicious, the security officer started questioning me, and I knew it was going to be a long and annoying wait. Just then, I heard an entourage of people heading into the airport behind me. I turned around to look, and it was the Mayor with his security personnel. I yelled, "Hello, Mayor William!" He came over and greeted me, "Mathews, we will see you later."

The security officer looked on in surprise. "You know him?" he asked. And since the pride in our hearts always looks for a chance to burst through, I proudly replied, "I know him, and I know your president, too." I instantly regretted it and repented about the brag in my heart, apologizing to the Lord. The officer observed me and asked me what my profession was.

"I am a servant of the Most High God."

"Does that mean you're a man of God?

"Yes!"

He took another long look at me and said I could leave. Security let me go and did not ask to recheck my luggage.

If I had turned down Pastor Henry's invitation to Sierra Leone, I would have missed so many divinely orchestrated opportunities. Seeing souls saved, seeing what the Lord was doing in a war-torn country for His glory, connecting with a believing mayor and president…it was incredible. It is the kind of work that comes when we decrease, when we lay aside our pride and foolishness, so that He may increase.

GOD'S TRANSFORMS YOUR MESS INTO A MESSAGE

My long-time friend Mike had gone through a series of painful experiences, culminating with the loss of his wife in a tragic accident. A few months after her passing, Mike was supposed to attend a business convention in Cancun, Mexico, but did not want to go alone. He asked if I would like to go with him to keep him company during such a difficult time of his life. I was scheduled to speak at a church in Maryland, but I felt that I needed to spend quality time with a hurting brother and encourage him. God's purpose for our lives is evident in this: We spend our valuable time with those who are hurting.

The trip was in October, just a month after September 11, 2001, so everyone was still very much on edge regarding their travel plans. Soon after we boarded in Richmond, Mike began having some difficulties. He was feeling nauseous and very ill. Before I was able to find something to settle his stomach, the plane took off. As we climbed higher and higher, all I could think about was getting him some help. I was so concerned that I forgot how it might look for a person of my complexion to draw any attention to himself on an airplane. I unbuckled my seatbelt and began walking toward the front of the plane. People instantly began to react with panic.

"Sir, where are you going?" The voice of the flight attendant glaring at me was sharp, and her words were less of a question than a warning. Suddenly, everyone was staring at me. "Go back to your seat, sir!" another attendant yelled from behind me. That's when I realized what the situation must have looked like to them, and I was so embarrassed. I went back to my seat and sat down. An attendant came and asked what the problem was.

"My friend is sick," I told him.

"I will get him something, but you must not get up from your seat until the captain says it is permissible to do so. Do you understand? You must stay seated with your seatbelt buckled."

"Of course. I'm so sorry." I felt humiliated enough already. But I was thankful no one tackled or tased me! The attendant brought some ginger ale, and we sipped it quietly. Mike began feeling better, but I began to question my trip. Why did I get on this flight? I should have stayed home and preached in Maryland, I thought. *Maybe I'm like Jonah. Maybe God doesn't want me in Cancun.*

I did not say much for the rest of the flight. I simply sat with my head down. I could feel everyone still glaring at me, wondering what my next move would be. They did not know that I was a believer and would never do anything to put them in danger. I tried to read my Bible, but it was hard to concentrate on the words.

Without any further embarrassing incidents, we landed safely, and our days in Cancun were quiet and uneventful. Mike and I relaxed on the beach, and I did my best to encourage him.

When we arrived at the airport for our return flight, we discovered that the plane had been delayed. We waited with everyone else in the small cramped gate lounge. I noticed that a woman who was sitting across from me on the benches kept staring. Finally, she spoke, "You know, I just want to tell you something. You are a good man."

I wasn't sure where she was going, but I answered as honestly as I could. "There is no good in me other than Jesus Christ, ma'am."

"No," she said, "I saw you on the flight over, and I was afraid of you at first, but now I know that you are a good person."

I wondered how many other people sitting there recognized me. Still, I refused to let embarrassment get in the way of an opportunity to lift up Jesus' name to a possible unbeliever. So again, I said, "But there is no one good other than Jesus."

"Why do you think like that?" she asked.

"Because I come from India. People in my country worship 33 million gods and goddesses…»

I started sharing with her stories about my life, and she began asking me questions. I could see that my friend was hoping I would quit my preaching soon, but I was finally beginning to feel good again.

Before long, I was sharing God's plan of salvation and more stories about His faithfulness in my life. Several times, the woman walked away, and then came back, asking me questions and starting conversations loud enough for everyone waiting to hear. Once again, I testified about everything from the pigeons in India, to the blessing of vehicles when we needed them, and even the provision of toilet paper for my family.

When it was nearly time to board the plane, the woman approached me once more. She very quietly said, "Mr. Mathews, I want you to know that I am a Christian, too. I just wanted all these people to hear who Jesus is. You did a great job. Thank you. Do you have a business card?" I laughed at how clever she had been and gave her one of my cards.

When we returned to Virginia, she began communicating

with us and supporting our ministry. She even took a trip to India with one of our teams to help us with the children's ministry. How God orchestrates our steps to fulfill His purposes is mind-boggling.

SAY "YES, LORD," AND BE OBEDIENT TO HIS CALL!

Life in the Father's business always has challenges. We were in the process of constructing a children's home and training center in North India and were desperately in need of funds. Even after trying different avenues to raise funds, nothing seemed to thrust the project forward. I was becoming very disappointed and spent hours seeking God and praying about what appeared to be a massive mountain of difficulty.

In the midst of that difficulty, I got a call from a friend, Pastor Terry. He said, "Hey, Bennie, I have a ticket to Israel that someone donated. I was thinking of you and wanted to know if you would be interested in joining us on this trip."

My first thought was, "I have so much important work to do, how can I stop to take a trip to Israel?" I told him that I would let him know after discussing it with Lina.

As always, Lina's words were very loving and precise, "When it is a call from God to give or to go, you just need to do it. You don't have to ask me. If it's a call, you answer the call." Lina, as you can tell by now, has always been my source of encouragement and support. I cannot thank God enough for bringing her into my life. When she speaks, her words and thoughts give me more confidence and courage to do anything. So, I prayerfully agreed to go, thinking the trip might help ease some of the pressure and give me a welcome break.

I saw the hand of God before I even boarded the plane from New York to Tel Aviv. My regular coach class tourist group ticket got upgraded, which surprised me as well as the entire team of 30 people on the trip. I was thankful for God's favor and that He gave me such great peace about taking the trip when I was slammed with work. I believe it was the Lord who was calming my spirit as I sat comfortably in business class. He lifted my burdens and let me know once again that He is large and in charge.

We landed in Israel, rested for a bit, and then began our daily tour. Everyone on the bus was seated with their spouses, which made me miss my wife even more. I finally spotted a single empty seat beside one man, Andrew.

As I introduced myself to Andrew, I told him I was from Lynchburg, Virginia. Surprised, he told me he was born a few miles north of Lynchburg in Madison Heights. I said, "Man, I thought no one would recognize Madison Heights. I actually live in your birthplace." Andrew said afterward that he had attended Amelon Methodist Church, and I shared how I had spoken there before. He was so excited that he wanted to know more about me and the ministry. Andrew treated me to lunch so we could talk and ask more questions. I spoke of India, our culture, and all the great things the Lord had done in my life. I told him about the time my father baptized over 1,510 people in West Bengal. Andrew wanted to know more about baptism by immersion, which led to another great conversation. Several in our group had plans to get baptized in the Jordan River near the end of the trip. Andrew asked me, "Can you baptize me?" I was happy to agree. I still remember getting into that cold water and baptizing my new friend. It was a remarkable experience.

Richard and his wife, Margaret, who sat across the aisle,

became close friends as well. Richard would take me to lunch and discuss missions and the ministry. I later found out he worked in finance, and he loved to teach others about finances. I asked him to come to India and help with our annual conference. Richard said, "People make promises like that, but they usually always forget to call. Sometimes when things are out of sight, they are out of mind. Will you remember to call?" I promised him that he would hear from me.

It was several months later, and my mind was once again consumed with the challenges of building the children's home, training center and organizing upcoming meetings. I had plans for my pastor friend, Bishop Brown, to come to India, but because of his visa and other issues, he was not able to make it. Then I remembered my promise to Richard. I called him to ask if he could come, and he gave me a hard time for taking such a long time to call. He gladly accepted the invitation and brought his wife so she could also teach. I took them to two different regions of North India. The Lord used them greatly and allowed them to see what the Lord was doing in Saggoli.

They were so impressed by what God was doing that they wanted to know how much we needed to start the construction. We needed a total of $65,000 for the building. Before they left India, they called me to the hotel and said, "Bennie, the Lord wants us to help with this project in Saggoli. We are in the process of winding down one of our businesses, and we want to give you $65,000 to complete this project."

Can you imagine if I had said no to the Israel trip? What if I had a wife who did not support me in answering the call of God? I would have missed the golden opportunity to baptize someone in the Jordan, or the chance to meet the person who would help with the building of Alpha's vision.

Lina always stood in His gap, she was unseen but doing significant work for His kingdom. I know she has her ears close to His heart, and that is the reason I am blessed.

It is important to be obedient and say, "Yes, Lord, I am willing, and I am available!" He works out His grand plan in our lives. His ways of providing are amazing! He continually proves that He will do great and mighty things in His time, if we only wait for His opportunities.

Every day He reminds me that it is He who lifts people up and brings them down, and I do not take that lightly.

When I was young, I thought I could be a success on my own, make money, and pull myself out of poverty. I was haughty and took pride in telling people I was a self-made man, but God humbled me. When I chose to give everything up for Him, He blessed me and lifted me into circumstances beyond my wildest dreams. I do not have to just read about His goodness from a book—I experience it every day of my life. I give Him all the glory and honor and praise.

As the Bible says, "Through the Lord's mercies, we are not consumed, because His compassions fail not. They are new every morning. Great is Your faithfulness" (Lamentations 3:22-23).

I have received nothing except what has been given to me from Heaven, and as I have decreased in my efforts to accomplish things on my own, God's testimony as a faithful Father has increased. Whatever good things are in my life have come only from His hand.

CHAPTER 11

APPLICATION POINTS

Whether you feel qualified or not, your Heavenly Father delights in showing His goodness through your life—but be careful!

Disappointment and rejection can dig a hole that becomes a rut of hopelessness and despair. Languishing there turns us from the perfect plan of God, when all along He is using those events to lay a deep foundation upon which He will build great things.

Difficult seasons teach us what life really is about.

Sometimes when we're down, we look for encouraging words from others, though what we need to hear is the word of the Lord. I gained an understanding of Kingdom work and what it meant to have a Kingdom mindset. I understood the meaning of "Not my will but Thine, O Lord." I learned to have a loose grip on things and that in any storm, I needed to know God was in charge.

You never know what will happen and how, but what you do have are His promises:

> *"I will never leave you nor forsake you."*
>
> **—Hebrews 13:5**

- Going through the furnace of affliction is always for refinement. One of God's purposes in allowing difficulty, tribulation, calamity, infirmity, and persecution is to rip the pride of self out of you.

- As we go through the fire of refinement, the light of Christ will shine in the darkest corners of our hearts, bringing out the hidden things.
- The Lord communicates His perfect plan to us and helps us so we may help others walk with Him through their trials.
- Each new day, we are presented with the opportunity to do something that will outlive us for eternity when we lay aside our pride and foolishness so that He may increase.

CHAPTER 12

I MUST LIFT JESUS UP

Most assuredly, I say to you, We speak what We know and testify what We have seen, and you do not receive Our witness. If I have told you earthly things and you do not believe, how will you believe if I tell you heavenly things? No one has ascended to heaven but He who came down from heaven, that is, the Son of Man who is in heaven. And as Moses lifted up the serpent in the wilderness, even so must the Son of Man be lifted up, that whoever believes in Him should not perish but have eternal life.

John 3:11-15

God has given me countless amazing experiences and tremendous blessings over the years, but He has also allowed me to understand what it means to suffer for His sake and for the sake of the Kingdom. One does not go into the Father's business because it is considered a 'lucrative career move' by the world's standards or even to secure a stable, comfortable lifestyle. Great sacrifices are often required. The cost can seem overwhelming; however, those who know the Father well know His benefits far outweigh any cost.

If I had not so often been in need, I would not have had so many stories of God's provision to tell others. As Alan Redpath once said, "When God wants to do an impossible task, He takes an impossible man and crushes him." Proverbs 17:3 says, "The refining pot is for silver and the furnace for gold, but the Lord tests the hearts."

Whenever God showed Himself as an on-time God, I would say to the pastors in India, "Don't think that I have a tree in my backyard with dollars for leaves. I don't just shake it, rake it, and bring it here. Like you, I am trusting God to provide for all of my needs." During our first ten years in Lynchburg, we did not receive a regular salary or stable income to provide for our growing family. We simply had to trust God to give us the things we needed. Though it was difficult, it gave us the authority to encourage others: "God has done all these things in my life, we have experienced His faithfulness, so you can trust God, He answers prayers." Learning to trust in the Lord's provision is not easy.

The ministry continued to grow in India. My father had prayed for God to enlarge his territory years before "The Prayer of Jabez" became popular in the West. Although he started out as one man—one missionary willing to go to North India to plant one church—God spread his ministry not only through North India, but also across Nepal, Burma, Sri Lanka, Haiti, Thailand, Sierra Leone, and other parts of West Africa. As Jesus was lifted up in India and all over the world, the enemy began to fight back. As God's church grew, so did persecution against God's people. We saw and experienced persecution firsthand numerous times on the mission field.

ATTACKED AT NIGHT—HE TRANSFORMS YOUR MESS INTO A MESSAGE

> "We are all faced with a series of great opportunities brilliantly disguised as impossible situations."
>
> **—Charles R. Swindoll**

Ministry in India—especially North India—saw an increase in persecution against Christ's followers. Sharing the Gospel in predominantly unreached and unengaged areas was dangerous, but teaching and discipleship were important to us, so we continued to do so. We often invited teams of American pastors to lead training with us, giving them opportunities to fellowship with and instruct our native pastors.

In November 1998, we arranged a very large training conference involving many Indian and American pastors. To our surprise, more than 500 native pastors arrived on the first day. The response by the local pastors required us to rent another facility to house everyone quickly. The one we rented was a non-Christian school, and we were unaware that the religious fanatics sent someone to spy on our event.

The first few days passed without incident, but it was not long before someone from the school spread a rumor that we were forcing the people to eat meat and eggs (devout Hindus are strict vegetarians) and converting them to Christianity. The rumor, of course, was not true, but the truth did not seem to matter. The rumors went straight to the ears of the militant religious fanatic leaders.

The next night after everyone had gone to bed, a large group of militant religious fanatics broke into the rented facility. There was a tremendous uproar as they started pulling our pastors from their beds and throwing them out of windows and down the stairs. Some of the native pastors were brutally beaten, and about forty people sustained severe injuries like broken hands and legs.

One of the pastors was able to escape the attack and reached our home to inform us of what was happening. As we were discussing the matter, my mother got up to leave, saying, "Let me handle this." She went with her brother before we could argue or disagree. She placed a large padlock on our front door, so it looked like no one was home, and then ran to the school to protect our people.

When she arrived, she found the police standing around watching instead of arresting the rioters. When the radicals saw my uncle, they mistook him for me since we look very similar. They charged at him, yelling, "That is her son, and he's the one who arranged these things—beat him!" They started hitting and kicking my uncle, but he managed to get away and jumped into the police van for safety.

My mother was furious. She said to the police, "Why are you just standing here? You should do something! You should arrest them! Stop these men from beating our people!" When she is full of righteous anger, she is fierce. However, the policemen were not intimidated. "Ma'am," they said to her forcibly, "You're under arrest. Get into the Jeep." They took my mother and my uncle to jail!

Meanwhile, the rest of us were locked inside the house with no way to communicate, and we had no idea what was happening to our friends and family. I was on my knees crying out to God, essentially begging Him to intervene and make a way. It was a frightening day.

The next morning, a church member told us that my mother and uncle had been arrested and taken to jail. He broke the padlock so we could get out of the house, and we gathered together to pray and strategize, knowing the police were going to make their release difficult. The situation was grave, and the possibility of things getting even more violent was very likely.

The American pastors had been staying at a nearby hotel and knew nothing of the raid until the following morning. When some of the pastors from North Carolina found out what happened, they contacted their U.S. Senator, who, in turn, reached out to a few influential individuals in Washington, D.C., who put pressure on India for their release from prison. Our lawyer went and fought for us as well, and with the added pressure from the State Department, the police decided to let my uncle and mother go for "medical reasons." Once again, God gave us the miracle we asked from Him.

Once my mother was released from jail, they forbade us from continuing with our meetings. However, we are obligated to a higher Authority. We stood together as one in boldness, unafraid of their tactics to silence us. We said that even if they wanted to come and beat us all, we were going to continue. "We are not converting anyone," we explained and invited them to come to watch if they did not believe us. We knew if we simply packed up and left, we would never be able to establish a ministry in that place again. God gave us the courage and the boldness to stand firm in our decision.

We held our meeting that night, and my brother Finny preached. My father stood with him and proclaimed, "We need to proclaim His name. We are not quitting; we are not leaving. If they kill us, they kill us. We are going to face this giant, and because this giant is in our way, it is also in God's way because we are heading in God's direction. God is our helper, and He will give us boldness to face anything that comes our way."

My mother boldly said, "We will continue to do what God called us to do—to love, serve, and share the Good News of Jesus Christ. Children, we are not leaving. God sent us here, and we will stay here until He wants us to leave. If they kill me, that's fine, let my body be fertilizer to the soil where God sent me." She boldly stood with my father and encouraged us and everyone with us.

When I think of this moment, I am reminded of Abraham Lincoln's statement, "No man is poor who has a Godly mother."

On the last day of the conference, everyone, including the 40 people who were injured, came to the meeting. They all testified, saying, "We were blessed to suffer for Jesus Christ." We were all empowered by a sweet time of prayer and encouragement. Many of the American pastors were deeply moved. It was a turning point in all of our lives, and a moment I have never forgotten.

That was the first violent persecution we dealt with in the North, but God gave us the strength to stand and witness His faithfulness. The militant religious fanatics were persistent and thought that if they pushed hard enough, we would leave. So the persecution continued.

One night, as my parents slept, someone threw a firecracker bomb through their window—it landed near their feet. My mom felt someone nudging her in her sleep. To her horror, she was awakened to smoke and heat from the flames engulfing the tiny room. She knew it was an angel of God who woke her up. She quickly took a blanket and smothered the fire around my dad's feet as she pushed my father off the bed. Dad suffered minor burns from that incident, and we praised God; they made it out alive. It was pretty terrifying to know how easily the entire house could have gone up in flames with my parents inside. We never found out who set the fire, but we knew Who protected my parents.

The persecution continued and subsequently extended to other areas. On January 23, 1999, Graham Staines, an Australian missionary and his two sons, Philip (10) and Timothy (6), were burned to death by a gang of militant religious fundamentalists while sleeping in his station wagon at Manoharpur village in Kendujhar district of Odisha. It was a horrific attack that made international news. While all of the attention on the incident certainly raised awareness of the persecution Christians were facing, it did not stop the radicals.

Persecution always rises as people answer God's call on their lives. As the ministry in India continued to grow and expand, people became not only believers, but also coworkers in the Father's business. Their incredible stories of salvation, in turn, came with stories of persecution. Every story was a testimony of God's faithfulness and the believer's desire to serve Christ—no matter what—revealing how He can work through any situation for His glory.

TENT, TEARS, AND TURNAROUND

> "The Lord's strongest weapons are formed on the anvil of adversity."
>
> **—Regi Mathai**

As time went on, the Alpha Ministries family continued to grow. Many church leaders began to request time to spend with my father for a deeper understanding of his vision. He explained that to the core of his being, he believed training frontline messengers was crucial due to the persecution, poverty, hunger, exhaustion, lack of education, and general lack of resources that pastors in Asia face. He explained that all of these stressors could quickly build incredible strains and, if not adequately addressed, the stressors could destroy a pastor's spiritual life, marriage, family life, and personal health. The ultimate vision and desire were to teach, strategize, and initiate the church-planting movement in Asia. Each pastor and leader who attended agreed to train two others and plant two new house churches within the next two years.

We, as an organization, realized the great urgency to own property as a training ground for these frontline messengers. The hope was that by avoiding future entanglements with religious fanatics, less exposure to them would also reduce the risk of subsequent attacks. We greatly revered the one urgent prayer request Jesus made in Matthew 9:30, where He said, "send forth laborers into the harvest." We believe that the burden we feel to train and equip pastors to go into the harvest was placed there by God Himself. Through this desire, our vision to plant 100,000 churches where no churches existed, although daunting, was birthed from God. In order to succeed, we had to own our own facility to develop and train pastors and leaders.

We began searching for a suitable property that was both affordable and provided the adequate security measures we needed but came up short in funds each time. We were desperate for a facility, and something had to be done quickly. I knew we had an urgent need for funding but had no clue where it would come from.

It was a stressful time for my parents and myself, and I was beginning to grow weary. One morning, with a heavy heart, I went to make a quick run to the post office to pick up our mail. As I began to thumb through the different letters and advertisements, I noticed one that was addressed to me specifically. I never received personal mail in our ministry inbox and was shocked to see the little envelope there with my name on it.

I opened the letter while still standing there and was stunned to see that it contained a cashier's check from Nebraska in the amount of $30,000. None of us at Alpha Ministries had ever been to Nebraska, much less know anyone well enough for them to give such a large amount of money. Standing there, speechless, I quickly read the attached letter, which simply said, "Bennie, be faithful to the call of God and use this for the glory of God." Without name or return address, I hadn't the slightest clue of who could have sent me that check.

There in the post office, the key still hanging in the mailbox, I knelt down to the ground and began to cry in gratitude for what God had done. I can only imagine the assumptions made by others at the post office that morning, but I was too amazed at His faithfulness in answering our prayers to really care too much. I immediately called India and shared the good news. My parents, at that time, informed me of how God had been moving in India as well by directing a member of our leadership team to an excellent property. We acted in faith to immediately pursue purchasing it. For a long time, I tried hard to find who had sent the check, but to no avail. I could only thank the Lord for what He had done. This miraculous provision helped us purchase that land.

My gratitude for what God was doing was sincere and genuine—but also flawed. I was thankful He was providing for *our* ministry rather than seeing God was naturally providing for His ministry to move in the direction of His choosing. As well-intended as I was to serve Him, God would soon work in my life to establish my proper calling to be about my Father's work rather than grateful the Father was blessing our work.

My dad soon shared his heart's desire to start training leaders on that property. He stated firmly, "God gave this land to us for this purpose, so we must go ahead." We prayed, and the Lord gave us peace about it. We hired the local event places to house our delegates and conducted our first leadership conference.

We had several successful training sessions for pastors and children's camps—huge events that were trouble-free because they were held on our own property. It was the most exciting time of our mission and ministry.

I remember the first conference theme very clearly: "Tent and Tears." The Lord impressed on my heart a vision: If His people came and dwelled in tents and cried out to Him, their tears would soften the land for His purpose. He would provide the funds to build a safe haven for His people on these grounds.

For the first two conferences, we housed people in local event centers around that area and bussed them to the event. It was an unforgettable experience to see hundreds of frontline messengers kneeling in His presence with thanksgiving for the land and crying aloud toward Heaven for the provision of a place to house and train His people.

It was around that time that I met Brother James, a contractor, and builder like Joseph. He suggested we start the expansion by faith. James managed his own construction company and, by faith, began the work, convinced that the funds to finish the job would follow. James had one of his draftsmen draw up the plan and quickly had it approved. The construction team arrived and excavated the ground to lay the foundations. To some, it probably looked like a mess with the land torn up and massive piles of dirt everywhere, but we envisioned hundreds of missionaries being trained, equipped, and sent forth from that training facility. During our annual leadership training session, we all stood together on those dirt mountains as my father and brothers prayed with other visiting American team members about the promise those holes and piles of dirt represented.

James called me aside and asked, "Did you receive any funds yet?" I told him I had not, but I believed people would help once I shared the story and showed them the building plans in our newsletter. I reassured him and asked him to pray as well.

Soon after the newsletter hit the mail, I got a call from a friend. He told me he wanted to remain anonymous and help us with the project. He was about to receive some insurance funds and wanted to donate the money for construction. His donation provided enough to finish the first phase of construction, purchase the adjacent land, and purchase our own church building in Baroda. It was incredible watching the workers tear down the previous boundary walls—extending and widening our territory to the newly purchased property line. I still remember my father's words that day: "Your mother and I spent several nights on this land praying as we built the first walls for it; today, others are doing it for us. See the faithfulness of our Lord; He will provide for the rest." As we witnessed the hand of God, our faith increased at each phase as the project unfolded.

The world is focused on filling barns and building homes that others will enjoy after our short lives. For God's economy, our faith was increased to see how He would provide for a vision by sharing that vision with others.

It was the most splendid time in our ministry, but I knew that for a more significant impact, big changes were necessary. We needed a new board with a fresh vision—a board actively involved and invested in that vision. My brother Finny and the entire family agreed. I had an international name in mind and so began the groundwork to form the bylaws to get this new organization registered. The new board for the international ministry was very much in sync with our mission.

Things were going so well. God was blessing our ministry tremendously, and we were making strides and significant advances on how to capitalize and take full advantage of every opportunity we had. All seemed to be going according to plan, and the long-awaited fruits of my family's many years of toil seemed tangible more than ever before.

However, things soon took a complicated, unforeseen turn. One day, out of the blue, I received some devastating news regarding the ministry. Finny wanted to lead the newly formed board and to implement his vision for the ministry. He sincerely believed in his heart that he could take the new organization to a higher level and create more opportunities for the Gospel to advance. I always considered the Father's Business to be a family affair, and working together was always the intention.

I knew my brother's heart well and understood, even then, that his intentions were never to hurt me or create any form of hostility in my family or within the ministry. He was simply doing what he felt would be best for the newly envisioned international ministry as part of the call upon his life. While I was struggling to share in this understanding with him, I felt even more torn over the fact that others were speculating the worst. The entire situation taught me much about grace and moving forward when left feeling confused about what God was up to.

However confused and concerned I was, I vacated the lease on our Alpha Ministries office in Madison Heights, Virginia, and decided to move all the furniture and files into storage. My pastor offered me a place at our church for an office and storage space in the gym. We had been given a big, beautifully designed sign with the new ministry's name on it, and he asked me to place the sign on the church property. It would cost a lot more to ship the sign to Texas, where my brother lived, so I agreed to keep it on the church property for the time being.

After praying and seeking God, Lina and I decided that we would move to India with the family, as Lina's mother, Nani, was in India. We spent a year there with her in Bangalore, homeschooling the kids, and going on mission trips with the entire family.

As we often do while going through a difficult valley, I reverted back to relying on my own understanding. All I saw before me was a gaping hole in my life. I did not know how I could move forward. I could not see how the original Alpha Ministries could continue for more than a year. I did not know how I could possibly support all the frontline messengers and children who depended on Alpha every month—who depended on me. I had not attended a seminary, so I did not have the preacher friends and connections I felt I needed. I was uncomfortable calling and making appointments for myself to ask for funds.

In my heart of hearts, I wanted to slowly wind down the work of Alpha Ministries and find an alternative ministry I could invest my time and energy in. I began drafting plans in my mind and attempted to gain a new vision. I knew I wanted to help raise funds for persecuted believers through M.A.P.S. (Mission Assisting the Persecuted Saints) and help our long-time friend Dr. Ruth Onakuwe who was a physician and missionary in South Africa. She had closed her practice in New York, moved to South Africa, and was continuing the work of Bethel's Mission that had started there years ago.

While in India, I made a special trip to visit my parents and ministry leaders to share my new "exit" plan. I was ready to let my parents know that I was leaving Alpha Ministries. Somehow, news of my decision to leave had reached my mother's ears even before that meeting. She simply said, "I hear you are leaving the ministry. Why?"

I explained that I did not have the resources beyond one year, and after that, I had no idea how we could continue.

"Do you mean to go back to fishing like Peter and the disciples did when they were discouraged?" She asked sharply.

"I want to help the persecuted believers and help Dr. Ruth with her ministry in South Africa," I replied.

My mother was having none of it. "I gave birth to you, and you have to be here and help your father's ministry; you have to make sure our ending will be better than our beginning. You are the oldest, and you should do what you have been doing all your life. Take the lead, lend your shoulder, and help navigate this. The Lord will provide."

In my hurt and introspection, I still protested. Many close friends counseled and requested that I not leave, but I was adamant, and no one could persuade me to change "my plans." I knew my calling lay in administration and leadership development. I could not speak at events and raise money because I was not a fundraiser, but I knew I was a people-raiser.

Shortly after, I was visited by Pastor Thomas, a relative from my mother's side whom we befriended after we helped him in circumstances of dire persecution. We met together from time to time to pray. Thomas knew some of the things that were weighing on my heart and had been praying earnestly for me. We talked for a while, and he asked me why I wanted to quit the ministry. I told him I did not see any hope at all. All I could see was a gaping hole in front of me, so big I could never dream of filling it. The presence of this hole made me feel empty and lost.

As my friend began to speak to me, his words immediately began to break through the confusion and hurt I'd allowed to fester. He said, "Brother Bennie, that big hole you see before you is a deep foundation for a skyscraper. It is not something that will consume you. Before you build a tall skyscraper, you will dig deep and develop a strong foundation. The secret of a tall building is its firm foundation. The Lord is working in and through this situation to do something big. Meanwhile, you must humble yourself, stay the course, listen to your mother, and see what God will build."

I asked if my mother had told him about all this, but he assured me, "No, but I know she is a godly woman, and she will direct you right."

That night, I prayed and asked the Lord to show me the way I should go.

A few weeks later, I stumbled across an article about Manhattan, and how there is an entire 'city' underneath Manhattan with sewers, subways, streams, canals, water tunnels, wires, pipes, and all sorts of cabling that can cover the distance between NYC to Chicago twice. Manhattan is far more than the tourist-filled sights we see above ground. I knew this was the Spirit of God's way of confirming that He was working within me to raise up something big for His glory.

As I started to praise Him, joy finally filled my heart again, and I began to see how this was drawing me closer to Him.

We returned to Virginia, and our friends Steve and Linda called to offer us the use of their cabin in the woods near Fredericksburg. "Bennie," Steve insisted, "It will be good for you to take a break and clear your mind with your family. Rest is important; Jesus took breaks, and so should you." We accepted their invitation, and their place was a welcomed respite.

That Sunday, we knew we could not skip church, so we headed out, found a church, and attended the service. We were sitting in the very back row so we could exit as soon as the service was over. After the altar call, the pastor asked the prayer team to go around and pray for people. A couple approached us and asked if they could pray for us. I wanted to say no, but instead, I just nodded. The couple took my silence as agreement and prayed for us. After prayer, the lady told me she had a word for me: "The Lord's calling is upon you. Do not take it lightly. You have an apostolic ministry ahead of you."

In my mind, I thought, "I don't see any ministry or any such prospects."

As these thoughts ran through my mind, she interrupted them with a question: "Why are you quitting?"

I went completely numb. I was shocked. It was like she had read my mind.

She continued, "God has a higher calling for you. You must submit yourself to your elders and to the Lord. The word I encourage you to read is 1 Peter 5:5-7."

I was squirming and wanted to get out of the church as fast as possible. Then she said, "Don't uproot it; let the roots grow deeper, and it will blossom again." My heart was just about to give out, and I was in tears as I fell to my knees.

Afterward, as the worship music continued to play, Lina and I stayed in the building, trying to find the couple. After a little while, I left the church sobbing. On our way back to the cabin, Lina and I were quiet as we processed the events of the evening. Lina was a woman of prayer, and she felt that God had reassured His purpose and anointing on our lives. She desired that the Lord would speak to my heart, but I was not ready.

Still desiring to protect the rawness of my heart, I retorted that it was just a blind man's lucky aim at a fruitful mango tree. As they say in America, 'Even a blind squirrel finds a nut once in a while.' She warned me by saying, "Don't take it lightly; it's the Spirit of God talking to you."

I came home and read 1 Peter 5:5-7:

Likewise you younger people, submit yourselves to your elders. Yes, all of you be submissive to one another, and be clothed with humility, for "God resists the proud, but gives grace to the humble." Therefore humble yourselves under the mighty hand of God, that He may exalt you in due time, casting all your care upon Him, for He cares for you.

I was brokenhearted and yielded myself to His will and His plan and prayed for His direction.

Weeks and months went by—no direction or leads came. I once again began to feel disappointed and entertained thoughts of quitting. Then, just before Easter, as I was praying and seeking God, I received a surprise text from my friend Pastor Dale. It read:

> Joseph of Arimathea was a biblical figure who played an important role in the burial of Jesus Christ. He is called "Joseph of Arimathea" because "he came from the Judean town of Arimathea"; and to distinguish him from other Josephs in the Bible. On Good Friday, he received a body that was dead, but life came back into it on Easter morning. The thing that you see as dead will soon be brought to life.

I texted him back to ask if that was his sermon for Sunday. "No," he assured, "that's a word for you today. God is bringing life into dead things. Just wait; the world might be saying it is over, but Sunday is coming."

I started sobbing as I read his reply. I knew I had to lay down all my regrets and excuses and trade them for the joy God had in store for me. He was the only one who could bring life from this death. Hope came alive in my life once more.

NO TURNING BACK—FOLLOW ME (MATTHEW 4:19)

> "Time is not a healer but a revealer of how God does the healing."
>
> **—Anonymous**

I called my mother to share the news, and she was overjoyed. After she told my father, he called me to say, "It was an answer to my prayer!" My father is a man of few words with people, but he continually communes with the Lord. "He has been an Ebenezer to us," he said. "I am praying the Lord will restore and use you greatly because you have kept God's interest and investment with accountability and a clear conscience."

I was elated to hear those words from my parents.

And she was right—I have seen the hand of God multiply that dollar several times over. Through all of the challenging times, Lina never left my side. She was always encouraging, uplifting, and supportive, saying, "I am with you. God will never leave us nor forsake us, and He will direct our path." We stepped out for ministry and vowed never to turn back, pressing on to finish the task set before us.

Ravi Zacharias credits it to an "Author Unknown." The poem, as he quotes it, is as follows:

> *When God wants to drill a man*
> *And thrill a man*
> *And skill a man,*
> *When God wants to mold a man*
> *To play the noblest part;*

When He yearns with all His heart
To create so great and bold a man
That all the world shall be amazed,
Watch His methods, watch His ways!

How He ruthlessly perfects
Whom He royally elects!

How He hammers him and hurts him,
And with mighty blows converts him
Into trial shapes of clay which
Only God understands;

While his tortured heart is crying
And he lifts beseeching hands!

How He bends but never breaks
When his good He undertakes;
How He uses whom He chooses
And with every purpose fuses him;

By every act induces him
To try His splendor out—

God knows what He's about!

As I look back, I can say that I learned invaluable life lessons in that season beyond anything I could have obtained at a school or in college. I gained an understanding of how the Kingdom works and what it meant to truly have a Kingdom mindset on things. I had to go through the process—even though it was painful to my flesh, my will, and my emotions. He must increase, I must decrease. I had a new understanding of "Not my will, but thine, be done, O Lord. Holy Spirit, precious Spirit, have your way."

I learned to have a loose fist instead of a tight grip. As Regi Mathai said, "I have my fingerprints on lots of things, but I don't hold anything."

Employers typically appreciate an employee who takes "ownership" of a problem, which is demonstrated by their commitment to seeing the problem solved. It is quite another for the servant to assume ownership of the venture. To be about my Father's business, I could not be about my business or even my family's business. God humbled me in love to see His ownership of the plans to spread His good news to those He was calling.

As a servant permitted to sit with a particular vantage point, it is my blessing to see how God moves to accomplish His plans. My job is to go and open letters to find the checks He has placed inside. My friend Dwight reminded me what his Pastor Waxer often shared, "God is large and in charge!"

Pastor Waxter's saying became my favorite life-phrase or motto after that season. The Lord was teaching me, building me, molding me, and making me a better child, a better son, husband, father, brother, and servant/leader. God gave me the freedom to know that the pastors in India were not counting on me—I did not have to be adequate, as their promises came from God alone.

I had to go through the fire to be refined and to be used for higher Kingdom purposes and to rest in the knowledge that God is faithful. He was faithful for the beginning, the middle, and the end of what He purposed. What God authors, He perfects.

Going through the furnace of affliction is always for refinement. As we go through the fire, the light of Christ will shine in the darkest corners of our hearts, bringing out the hidden ugly things. The Lord communicates His perfect plan to us and helps us, so we may help others walk with Him through their trials. Every stop is like a stop sign on the road. It is placed there to protect us from oncoming traffic, or to take us in new directions. On that road, we can take comfort in God's many promises, like..."I will never leave you nor forsake you" (Hebrews 13:5) . . . and "'I know the plans I have for you,' declares the LORD, 'plans to prosper you and not to harm you, plans to give you hope and a future'" (Jeremiah 29:11). His plans are for our good and for His glory—to use deep holes to build amazing works of His creation in our lives. God did not want me to own the building, but to find His peace in the hole.

Today, the Lord is using both ministries in powerful ways in different parts of the globe. Each new day, we are presented with the opportunity to do something that will outlive us for eternity. Our endings will be better than our beginnings when we step out in faith and humility that God is large and in charge. All of the means, the holy desires, He establishes to help guide us, and the results are His. God has been teaching me to rest and to trust in His faithfulness to perfect what He authors.

RESTORER OF MY SOUL
HIS AMAZING HAND OF PROVIDENCE

> "Living for someone else and seeing others grow is the most joyful thing."
>
> **—Regi Mathai**

I once heard the late Dr. Billy Graham share a story about Albert Einstein, the great physicist, who was hailed by *Time* magazine as the Man of the Century. In the story, Einstein was traveling by train from Princeton when the conductor began walking down the aisle of the car, punching the tickets of every passenger and ensuring everyone on board was supposed to be there. Einstein went to retrieve his ticket from his pocket and was shocked when he realized it wasn't there. He frantically searched his entire luggage and seats around him, but to no avail.

The conductor, noticing the famous passenger on his train, was visibly struggling to locate his ticket, assuredly smiled, and said, "Dr. Einstein, I know who you are. We all know who you are. I'm sure you bought a ticket. Don't worry about it."

Einstein nodded appreciatively. The conductor continued down the aisle, punching tickets and going about his business. As he was ready to move on to the next car, he turned around and watched as the great physicist lowered himself down onto his hands and knees and continued looking under his seat for his ticket. The conductor rushed back to him and said, "Dr. Einstein, Dr. Einstein, don't worry, I know who you are; no problem. You don't need a ticket. I'm sure you bought one."

Einstein looked at him and said, "Young man, I, too, know who I am. What I don't know is where I'm going."

Similar to Dr. Einstein, I knew who I was as a follower of Jesus Christ. I had tasted the goodness of the Lord and understood that I was His. However, I had no idea where I was going with the ministry He had entrusted me with or how I would take on the colossal task of what it takes to lead such an important organization. My prayers began to change tone quickly and began to sound like, "Lord, all of the strength I need is in Your hand. I need You to move mountains."

The Lord then impressed upon my heart to call a dear friend, Brother Nathan, and ask him if I would be able to visit. Nathan had business know-how, and I desperately wanted his advice on how I should move forward with the ministry plans I had in my heart. He told me, "Bennie, come over to my house, take a couple of days' break and let us pray over the matter."

So I did just that. I packed a small bag and went to his home in North Carolina, where we were able to catch up on life. After dinner on that first night, he looked at me and said, "Let's go outside to that brick wall near the pool." We went out, took off our shoes, and stood at the wall, and prayed. I shared the situation about how the ministry was changing, and what I was hearing from the Lord, and we prayed some more. He recommended that I add fresh perspectives and life to the board of Alpha Ministries with new members, get a new logo designed, and begin to move forward officially.

On my way home, I passed through the town where my friend Jamie was living and decided to give him a call. We met for lunch, and I shared the advice I received from Brother Nathan about moving Alpha Ministries forward with some tangible new steps. Jamie became very excited over the ideas and immediately agreed to be on the new board of directors for the organization. While keeping this momentum, I then called Spence, who, without batting an eye, also agreed to be on the new board. Spence took time to redesign our website and launch it with a fresh new look and made it much more accessible for our partners and those looking to learn more about the organization. Jamie also helped us start the necessary paperwork for the ECFA (Evangelical Council for Financial Accountability) membership, an essential step for our ministry.

We needed the recommendations of two organizations in order to obtain approval for our application, so I contacted my longtime friend and mentor Ben Manis. After consulting with

Ben, his son Dustin, and their ministry CFO, Robin, all of the official paperwork I needed was drafted and ready to be submitted.

Interestingly enough, Ben knew of a local physician who was passionate about medical missions. He suggested we connect with Dr. Brent Brown in order for me to share our vision and see if he would be interested in being a part of all that God was doing through Alpha Ministries. We spoke in-depth about our vision for medical missions, and Dr. Brown was thrilled to step in and head up the medical mission board. Things were really coming together quickly, and I was so grateful.

ECFA required two letters of recommendation as well, so I texted my dear friend Dr. Vernon Brewer of World Help. I shared about the new direction of our ministry, and Vernon, without hesitating, agreed to sponsor all the children in our children's home while also agreeing to come alongside Lina and me with monthly support. I never asked for personal support, but he (accurately) sensed the need, and graciously stepped in to help.

Sometime after that, I received a phone call from Dr. Heard. He called to check in and catch up, as it had been a long time since we had spoken. I was able to share with him all of the amazing things happening with the ministry and what God was doing and was shocked when he immediately purchased a plane ticket to fly me to Houston. After being able to speak with him in person over our ministry's needs, Jeff, Rashall, Mike, and Mo stepped in and took responsibility for the monthly support for 130 frontline messengers. The timing was so right because I did not know how I could raise the money needed to support our frontline workers, and raising funds for missionaries was just as difficult then as it is now. Mike said, "Brother Bennie, we are standing with you. You have our support and prayers."

Soon after that, the Lord inspired Pastor Butch and his

leadership team to arrange a missions event at their church, where they asked me to speak. After the event, Pastor Butch took me out for lunch with his church's board of directors and asked me to share our vision as a ministry. As I returned home, Pastor Butch called and said, "Bennie, the board has agreed to pay rent for your new office, help hire an assistant, and adopt a region with church-planting efforts." This new partnership was a crucial and fundamental component of the growth Alpha Ministries has experienced. God was intricately designing the framework.

Meanwhile, persecution against Christians around the world continued to escalate—a growing number of attacks caused by hostile individuals and government authorities were becoming commonplace. The governing bodies in these regions turned a blind eye to the brutality believers were facing for the sake of the Gospel. It was very frustrating and painful to see the crucial work of spreading the Gospel hindered.

People all over the world were unaware of these attacks, and the news never appeared on the pages of newspapers and magazines here in America. People had no clue as to how much was happening or what our frontline messengers were facing on a daily basis. At times, it felt as if we, as a ministry, were the only people in the world aware of how our staff was risking their lives to advance the Gospel despite the dangerous circumstances.

At that time, the International Day of Prayer (IDOP) occurred, and Voice of the Martyrs, extremely aware of how uninformed people in the West were, produced a video entitled *Suta*; it shared the true story of a frontline church-planter in India. The Annual Open Doors World Watch List, an ongoing effort to highlight the persecution of Christians around the world, expounded upon the worsening situation in South Asia around this time as well, which acted as a huge encouragement and gave believers the understanding they needed to pray for the persecuted church in India. The *Suta* video became an essential tool our ministry used to share the urgency and need for prayer and intercession on behalf of our persecuted brothers and sisters in the faith. Forgiveness, prayer, and perseverance of God's people will continue to advance His kingdom when everything seems to be against it. Amen!

BACK TO HIS BUSINESS TO EVERY TRIBE AND NATION (REVELATION 7:9)

Part of the outreach of Alpha Ministries in India & Myanmar is to children. Over 440 million of India's population are children—a number higher than the entire population of America. These alarming numbers sadly mean that not all children who are born are even given a chance to live, let alone be children. A startling 60% will be used in child labor, and many faces much worse. This is partly why Alpha Ministries has children's homes throughout the country. Of course, we cannot change millions of lives, but we try, every chance we get, to help every child who is entrusted to us by our Heavenly Father.

Such was the case for baby Moses. In 2014, a 15-year-old girl from one of the villages gave birth to a baby out of wedlock. In the Hindu and Muslim culture, a child born out of wedlock, regardless of the circumstances, is a disgrace and a bad omen for the family. Keeping such a child would bring bad luck and shame to the rest of the family. Those beliefs make finding a family to adopt such a child nearly impossible. In fact, if the girl's family had known she was pregnant, they would have forced her to have an abortion, or worse. Thankfully, her family did not know about the pregnancy until the very end. The young girl was reluctantly taken to the hospital, where her family forced her to abandon the baby right after he was born. No one was allowed to intervene. In India, such cases quickly become police matters, and getting involved with the police would only mean more trouble. One of the nurses in charge of the young girl's care was a friend of our family, and she secretly contacted my mother, knowing she would find a way to save the baby. The Lord's hand was at work once again.

Although my mother was about 76 years old, she did not take her age into consideration, or anything else for that matter. She saw an urgent need, and she said, "Yes!" My entire life, I've seen my mother volunteer and jump in to help, no matter the need. She extended her hand whenever she saw a need, believing the Lord would help her navigate through. However, a newborn baby was a different story.

I happened to arrive in India the same day my mother brought baby Moses home. I reached their house around 6:30 p.m., but Mother did not come out to greet me like she usually did. I was kind of surprised and asked the driver, "Why is sister Grace not out today? Is she not feeling well?"

He smiled and replied, "You'll soon find out why." As I walked into the house, I saw my mother sitting on her bed. When she saw me, she got up and greeted me with a bright smile and a warm hug. I sat down to take my shoes off, and one of my mom's helpers came to greet me and bring me a glass of water. She was smiling too. As my eyes began to adjust to the light in the room, I noticed something moving on my mom's bed.

Alarmed, I asked, "Is that a baby?"

She replied, "It is a baby…and he is mine."

"Mom! You guys are not Abraham and Sarah to have a baby

at your age!"

With a grin, she began explaining the whole story of the call from the hospital, reminding me that people do not adopt such babies, and that they often end up in adverse, abusive situations. She excitedly said, "I saved him, so I have named him Moses."

I was tired from my trip and quite surprised by the presence of little Moses, so I did not say much. Instead, I went upstairs to shower and get some rest. Later, I came down and heard Moses crying. Mother was trying to feed him some milk, but I suggested he needed a diaper change. She retorted, "Son, don't teach me how to raise children. I have raised seven, and I can do this." When mom talks, we cannot argue with her. Even so, I tried. I reminded her that newborns must be changed every hour and took the liberty to check his diaper. Sure enough, it was full.

I said, "See, I told you," as I gently cajoled her and changed his diaper. My mother laughed, and I convinced her to either send Moses to one of our children's homes or to a young family who could adequately take care of him and give him a future. She reluctantly agreed—her mother's heart had gone into full power mode for that helpless, tiny infant. When I called and related Moses' story to Lina, she said she wanted to adopt the baby. We were all very excited about the new addition in our family until we found out that the Indian government did not allow male baby adoptions out of the country. Lina was totally disappointed. I then called a family friend to come over and explained the situation to him and his wife. They were delighted to take Moses and raise him. We gave them the baby with one request; that every time Mom wanted to see or play with Moses, they would bring him over. They agreed, and we handed Moses over to his new parents that evening.

Moses' future could have been death, abuse, or child labor—

he could have been one of the malnourished children of India. But God was orchestrating the life of little Moses even before he was conceived. Just like Moses was rescued from the cruel Egyptians, our baby Moses was rescued from certain death. Baby Moses now had a new life and would grow up knowing the power of a resurrected life, not just now, but for eternity.

Sometimes, we must wait for God's will and timing before we act, but when it comes to saving souls, His will is always that "none should perish."

RACISM AND PERSECUTION

We talk about racism as a predominantly black-and-white issue in America, but when I travel the world, I see a much worse and varied form of racism. All over the world, there is racism between tribes, grades of skin color, languages, ethnicities, and general upbringing. In fact, I spent over three decades in America, and I have never experienced racism as I have in Europe and many parts of Africa and Asia. To this day, I do not like flying through England or France because I'm often treated rudely, like a second-class citizen.

I fly close to 200,000 miles every year. I love Delta, Emirates, and our national Jet Airways, but I often encounter difficulty flying Air France or any European airlines. After speaking at a Voice of the Martyrs conference in California, I was exhausted, and the three-hour drive from Riverside to Los Angeles International Airport (LAX) did not help. Add to that the shuttle ride from LAX rental car drop-off to the terminal that took 40 minutes because of traffic. Needless to say, I was eagerly looking forward to what would be my first flight on Virgin Atlantic Airways to London. I had read a lot about their service, flights, and founder, Richard Branson. With great expectations, I went to check my luggage but found the well-dressed English gentleman at the counter to be quite rude. He never greeted me, and it was clear by his actions that he was uninterested in helping me, as were the other two ladies at the counter. Though I showed my Diamond Status frequent flyer credentials, I noticed he did not place a priority tag on my baggage. When I asked, he informed me that they did not recognize my status. I let it go and requested an empty row or a seating upgrade, but he dismissively said, "It's a full flight." I asked if I was authorized to use the Clubhouse, only to be told, "No, you are not flying Upper Class."

A bit hurt by his treatment but too tired to argue, I proceeded to TSA check-in and then grabbed some lunch. Afterward, I decided to check with the Virgin Clubhouse attendant to see if I could, in fact, enter the lounge. The lady greeted me at the counter with a warm smile. By her accent, I believed her to be from South America. I presented my boarding pass, and she told me to go right in. I paused to explain the issue I'd just had with the man during check-in, and she apologized. Even though I knew in my heart that racism was at the root of the animosity, I felt from some of the British attendants, and I chose to let it go and enjoy the peace and quiet of the lounge before boarding my flight.

During a different flight that was particularly long, I was thumbing through a magazine and noticed an article about racism. It referenced survey results published in 2016 about the most racist countries in the world. It combined the results of a couple of surveys done by two different sources. One asked if people would mind "having people of other races as neighbors." The other asked if people "had personally witnessed or experienced racism." Based on the survey results, 46.6% of people said they would not like having people of different races living next door to them, while 64.3% said they had witnessed or experienced some form of racism.*

I was not surprised to read that India was ranked as the #1 most racist country on the list of "the top 25." White supremacist ideology is unfortunately common in India, where lighter skin is glorified by the movie and advertising industries, among others. There is also discrimination between different regions of the country. The harshest forms of racism I've ever faced were in my motherland. People called me *Madrasi* because my family came from South India. Our neighbors were Brahmins, and they hated us and called us all sorts of names because we were not vegans. If you look at the Sunday newspaper's matrimonial sections in India, you will see the expectation of parents for their children as mates: fair looking, particular caste, particular state, and language. Even if you are from the same caste, it is expected that you match the language and people group. It would take far too long to explain all the dynamics of the racism that is so profoundly woven into Indian culture.

People all over Asia and Africa face similar problems. When I was visiting Kenya, my host was taking me out for lunch—but he had to go to four different restaurants before finally choosing one. I asked him what was wrong with the other three, and he said, "The owners belong to another tribe," meaning, my host would not have been allowed to eat there.

Racism definitely adds another layer of resistance to the message of the Gospel reaching the unreached. However, God continues to raise up men and women who will not be stopped—

* **Source:** https://businesstech.co.za/news/lifestyle/116644/the-most-racist-countries-in-the-world/).

no matter the level of persecution they might face. As Jesus said, "And I, if I am lifted up from the earth, will draw all peoples to Myself" (John 12:32).

I have the pleasure of knowing men and women all around the world who risk everything to lift Him up.

A young Burmese man named Chola had been a staunch follower of Buddhism until he became a Christian through the ministry of a local frontline messenger in Myanmar. Chola's passion was completely diverted from Buddha to Christ. He could not get enough knowledge of his new-found faith, so he joined the Bible Institute. Chola met a Christian girl there—she was from the Chin people group. The two fell in love and planned to marry, but their families fiercely opposed their union. In Burma (Myanmar), the Chin people are one of the most racially persecuted groups.

Eventually, the Lord worked things out; they were married and started serving God full force. The couple knew He was calling them to children's ministry since they were surrounded by many children who had no food or education. They established a ministry home and plunged into tutoring the children and feeding them one large meal a day.

The ministry home is located in the middle of a swampy region. It is elevated like several other makeshift bamboo homes scattered over stagnant, sewage-ridden water. Cyclone Nargis severely damaged the area in 2008—the worst cyclone in the history of Myanmar, with 80,000 deaths considered "underreported." Myanmar is one of the poorest nations in the world, with "1.5 million stateless and internally displaced" Burmese. Recovery seems impossible as far as the physical conditions are concerned. It even seems hopeless in some respects, but within the home of this couple, there is an abundance of hope and joy. They exude joy in their service to the children and impart the joy of the Lord to everyone around them. The Lord can do so much with one changed life! Two of Chola's brothers have since been saved, though his parents are still against his marriage and service to the Living God.

God has great plans for people groups we do not think about—or even hear about—in our prosperous nation of America.

In 2016, sprinkled throughout political headlines were stories of a drought in India's western region of Maharashtra. What is left out of the articles, though, is the untold peril of Christian persecution, adding to the weight and severity of the drought situation. Christian families in that region have been restricted from drawing water in their villages. They are forced to travel long distances on foot to try and find water elsewhere. These dedicated believers alternate traveling between limited water supply at government-run schools and receding ponds plagued with health risks.

Pastor Nag shared, "We have to wait for a month and a half for the monsoon rain to arrive. Almost all the rivers are dry right now. People have to go farther and farther to find water. Right

now, the nearest available water source is two miles away. For most people, they have to do this trek on foot."

The Christian persecution in this area has also escalated in recent years, specifically in the Chiroola village, following a series of events that began in 2014. A couple of years ago, Pastor Saila began ministering in the Chiroola village, located on the border of Maharashtra and Madhya Pradesh. Ashok, a blind man, was the first to accept Christ as his Savior among the villagers. Through God's work there, other members were saved, and a prayer fellowship began with three families in attendance. As the prayer fellowship continued, they were able to reach other members of the community for Christ.

In 2015, the Chiroola village chief and temple priests began collecting funds for their religious festival. Those who had trusted Christ as their Savior refused to contribute to the celebration of the idol worship. The village chief was furious and threatened Christians with severe consequences. By the grace of God, they were spared any retaliatory incidents at that time.

The following year, however, the demand for financial support of the festival and installation of idols came with a severe warning from the village chief. He declared that any families who did not participate in giving toward the holiday would not be allowed to draw water from the village well. With the exception of one family denouncing their faith out of fear, Ashok, his family, and a number of other families stood firm in their belief in Christ and His provision. Ashok and his elderly mother decided they would rather travel many hot and dusty miles to find water, rather than bow to the threats of those who refuse to acknowledge the one true God of Heaven. The testimony of Ashok's family is just one example of the persecution many Christians are facing across India.

In North India, fewer than one person in a thousand is a Christ-follower. In fact, it is actually illegal for Christians to share their faith with others. On weekdays, prayer meetings and Bible studies take place in believers' homes during late evening hours. Militants target such gatherings, barging into homes and roughing up the men in front of their wives and children. They create a commotion until a crowd gathers, and the police are called. The Christian leaders are then accused of converting the residents, so the men are handed over to the police under false charges. The women and children are then usually left alone to defend themselves. It is a way of mentally torturing Christian families.

One of our missionaries, Sashi, who had already endured

many hardships and physical torture for the sake of Christ, was the target of a bizarre attack. He was in a village proclaiming the Gospel when an anonymous caller informed his neighbor that Sashi's body had just been discovered. The stunned neighbor told Sashi's wife, who frantically called the missions office for help. Our staff promptly began a search that lasted well into the night but was unsuccessful. People were just beginning to fear the worst when an oblivious Sashi showed up at his home to the delight of all. The call turned out to be a shocking prank played on the unsuspecting wife of a missionary.

A few days later, another missionary and his family were the targets of a premeditated attack. Pastor Joseph was traveling with his wife and two children on their motorbike to Baroda when a car deliberately hit them. The assailants fled, but Pastor Joseph and his two children sustained injuries and were rushed to the hospital.

Prakash, another missionary in India, was leading worship in his church when a group of militant religious fanatics attacked the small congregation. They ransacked the building, pulling down posters, Scripture verses, and anything remotely Christian and burned them. Prakash and his wife were forcibly taken to a nearby police station where they were falsely accused of bribing people with the intent to convert them to Christianity. False witnesses were brought in to testify against them. The police ignored the couple's pleas of innocence and took them into custody to appease the angry mob. Criminal proceedings were filed against them and a summons issued for a court hearing.

Religious extremists arrested another pastor during his morning worship service. They brought the police to his church and had him arrested while he was standing in his pulpit. The militants beat him in front of his congregation, then took him to a local temple and ordered him to bow down and worship their idols. He refused, so they severely beat him again and took him away to jail. For two days, he sat alone in the dark, extremely discouraged, in solitary confinement. Then, some of his pastor friends and other Christ-followers began to visit him in jail. Different groups of believers came each day to encourage their pastor. The jailer assumed that the pastor was a man of some importance, so after 18 days of solitary confinement, he allowed the pastor to begin a Bible study for the prisoners. When he was finally released, many of those criminals had become believers, including three of the religious extremists. Just like a modern-day Paul and Silas, this pastor demonstrated that man cannot chain up what God has set free!

Orissa, one of India's poorest states, has a long history of communal violence. Kandhamal District is known for the tension between various tribal groups. It is also the state where Australian missionary Dr. Graham Stains and his sons, Timothy and Philip, were brutally murdered by radicals in 1999. Orissa has 62 distinct tribal groups, making it the largest collection of tribal people in any single state in India. These tribal people are considered the untouchables, or Dalits. For centuries, no one cared for them. They were given no rights and were considered lower than some animals. When these tribal people came to know the true love of a Living God, many thousands of them turned to Christ.

The religious fanatic activists spent much effort trying to scare the tribal people away from their faith. Having little success, they resorted to violence. On December 25, 2007, the anti-Christian activists orchestrated a deliberate attack, using widespread violence to destroy churches and Christian homes in the Kandhamal District of Orissa. A mob of about 4,000 militant extremists, many bearing symbolic religious marks on their foreheads, attacked over 450 homes and 48 churches. As they entered each church building, they would put all of the furniture, Bibles, and hymnals into the center of the church and torch them. They used the Bibles and Christian literature as fuel to burn Christian properties. Two people were killed, and hundreds were seriously injured. One victim's body lay in the street, unattended for several days.

Prior to the attack, the radicals cut the power and severed telephone lines to the area. Police officers either refused to come to the aid of the Christians or stood idly by, watching the horrific violence happen.

While attacking the Christians and their places of worship, the militants chanted, "Become Hindu or die. Kill them. Kill Christians. Kill them. We want Gita (Hindu holy book), not the Bible. Destroy their faith." Crude handmade bombs and propane gas cylinders were used to set homes and churches on fire. In Barakhema village alone, 322 homes of Christians were torched. In total, more than 700 people became homeless almost instantly.

Unable to find safety anywhere, the terrorized Christians ran to the jungles to find refuge. December and January are cold months in North India. At night, temperatures drop below 40 degrees, which can be extremely dangerous if there is no access to adequate shelter. The believers huddled in the jungles for days with no protection from the cold weather. They clung to the only protection they trusted, Psalm 91:1-2: "He who dwells in the secret place of the Most High shall abide under the shadow of the Almighty. I will say of the Lord, 'He is my refuge and my fortress; my God, in Him I will trust.'" Many of those precious saints shared with me later how they felt warmth in the jungles even though it was the coldest time of the year.

The media eventually showed the atrocities committed against these helpless people, so the government was forced to step in and open a refugee camp. Though the camp did not have adequate facilities for so many people in such great need—food was scarce, and the living conditions were deplorable as the refugees were considered low caste by the religious extremists—the Christ-followers still praised God.

On February 28, 2008, I had the opportunity to meet 54 of those believers from Orissa who had suffered and were tortured for Christ. They had nearly nothing, to begin with, and whatever little they did have had been burned and looted. Even so, each individual gave an incredible testimony about God's protection and guidance in the middle of nowhere. I had a rare front-row seat to see champions and great giants of the faith take turns sharing their stories of God's faithfulness; tears flowed freely all through the service.

I met three widows whose husbands were martyred, and a young 13-year-old boy who was struck in the head with a machete. I met a brother who had been stabbed nine times and was left to die. His wife dragged his body to a nearby hospital where the staff refused to treat him. She waited helplessly under a tree, praying to God for healing. Though the doctors ignored him, the Lord touched him, and today his scars tell the story of his miraculous healing. Each one is an awesome testimony for God's glory.

After the service, I asked the leaders of the group how we could help them. I was sure that these people living in a refugee camp with nothing but the clothes on their backs would ask for food, clothing, or shelter. But their first request was for Bibles to sustain them. Humbled by their ability to clearly see what was most important, I left the place with a greater desire to live my life for Jesus and lift His name up, no matter the cost.

In the Mahkjung village of Madhya Pradesh, Pastor Ramlal was conducting a Christian house group meeting one night when a group of radicals rushed in and dragged the men out, stripped them, and beat them for about six hours. The police finally arrived and took the men to the hospital, only to arrest them after their wounds were treated on the grounds of "forced conversion."

Religious fanatics and radicals are aiming at erasing Christianity by 2021, but God is on our side. Our prayers are the greatest support they can get. (Would you please set aside some time to pray for these issues?)

THE POWER OF SUFFERING—PERSECUTION WILL FOLLOW PROCLAMATION

The Father's Business offers no guarantees about riches or safety. I have never been promised that I would make a certain amount of money, or meet important people, or go to prestigious events, or keep everything I believe is mine. Even my life is not my own, and when I trust that life to Christ, I give Him the right to do whatever He wants with me. But no matter the loss—in my own life or in the lives of other believers I have known—it is surpassed by the richness and joy found in knowing Christ.

At the beginning of this book, I told you the earliest image I had of my father: pressed up against a wall with the hand of a militant extremist violently gripping his neck as he punched my father repeatedly in the face. Back then, I saw a weak man incapable of protecting himself, his family, or me. I did not yet understand "power made perfect in weakness" or the strength it took to offer grace to those who neither wanted it nor deserved it.

I am thankful the Lord was patient enough with me to remove the blinders of pride from my eyes eventually, so I could finally see my father's "superhero status." Like him, to my dying day, I will seek only to be about my Father's business. In good times and in difficult times, from Lynchburg, Virginia, to Orissa, India, and everywhere in between, I have learned what it means to live these words written by the Apostle Paul:

> *But whatever were gains to me, I now consider loss for the sake of Christ. What is more, I consider everything a loss compared to the surpassing worth of knowing Christ Jesus my Lord, for whose sake I have lost all things. I consider them garbage, that I may gain Christ and be found in Him, not having a righteousness of my own that comes from the law, but that which is through faith in Christ—the righteousness that comes from God on the basis of faith. I want to know Christ—yes, to know the power of His resurrection and participation in His sufferings, becoming like Him in His death, and so, somehow, attaining to the resurrection from the dead.*
>
> **—Philippians 3:7-11**

CHAPTER 12
APPLICATION POINTS

It's time to join the business!

Today business degrees are some of the most sought-after degrees in higher education. People spend lifetimes going to school and learning about budgets, management systems, and networking in order to become successful businessmen and women. They watch the ever-changing economy and make decisions based on principles they learned in class and are living out in the boardroom.

I did not receive my business education on a university campus, but rather in the dusty streets of India, in the neighborhoods of Virginia, and in village homes and churches of faithful Christ-followers all over the world. My textbook was not written by Donald Trump or Bill Gates, but by a collection of men who learned, by experience, that the only business worth working for is the business of their Heavenly Father.

And what is that business? It is investing what you have been given by God into the plan of God to bring the hope of Jesus Christ to a world living in hopelessness. It is the greatest job in the world.

It also has endless employment opportunities—are you interested? Here's how to get involved:

Recognize the deficit. (Matthew 9:37)

There are over 6.87 billion people in the world, and over 2.88 billion are unreached with the message of Christ. Currently, 56.1% of the world's population doesn't even have adequate knowledge of the Gospel. One billion of them have little or no chance to hear it because of the circumstances in their countries. Despite Christ's command to evangelize, 67% of all humans from AD 30 to the present day have never even heard His name.

Many people do not even know who Jesus Christ is.

(Jonah 4;11)

Although efforts are being made to reach these unreached people, fewer than 10,000 of the 135,000 actively commissioned North American missionaries are actually working with them. Christian churches worldwide devote more than 85% of their resources—personnel, finances, prayer, and tools—to their own development, and 96% of Christian media is geared toward predominantly Christian nations. Countries that are already 95% evangelized are the targets of 91% of all Christian outreach efforts.

While there are people everywhere, in every country, who need to hear the Gospel of Jesus Christ, these statistics show that the 2.88 billion unreached people are currently receiving:

- 0.1% of Christian broadcasting
- 15% of church resources
- 0.4% of annual Scripture distribution
- 9% of all Christian outreach

The average North American Christian gives 50 cents a week to global missions. How many businesses do you think could turn a profit with that kind of investment strategy?

Hopefully, however, the stories in this book have shown

you that while serving God includes reaching those around the world, it is not limited to ministering only to the unreached. Coworkers in the Father's business have blessed us with cars, trips, finances, and homes, even as we sought to bless others with the knowledge of the Good News of Christ.

Are there people in your life who do not know Christ or believers who are in need of a blessing that you could provide? Jesus said, "The harvest is plentiful, but the laborers are few."

What can you do to tip the scales?

Allocate the spending.

The missionary and martyr Jim Elliot said, "He is no fool who gives what he cannot keep to gain what he cannot lose." In the West, it is almost a cultural norm to spend our time and money on leisure activities or on items we can live without. In fact, there are many things we feel we *must* have or must do. We use the word "must" several times a day, but what is it—really—that we must do?

- I must have coffee to wake me up
- I must read the newspaper first thing in the morning
- I must watch the news
- I must go shopping
- I must have time off
- I must take a vacation
- I must have some chocolate
- I must watch a movie

Some of these *musts* can convert to supporting the "musts" of missionaries and their families. $100 a month can support a Frontline Messenger and his family and bring so much happiness to them. $25 a month can give another child a backpack filled with supplies that continues to give throughout the year.

Perhaps you can consider going without one of your musts this year. Perhaps your sacrifice can make a lasting difference in a tiny unreached community in North India. Just sharing your resources can make a difference.

> *Jesus said, "I must preach the kingdom of God to the other cities also, because for this purpose, I have been sent."*
>
> **—Luke 4:42-43**

Jesus knew why He was sent, and He was clear about the purpose of His mission. He was focused. As He walked through the streets and as He met people, He simply shared with them about the Kingdom of God. His life was a picture of spending what He could not keep, helping others gain what they could not lose.

He spent His time, He spent His resources, and He spent His life taking every opportunity to show the world that God would satisfy them more than anything they thought they "must" have.

Increasing our spiritual spending does not always mean traveling to the other side of the world to tell people about Jesus (though sometimes it does). It means having eyes to see the needs of others and the willingness to meet those needs. It means having the courage to speak encouraging words of life when discouraging words come more naturally. It means trusting God to provide when He asks us to give away more than we feel comfortable letting go.

Spending our lives—our time, our gifts, and our finances—on behalf of others may sometimes feel tedious or discouraging, but it is the way Jesus did things, and it is what He trained His disciples to do.

After all, everything we have is simply a gift from Him. What do you think He gave it to us for?

Invest Wisely Mission Not a Choice, But a Command

Ultimately, being about the Father's business is the practice of investing what we've been given into the work God made us to do. We cannot be passionate about the Christian life until we are passionate about Christ, and recognizing that He is our greatest treasure is the first step toward investing our lives wisely.

For much of my life, I thought this way of doing business was foolish. My parents did not make much money, and I could not understand why it did not bother them. I thought it was my responsibility to provide for my family and for myself. As hard as I worked, though, I could never produce as much as God did when my family simply trusted Him to provide. Eventually, I learned to stop investing in my own efforts and, instead, invest in the needs of others. When I changed tactics, God showed Himself to be faithful, and over and over again, He gives me more than I could dream of attaining for myself.

Being about the Father's business is simply choosing God's way over any other way. My father knew it long before I did, and I hope my son and daughters will continue to realize it long after I am gone. God's business plan may look different than any other on Wall Street, but its success is not shown through ever-fluctuating markets or busy boardrooms. It is broadcast instead through the rock-solid testimonies of those who have lived through the lens of 2 Corinthians 6:4-10, who can attest to God's faithfulness, to His goodness, and to His habit of being right on time.

I will gladly carry on the work of my father. It's not light work, but nothing worth doing ever is. Would you be willing to join me in my Father's business? I hear He's hiring.

> *But in all things we commend ourselves as ministers of God: in much patience, in tribulations, in needs, in distresses, in stripes, in imprisonments, in tumults, in labors, in sleeplessness, in fastings; by purity, by knowledge, by longsuffering, by kindness, by the Holy Spirit, by sincere love, by the word of truth, by the power of God, by the armor of righteousness on the right hand and on the left, by honor and dishonor, by evil report and good report; as deceivers, and yet true; as unknown, and yet well known; as dying, and behold we live; as chastened, and yet not killed; as sorrowful, yet always rejoicing; as poor, yet making many rich; as having nothing, and yet possessing all things.*
>
> **—2 Corinthians 6:4-10**

ABOUT THE AUTHOR

On the jacket of most book titles, there is a blurb about the author. What would the blurb of your life's story say about you?

Brother Bennie was born and raised in India by devout Christian parents and eventually relocated to the United States. Reluctant to accept his parents' faith in Jesus at times, Brother Bennie wrestled with his personal beliefs for years until eventually accepting God's call on his life to join full-time ministry like his parents. In 1994, he resigned from his hard-earned job in the medical field in New York City and began devoting his energy and efforts toward the work of Alpha Ministries. During this time, he received a personal invitation from Dr. Jerry Falwell to join the Liberty Bible Institute as a new student in order to study under some of the nation's leading Christian leaders and thinkers. Through a series of life-changing experiences under the leadership of Dr. Harold L. Willmington, Brother Bennie has been faithfully walking and serving in the God-given call on his life since. Bennie has been married to his wife, Lina, for 30 years, and they have been blessed with three children.

Describe your involvement with Alpha Ministries?

Since 1995, I have been striving to serve full-time as the "hands and feet" of my Savior through the work of our ministry—focusing on strategic planning, leadership training, and the raising and stewarding of resources for utilization internationally to preach Christ and mobilizing natives to accomplish God's global agenda among the least-reached. My role within the organization has evolved greatly over the years and is always presenting me with new and exciting challenges and opportunities. As the President of Alpha Ministries, Executive Pastor of Alpha Bible Churches of India, and Chairman of Leadership Development at the ministry's Alpha Impact Leadership Seminars & Church-Based Bible Institute (M-28Training), I have been honored to see the new generation of young believers grow in their passion for God and people while also equipping leaders and church planters on the front lines of the world's mission fields.

What are you most passionate about?

I am very passionate about missions work. To make Christ known in places where people have never heard the Gospel, mobilizing nationals to accomplish God's global agenda among the least-reached, is what really feeds my soul and gives me purpose.

What are some of the things that every person needs?

A deep love and healthy understanding of their spouse, a supportive family, a biblically sound church, and godly friends.

What ten words do you use to describe yourself?

I would describe myself as helping, honoring, driven, caring, friendly, honest, sensitive, creative, fun, and compassionate. These words are a mix of the years I've spent working to become who God has called me to be with the steadfast faithfulness He has shown me in developing them within me.

What is the single most valuable thing you've learned in your life?

I've learned the importance of holding things loosely in your hands (metaphorically speaking, of course). Nothing in this world is permanent other than what you do for Christ, and the sooner we truly learn that, the sooner we can begin to prioritize the things that truly matter. Every day, I pray that God may be glorified in my life, at my own expense if necessary.

Pastor Cherian and Grace Mathews
Founders of Alpha Ministries

Brother Bennie's family, L to R: Laramie & Faith-Hannah Huggins, Bennie, Ben-Israel & Elizabeth, Lina & Joy-Ruth Mathews.

Pastor Cherian & Grace Mathews and their six children.
L-R Standing: Lovely Koshy, Jimmy, Davis, Denny, Finny & Bennie.

Pastor Cherian & Grace Mathews.
This was Papa Mathews' last interview in 2018.

Pastor Cherian Mathews with Brother Bennie at Alpha Northern Bible College Graduation.

A commencement ceremony for Alpha Northern Bible College graduates.

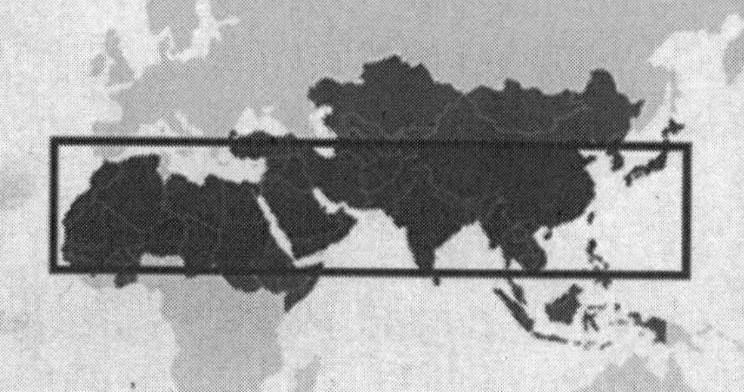

Where There is Darkness, We Bring the Light of Christ!

Two-thirds of the world's population—more than 4.4 billion people—live in the 10/40 Window. Eighty five percent of those living in the 10/40 window are the poorest of the world's poor. Half of the world's least evangelized cities are in this window.